In the Voice
of Others

Michigan Monographs in Chinese Studies
Volume 63

For my father
Gilbert J. Allen

In the Voice of Others

Chinese Music Bureau Poetry

Joseph R. Allen

Center for Chinese Studies ✳ University of Michigan

Center for Chinese Studies Publications
104 Lane Hall
The University of Michigan
Ann Arbor, Michigan 48109

Cover design: Shayne Davidson

Printed and bound by CPI Group (UK) Ltd, Croydon, CR0 4YY
5 4 3 2

Library of Congress Cataloging-in-Publication Data

Allen, Joseph Roe.
    In the voice of others : Chinese Music Bureau poetry / Joseph R. Allen.
        p.   cm.— (Michigan monographs in Chinese studies ; no. 63)
    Includes translations of 120 poems.
    Includes bibliographical references and index.
    ISBN 0-89264-096-0 (cloth : acid-free paper).
    ISBN 0-89264-097-9 (pbk. : acid-free paper)
    1. Yüeh fu (Chinese poetry)—History and criticism. I. Title. II. Series.
PL2309.Y8A43 1992
895.1'12409—dc20   92-1185
                                                                       CIP

ISBN 978-0-89264-097-3 (pbk : acid-free paper)

Contents

Dynastic Chart

Shang 商 (1766–1122 B.C.)
Zhou 周 (1122–249 B.C.)
Qin 秦 (221–207 B.C.)
Han 漢 (207 B.C.–A.D. 220)
Three Kingdoms 三國 (220–280)
    Wei 魏　Shu 蜀　Wu 吳
Jin 晉 (265–420)
Six Dynasties 六朝 (420–590)
    Southern: Sung 宋　Qi 齊　Liang 梁　Chen 陳
    Northern: Wei 魏　Qi 齊　Zhou 周
Sui 隋 (590–618)
Tang 唐 (618–906)
Five Dynasties 五代 (906–960)
Song 宋
    Northern (960–1127)
    Southern (1127–1260)
Yuan 元 (1260–1368)
Ming 明 (1368–1644)
Qing 清 (1644–1912)

Acknowledgments

Several people died while this book was being written—among them, my father. The news of his sudden death, which came to me in Taiwan in the fall of 1987, overwhelmed me with grief; yet grief is often oddly manifested. My immediate, and peculiar, reaction to that tragic news was to regret that my father would never see this book in print. Not that this book would matter much to him, but the dedication had long been planned as a note of gratitude from a prodigal son to a father who gave everything and asked so little. It would have been a small token, but since my father was a man who loved words, books, and stories, it seemed appropriate. But once again I was too far away and too late; for that I am deeply sorry.

Yet others, thank heavens, survived the wanderings that this book represents. Lauren, who has been my anchor for over twenty years, offered her support at every juncture from beginning to end. And my mother welcomed me home once again in the fall of 1989, at a time when I needed to be home. To these two women I also owe much more than these words.

There were many friends, colleagues, and students who read, contributed to, and improved this study. To name just a few: at the very beginning there was a small band of dedicated graduate students in my *yuefu* poetry seminar at Washington University; the hours we spent contemplating the intricacies of the *yuefu* genre were instrumental in defining the shape of this study. I am especially grateful to John Brennan, whose critical insights led the way for all of us. Next, Professors Ch'iu Hsieh-yu and Ch'i T'ing-t'ing of National Taiwan Normal University, with whom I read hundreds of poems in the fall of 1985, provided ballast for the study. Without their boundless goodwill and knowledge, I would have been lost before I began.

In the early stages of writing, Stephen Owen offered his encouragement and insight, especially for what now is Chapter 2. Those words of advice, to say nothing of his wonderful studies on Chinese poetry, buoyed me through some rough waters and dark nights. Bill Matheson has read these chapters in so many versions that he has lost count, but never patience. In the spring of 1988 Robert Hegel and Lai Chiu-mi read the entire manuscript, which led to substantial revisions. For those revisions, Anna Shields provided a marathon session of proofreading and comment. Stephen Durrant was my sounding board and biking companion through these and other deliberations; his company is greatly missed these days. And providing the glue that kept things stuck together (when they were always on the verge of falling apart), with her electronic renderings, intercontinental missives, and unfailing good humor, was Shaaron Benjamin.

The bulk of the research and writing of this study was carried out under a fellowship from the National Endowment for the Humanities in 1985–86. A Summer Faculty Research Grant from Washington University the following year helped bring the study to a tentative conclusion. My time as a Fulbright Fellow and Inter-University Program Language and Research Fellow in Taiwan, 1987–88, and as a Mellon Faculty Fellow in the Humanities at Harvard University, 1989–90, allowed me to steal time from other projects to attend to this manuscript at critical stages. To all these organizations and institutions I am truly grateful.

Introduction

The primary purpose of this introduction is to define and discuss certain key terms and concepts used in the study, thereby clarifying the assumptions that lie behind my arguments. Since much of the discussion here is a summary of others' thoughts, this will include the review of literary materials that might well be familiar to some readers; for that I ask your indulgence. In the case of the study's central concept, *intratextuality*, I do, however, expand its previous usage, and in doing so must anticipate some of my main arguments about the *yuefu* genre. In the concluding remarks to this Introduction I also describe the general plan of my work. This study is highly integrated and best read as a whole, but many readers will find certain sections of the study more or less suited to their needs. The outline is intended to serve as a guide so that they might find the most suitable route through my arguments and examples.

Genre

A genre, as an identifiable form within a literary system, is maintained by a contract between writer and reader. Each genre has its rules, its conventions, and its assumptions, which both the author and the audience must share, either explicitly or implicitly, in order for the genre to exist. The author accepts those conventions from the past, perhaps with some modification, and entrusts them to the future, to the audience. Heather Dubrow writes:

> A genre represents not only a pronouncement that a writer is making to and about the writers of the past, not only an injunction that he is delivering to the authors who may follow in his footsteps, but also a communication from the writer to his readers. He is in effect telling us the name and rules of his code, rules that affect not only how he should write but also how we should read.[1]

By accepting the generic code of a work, we read the work in its "proper" context inasmuch as we read with a set of expectations that we share with the author, expectations by which we understand and judge the work. Those expectations are not only the overt ones—the necessary rhymes in the sonnet or Chinese regulated verse, for example—but also the more subtle ones, such as the acceptance of magic in tales of King Arthur or the Chinese knight errant. In this way, the definition and existence of the genre depend as much on the competence of the reader as on the intention of the author. One might write a superb parody, but if the reader does not understand the rules of parody, or is not familiar with the work being parodied, then the parody ceases to exist and one has "written" another type of work, one that will no doubt not be considered very successful by the ill-informed reader.

Of course authors will often introduce innovations into their work, innovations that might challenge our expectations, but those innovations exist only because we accept the conventions of the genre. Jonathan Culler says:

> To write a poem or a novel is immediately to engage with a literary tradition or at the very least with a certain idea of the poem or the novel. The activity is made possible by the existence of the genre, which the author can write against, certainly, whose conventions he may attempt to subvert, but which is none the less the context within which his activity takes place, as surely as the failure to keep a promise is made possible by the institution of promising.[2]

In this way innovative poetics are sustained only within the context against which they turn; of course, if they turn too far they then break the context completely and are not "innovative" but only "other than."

If the Tang poet writes against the conventions of the regulated verse to such an extent that its context is denied, then the poem becomes something else, an "old style verse" for example, and is no longer innovative. These concerns with conventions and their disruption are extremely pertinent to our study of *yuefu* poetry, both at the generic level where we need to engage its functional conventions, and at the subgeneric level where we discuss intratextual expectations of given poems.

Genre studies are commonly of three types. The first, which is really a form of literary history, describes the development and nature of a historically recognized genre, such as the Western sonnet or the Chinese regulated verse. A variation on this type of study would be a synchronic description of a literary system in which certain genres were placed. Aristotle's *Poetics* heads the list of these studies in the West, as Zhi Yu's "Discussions of Literary Types" does in China.[3] This type of genre study, whether traditional or modern, is the most conventional kind, and provides us with much of our basic understanding of the literary world. The second type of genre study is one that is more recent, being based on comparative poetics. In this type, the critic sets out to describe a part of one literary system in terms of another, a method that has been used a great deal in Western studies of Chinese literature. Within this method there are also two variations. The first is where the target of the description is a recognized literary form, such as *xiaoshuo* being discussed as "novel." The second is where the foreign genre is used to identify and describe a theretofore undelineated part of the literary system, thus the search for the Chinese "epic" in twentieth-century studies. The third type of genre study, which is rare even in Western studies, to say nothing of Chinese studies, is carried out by describing a new generic type within any given system. In these studies one identifies the functional conventions that give rise to and maintain the theretofore unrecognized form; a new genre is brought into consciousness if not into being by such a description. This enterprise is the forte of structuralist criticism, and Tzvetan Todorov's study of the "fantastic" is our best example.[4]

My study seeks to fuse different aspects of these three basic types of genre studies into a hybrid method. The topic of study, *yuefu shi* (Music Bureau poetry), is itself a recognized historical genre and has been described in a number of literary histories, both Chinese and Western. Moreover, it has received a certain amount of attention in type-two studies, most notably the discussion by Hans Frankel and Anne Birrell of the balladic nature of the poetry.[5] The object of my study is also that historically defined corpus, but I want to use recent Western critical considerations not just to describe the corpus, but also to redefine the operating conventions of the genre. I believe that these conventions were essential in maintaining the genre, but that they have been generally overlooked in recent assessments of the poetry. By doing so I do not bring a genre into being, but rather revitalize a historical one by making it possible for us to participate in its functional conventions again. I offer an old genre in new clothes, and in this case, most importantly, in clothes that we can see.

Textual Relationships

Intertextuality, intratextuality and (textual) imitation all refer to relationships between two or more literary texts in a given literary system or environment, which may be as large as an entire literary tradition or as small as the two texts themselves (i.e., model and imitation). Most often, however, the environment is in the medium range, especially in the form of a given genre or literary type. In discussing these concepts the focus of attention turns away from the relationship between the text and the external (either natural, social, or biographical) world, and focuses instead on the text's relationship with other texts within its system. Thais Morgan, commenting on the general configuration of intertextual studies, which have come into prominence since the late 1960s, says:

> As a structural analysis of texts in relation to the larger system of signifying practices or uses of signs in culture, intertextuality seems by definition to deliver us from old controversies over the psychology of individual authors and readers, the tracing of literary origins, and the relative value of imitation or originality. By shift-

ing our attention from the triangle of author/work/tradition to that of text/discourse/culture, intertextuality replaces the evolutionary model of literary history with a structural or synchronic model of literature as sign system. The most salient effect of this strategic change is to free the literary text from psychological, sociological, and historical determinisms, opening it up to an apparently infinite play of relationships with other texts, or semiosis.[6]

While I would be the last to suggest that we should ignore author/work/tradition in the study of Chinese poetry, intertextual studies do give us an opportunity to look at the poem in a different light, thereby breaking the iron grip certain conventions have held on the understanding of that literature, conventions that conceal as much as they reveal about the text. I believe this is particularly true for the poetry that is the topic of study here. For much too long *yuefu* poetry has been understood by conventions that are inappropriate to it or unavailable to the reader. I believe intertextual and, more importantly, what I call *intratextual* reading will restore some of the lost integrity to this genre.

Intertextuality, intratextuality, and textual imitation are not mutually exclusive spheres, but are, in fact, elaborately interwoven. One heuristic model for the relationship between the three might be that each sphere is subsumed by the one surrounding it. They form mathematical subsets in total intersection, fitted inside of each other like "Chinese boxes," with imitation being a type of intratextuality, and both being a type of intertextuality. But unlike the mathematical or knick-knack model, the lines dividing the three concepts are often quite blurred, with relatively broad bands of ambiguity lying between two contiguous concepts. While this is true, it is convenient to discuss the three as separate entities, always being aware of how fluid the borders are between them. Since intratextuality is the central concern of my study, I want to first introduce the two related issues of imitation and intertextuality, which surround and help define intratextuality.

Textual Imitation

Textual imitation, or just imitation (but *not* mimesis) for our purposes, is identified by the deliberate modeling of one literary work or type on another. In its simplest form, imitation is the author's intent and is in the author's control; it is also fully present in the reader's understanding of the work, or so the author hopes. The author turns directly to a text, or a text type (the Shakespearean sonnet, for example), and reproduces a variation of it. The model is either specifically or implicitly announced, and the success of the imitation is judged against the model. Textual imitation is found in any literary tradition, and in the West it is most often associated with the Renaissance, especially with the poetics of Petrarch:

> The enormous prestige of Classical literature, and the similar prestige of Petrarch, encouraged, when it did not oblige, sixteenth century writers to return incessantly to the same sources. Not only allusions to Classical mythology and so on, but actual imitations of Classical (or Petrarchan) models were the rule rather than the exception in poetry, drama, satire and other ancient genres. Originality in the sense of doing something completely new, and sincerity, in a simple biographical sense, are irrelevant concepts for most of the literature under discussion. Variations on a theme and the ability to express emotion within the strict conventions of style are the Renaissance norms.[7]

The celebration of the classical model is something that is also found with ubiquity in the Chinese literary tradition up into the twentieth century. Anticipating arguments in Chapter 1, I would suggest that the Chinese were consistently more interested in imitative poetics throughout their history, and this was a consequence of (and partly responsible for) the continuity of their literary tradition.

Textual imitation can obviously take numerous forms, but there have always been attempts to classify the major types. These lists were created not only to help describe different types of textual imitation, or the "quoting" of a model text, but also to help delineate the edges of imitative poetics (i.e., where imitation stops and some other textual relationship begins). For pedagogical purposes in the West we have the Latin schoolmaster's list of *translatio, paraphrasis, imitatio,* and *allusio,* a typology that Thomas Greene says "tries to draw boundary lines as the version of the original becomes increasingly free."[8] This list has been refined by Greene into the *reproductive, eclectic, heuristic,* and *dialectic* types of imitation. But Greene warns us about the edges of these imitative poetics, wanting to distinguish between

> echoes so brief or peripheral as to be insignificant and a *determinative* subtext that plays a constitutive role in a poem's meaning. The imitative poem need not follow its "model" throughout, but the earlier poem must count as a major presence if one is to speak of imitation in a valid sense. The reader must also distinguish between the use of a single, specific subtext and a topos that conventional repetition has removed from the purview of any one author or work.[9]

In the Chinese materials we have similar possible (but no actual contemporaneous) lists for the classical imitative poetics, and in the conclusion of Chapter 1, I formulate such a list based on those sources. In that list there is also the difficulty of deciding when one leaves imitative poetics and moves into nearby, but qualitatively different, textual relationships.

Intertextuality

Intertextuality has a somewhat confusing history as a term in literary studies of the last twenty years, but it is first known in its usage by Julia Kristéva and with the interpretive strategy known as semiology or semiotics.[10] Thais Morgan reviews the configurations that intertextuality has taken in the arguments of various critics. In that review, Morgan offers a preliminary definition of intertextuality as simply "the structural relations among two or more texts."[11] In this sense, textual imitation and intratextuality (which I shall take up presently) are types of intertextuality. While that is true, intertextuality also transcends these relatively delimited relationships to include the more pervasive relationship that any literary work must have with all other works that surround it in a given system. Intertextuality is what Kristéva understands as the totality of knowledge that makes literary meaning possible by allowing a text to be read within a semiotic system.[12] Stamos Metzidakis takes a similar position on intertextuality, saying it "comprises all aspects of a poem the perception of which presupposes a certain linguistic *and* literary competence on the part of the reader."[13] Thus, intertextuality is the literary text's own creator and creation, which means, as Jonathan Culler says, that "literary works are to be considered not as autonomous entities, 'organic wholes,' but as intertextual constructs: sequences which have meaning in relation to other texts which they take up, cite, parody, refute, or generally transform. A text can be read only in relation to other texts, and it is made possible by the codes which animate the cursive space of a culture."[14]

This type of thinking leads Vincent Leitch to the more extreme claim that in any given text,

> its system of language, its grammar, its lexicon, drag along numerous bits and pieces—traces—of history so that the text resembles a Cultural Salvation Army Outlet with unaccountable collections of incompatible ideas, beliefs, and sources. The "genealogy" of the text is necessarily an incomplete network of conscious and unconscious borrowed fragments. Manifested, tradition is a mess. Every text is intertext.[15]

While I acknowledge that intertextuality subsumes all the possible relationships between two or more texts, I generally use the term here to refer to those relationships that are less self-conscious and less controlled than imitation and intratextuality. That is to say, I use the term in the manner of which Leitch speaks. To me *intertextuality* refers to those relationships that a given text has with any other, even a future, text in a given literary context by which the text is made more significant. While those relationships are in some ways the author's conscious creation, generally speaking they exist only as potentialities until they are activated by the reader's response to them, and that response very well may not have been, or might even be contrary to, the author's intent. The author offers the reader a text that, by definition, is full of incipient intertextuality, but it is the reader's responsibility to bring that text into significance, that is, to complete its intertextuality.

Intertextuality can thus be viewed against the spectrum of intention and consciousness, ranging from the most determined to the least in the encoding of the text. Semiosis is the process by which those codes are entered and interpreted. Morgan offers this assessment of intertextuality in relation to the power of the semiotic method to control significance:

Debate has also focused on whether or not the process of semiosis can be fully formalized and interpretation of signification made scientific. For the purpose of the present introduction to intertextuality, we may place semioticians into two main camps around the issue of limitability of meaning. In one camp, abiding by the "founding" theories of structural linguistics in Saussure and Roman Jakobson, assumes that the signification of a text or corpus of texts can be contained and fully explicated by description of elementary units and their systematic or recurrent relations. The other camp, critical of this "structuralist" enterprise, emphasizes the ambiguity of the basic sign relation (signifier-signified) and the infinite regression or *mise en abîme* of signification.[16]

Between the formal structuralists, with their charts and graphs, and the deconstructionists, with their gaps and slashes, there is a great deal of middle ground in this intertextual-semiotic critical world. That ground is occupied by such people as Robert Scholes, Harold Bloom, and Michael Riffaterre. It is in this range of intertextual poetics that I want to place my study. I believe that semiotic reading can bring control and significance to our understanding of a given text, but I also believe that much of intertextuality is out of the author's control, and it can lead to an undermining of intention and order. Not only do I believe that, but this study is formed on that process, with my readings ranging between controlled and more subversive types of intratextuality, on both an inter- and intra-chapter level.

My reading of *yuefu* poetry has been indirectly guided by the studies of Michael Riffaterre, who is explicit and clear about the semiotic method he uses. He emphasizes the limitations that intertextuality places on the reader's interpretations, believing that the significance of a text is achieved as "ungrammaticalities" (those places where the text cannot be reconciled with simple linguistic "meaning") that force the reader onto another level of understanding at which those ungrammaticalities are resolved, which is where significance is found. About this dual process he says:

> *Significance* is understood as the interpretation the literary text forces upon the reader. It combines two factors, a semiotic transformation and the inference the reader draws from it. The

transformation affects simultaneously a sequence of discrete meanings identified through a first heuristic reading. A second reflexive, comparative, retroactive reading makes the reader discover that the sequence must be seen rather as [an intertextual] network or system which converts its components into variants of a single representation.[17]

This significance-producing retroactive reading describes well the best way to read *yuefu* poetry. What is special about *yuefu* poetry is that the network it imposes on the reader is not intertextual, but intratextual.

Intratextuality

On a spectrum of textual relationships ranging from the least to the most determined, intratextuality lies between intertextuality and textual imitation, but intersects with each on their borders. As its prefix suggests, the range of intratextuality is more contained and uniform than that of intertextuality, but intratextuality is not as bilateral as imitation. Most simply, intratextuality can be understood as limited intertextuality, and much of the above discussion of intertextuality can be applied to intratextuality as well.

The term *intratextuality* has been used before by at least two critics to suggest an intertextuality with a limited sphere of reference. Thais Morgan uses the term *intratext* (along with *autotext*) to describe references that authors make to their own works, in this case Roland Barthes reflecting on his own literary theories.[18] Stamos Metzidakis, on the other hand, has a much more detailed theory of intratextuality, although the sphere of reference is different. In a discussion of textual "repetition," Metzidakis makes a distinction between textual references to something outside the borders of the text under discussion (i.e., intertextuality), and those references to something within its own borders (intratextuality). He summarizes:

> Intertextual repetitions occur then when an external or past model is re-presented by what one judges to be a copy in the text one is reading. The intratextual variety has a model one first perceives *within* the present text's margins. The latter can be thought of as a "future" repetition inasmuch as what was construed to be The Model in the initial connection between the present text's linguistic

units reveals itself *afterwards* to be also a less evident copy of something familiar from before. Thus, an intratextual model is the sign of an as yet undiscovered intertextual model.[19]

Thus Morgan limits his intratextual references to the works of a single author, while Metzidakis limits his to a single work. But I would note, as Metzidakis suggests, that the intratextual referent is always capable of becoming an intertextual one as well. That is to say, the outer borders of the intratextual web thin out, with strands leading into the broader intertextual world.

My use of intratextuality is similar to that of Morgan and Metzidakis, except the configurations of my "intratext" are more textual than Morgan's sphere of reference and wider than Metzidakis'. The intratext to which I refer in this study is defined by a "set" of *yuefu* poems that are identified with each other by shared or derived titles: what I call a "titular set." The intratextual referents of which I speak are found within that set of poems. In Chapter 2, I describe those sets of poems in detail, but for the moment let me just note that while their configurations vary greatly (from a single poem to a set of nearly a hundred poems), a "typical" set might consist of fifteen poems, with the same or derived title, by ten different authors, along with two anonymous poems, from a period of five hundred years. We naturally think of the "first poem" as the "model," and all those that follow as imitations of it, but the intratextual relationships within a titular set are usually much more complex than that.

There are many things that distinguish *yuefu* intratextuality from that referred to by Morgan and Metzidakis, but most important are: (1) the diachronic dynamics of the intratextual set; and (2) the heightened potentiality of "negative" referents. Any *yuefu* intratextual set was open-ended throughout the history of the genre, always capable of accepting new poems, "imitations," into the set. As each poem was added to the set, the set itself was reconfigured. Moreover, when read as part of the set, any poem is viewed in positive or negative relationship to all the poems that surrounded it. As with imitation, *yuefu* intratextuality often provides the reader with a determinative subtext (model), or more often, subtexts, but one also has an *intratext*, which is the array of the often heterogeneous, even mutually exclusive, literary referents that gather around the titular set. It is the potential of all of those referents against which the poem under consideration is written and read. The realization, reconfiguration, and *denial* of that potentiality is the formation of intratextual reading and writing. In intratextuality it is often the absence of the subtext, or even a signature-bearing topos, that distinguishes the poem. With the looming intratext, the peripheral, brief, and even non-existent relationship is determinative. The intratext, which is always in a state of flux as it is rewritten by its contact with the later texts, provides the walls against which the textual vectors ricochet.

Unlike the imitator's determinative subtext, the creation of the intratext lies much more with the "imitating" writer and the reader; but unlike free-flowing intertextuality, the configuration of that intratext is dependent upon the reader's consciousness of it. Imitation is author-controlled intertextuality; intertextuality is imitation without imitator or model; but intratextuality is a sprung imitation, a circumscribed intertextuality.

We can easily identify imitative, intratextual, and intertextual poetics in Chinese classical literature, especially in poetry, which has been the most central of the genres. We also have a continuous spectrum of those relationships throughout the literature, such that no genre has sole claim to any of these types; yet some poetic genres are more inclined to one end of the spectrum than others, and I believe that is especially so for intratextuality and *yuefu* poetry.

The Study

My intent here is to show that Music Bureau poetry (*yuefu shi*) can be best understood within the conventions of intratextuality. Intratextuality is by no means unique to *yuefu* poetry, but it is most distinctive to and generative of the genre. That is to say, intratextuality not only most accurately describes the central configurations of the genre, it also allows us to participate in the genre in a way compatible with the original act of composition. In pursuit of my proof, I have structured this study in a progression of essays that move from the broadest concerns to the most focused, and then out again. These essays are composed of three different types of material: the introductory, the historical/theoretical, and the interpretive.

The introductory material of the study includes this Introduction itself and Chapter 1. Like the Introduction, Chapter 1 is intended to provide a backdrop for the main arguments of the study, especially the historical/literary chapters. But unlike the Introduction, Chapter 1, which describes the literary world of medieval China in broad strokes, is written for the reader with little exposure to Chinese language and literature. Anyone familiar with the Chinese literary tradition might want to go to Chapter 2 directly.

The historical/theoretical materials are found in Chapters 2 and 7. Chapter 2, which is the core of the study, discusses in detail *yuefu* poetry as a genre, both in a historical and theoretical sense, especially in regard to the problem of its functional conventions. In Chapter 7, after the intervening interpretive materials, the genre is discussed again, but this time not as an entity unto itself, but rather as part of the literary system of medieval China. While Chapter 2 will be of interest to students of both theory and Chinese literature, the last chapter, along with the Bibliographic Note, will be most useful for those interested in the literary history of the genre.

The four central interpretive chapters, which are readings of different *yuefu* poems, form the illustration of the central thesis of the study presented in Chapter 2. Ignoring Culler's warning against confusing semiotics with interpretation, these are dual readings that describe the structure of the intratextual system under discussion as well as explore the "significance" of the work itself.[20] While each of the four chapters forms a self-contained unit and can be read as such (after reading Chapter 2), there are also a number of cross references throughout the chapters, which form a type of intratextuality of their own. Chapter 3 begins the interpretive readings with a discussion of thematic signatures in one relatively small set of poems, while Chapter 4 concentrates on four pre-Tang *yuefu* poets and their different relationships to genre: Cao Zhi, Lu Ji, Xiao Gang, and Bao Zhao. Chapter 5 explores the web of intratextuality in a large set of poems whose internal coherence is always on the verge of dissolving into wider areas of intertexuality. In Chapter 6, I speculate on how the radical poetics of

Li Bo made him the most productive and powerful *yuefu* poet in the tradition. Furthermore, I argue that Li's intense engagement of the intratextuality of the genre not only brought *yuefu* poetry to new heights, but also exhausted the genre, leaving only ashes in which later poets could rummage.

In these central chapters there is a general progression of arguments as I move from the relatively naive to more sophisticated forms of intratextuality, which means the critical probes in each chapter are progressively deeper and more daring. Since each essay focuses on a different type and different stage of intratextuality, not only is the poetry under discussion quite distinct, but the presentation of the material differs as well. Each chapter is intended to mirror, as well as discuss, the type of intratextuality that is its topic.

Note: Except for established usage with personal names, and where it is critical to the arguments, I transliterate all Chinese words into standard modern pronunciations. I use *pinyin* romanization throughout, including transcribing quotations from Western sources that use other romanization systems (but of course not in the titles of published works). Where I give Middle Chinese (Tang) pronunciations, they are marked with an asterisk; I follow Bernhard Karlgren's *Grammata Serica Recensa* reconstructions with some orthographic changes for convenience. Life and other period dates are given only on first citation; Chinese graphs for names and terms appearing in the study are found in the Glossary and Works Cited. A list of abbreviations used in the text can be found at the head of the Works Cited.

1

Patterns: Textuality in Chinese Culture

The continuous depth and breadth of the Chinese literary tradition assures a nearly chronic intertextuality to all its poetry. This is so between the Han and Tang dynasties, but is also true before, and even more so after, those ten core centuries. Of course, Chinese literature and culture do not form an unchanging monolith as is sometimes claimed; yet if one were to compare the disruption, change, and variation that occurred between classical Greece and Romantic Europe with that between the analogous Zhou dynasty and late imperial China, then one could understand how the "myth" of monolithic China, one perpetuated by the Chinese and accepted by the West, came to be. By European standards China does appear unified and enduring over the centuries.

The political and cultural continuity of China is best evident in, and largely accounted for by, its cohesive linguistic-literary tradition. While the legacy of classical Greece underwent a number of "translations" (both literal and figurative), first into Latin and then into the various vernacular languages of Renaissance Europe, culture in China was nearly always embedded in the same classical language, which required no "translation" for the literate elite of China for nearly two thousand years.[1] Even today anyone who can read Chinese, either thoroughly or marginally, shares a basic identity with the foundations of Chinese culture. Modern Chinese spoken language has evolved far from its classical sources, but the script it uses to transcribe that language has remained stable for centuries. Since that script makes phonetic and semantic distinctions on a level higher than that of an alphabet or syllabary (i.e., at what John DeFrancis calls the "morpho-syllabic" level),[2] even minimum literacy seems to allow one to share directly in the classical tradition. For example, it is not unusual to see the barely literate tourist (either Chinese or foreign) poring over Han dynasty bamboo strips or Tang stone inscriptions for graphs he can "read." He recognizes the words; whether or not he actually understands them in context is quite another question. At the same time, speakers of mutually unintelligible Chinese dialects are able to communicate through the written language that their dialects share. This script is therefore the cultural cloth that unites China both vertically with its tradition and its future, and horizontally with its furthest geographic and cultural reaches.

In pre-modern Chinese society that diachronic and synchronic web of language was strongest within the scholar-official elite, for whom the script was the very vehicle to a successful public career; attaining a position in the imperial bureaucracy depended on a thorough under-standing of the written language and a total absorption of the literary tradition. Nothing mattered so much in this training as the ability to actively reproduce, spontaneously and without reference, the major literary works. By the age of fifteen a young man on his way to an official career would have been expected to have memorized seven major texts totaling 431,286 graphs.[3] The goal of this memorization was the active command of any passage from those texts, so that it could be produced orally and graphically on command. Chinese scholars were not only veritable walking books, they were the same books, and the books remained relatively limited and unchanged for nearly a millen-nium and a half. Thus, those who aspired to such positions not only had to know the literature, they had to write so others knew they knew, and this knowing was the entry card into this elite club of the scholar-offi-cial.[4]

Script and Myth

The mythological foundations of Chinese culture are by definition interwoven with its script system, and that script in turn has been integral to the continuity of its mythology, including recent reconstructions by modern mythologists.[5] The script functions both as the vessel and the contents of Chinese myth—any consideration given to the origins of the script was necessarily immersed in the legacy of the myth itself. Only later, when the myth and script could be contemplated in another script/thought system—first Sanskrit, but more importantly in the alphabetic languages of modern Europe—could the vessel and its contents be separated.

While the history of Chinese script is relatively short compared to those of the ancient Near East, with irrefutable evidence dating it to the middle of the second millennium B.C., it is the only ancient writing system that has remained essentially intact up into modern times. In the twentieth century, archaeological discoveries have brought to light much more information about the actual beginnings of Chinese script; yet the mythological explanations and the archaeological evidence agree that this script is essentially, if not uniquely, Chinese.[6] Since my purpose here is to describe the function of language in patterns of intertextuality, the mythological trappings of the script are "truer" than the scientific data. While philology and linguistics more accurately describe the phonological, syntactical, and denotative structures of the language, they tell us little of the symbolic import the script had for those immersed in it. Here mythology is the better source.

The Chinese myth of the origins of their script affirms the close identity between the Chinese people and their literary heritage: to be Chinese meant to participate directly or indirectly in that script system, and perhaps vice-versa. Throughout the history of Chinese civilization, literacy has been the mark of acceptance into the Chinese world, from the individual visitor to the conquering nation, from Matteo Ricci to the Manchu rulers. This identification is operative even today, since language is the primary factor differentiating ethnic groups within China. That identification was and is especially associated with script, rather than with spoken language. In many ways one might say that China, as a cultural entity, is essentially a script system. Geographic, political, racial, and historical considerations are secondary to that identification with its written language.

The commonly recounted myth of the origins of Chinese writing identifies this script with visual manifestations of the natural world, including patterned markings *(wen)*:

> When in early antiquity Bao Xi ruled the world, he looked upward and contemplated the images *[xiang]* in the heavens, he looked downward and contemplated the shapes *[fa]* on earth. He contemplated the patterns *[wen]* on birds and beasts and their adaptations to the regions. He proceeded directly from himself and indirectly from objects. Thus he invented the eight trigrams in order to enter into connection with the virtues of the light of the gods and to regulate the conditions of all beings.[7]

Here is the beginning of Chinese script as known by the pre-modern tradition, and it is significant that what is first produced from this discovery of "meaningful traces" is not language *per se*, but rather oracular signs, which in turn lead to script. *Wen*, these signs turned script, soon comes to stand for "literature" and even "culture," leading quickly to a cosmologically laden concept. James J. Y. Liu, in his lengthy discussion of various nuances of the term *wen*, translates the following passage from Liu Xie's (465–520) *Wenxin diaolong*. The translator covers the polysemic text by including the different possible meanings in brackets, in addition to several notes (which I have deleted):

> The power of *wen* [configurations/culture/literature] is great indeed! It was born together with heaven and earth. How so? [At first] the dark [i.e., heaven] and the brown [i.e., earth] interspersed their colors; [then] the square [i.e., earth] and the round [i.e., heaven] separated their bodies; the sun and moon, twin jade discs, suspended their signs attached to heaven; the mountains and rivers, shining like fine silk, spread their orderly arrangements over the earth—these are really the *wen* [configurations/embellishments] of the Dao. Looking up, one might contemplate that which emitted lights, and bending down, observe that which contained compositions *[zhang]* within. When the high [i.e., heaven] and the low [i.e.,

earth] each had its position fixed, the Two Forms *[Liangyi]* were born. Man alone made a third, being the concentration of natural spiritual power *[xingling]*. These are called the Trinity. [Man] is the finest essence of the Five Agents, and truly the mind of heaven and earth. When mind was born, then language was established; when language was established, then *wen* [literature/patterns] shone forth. This is a natural principle *[dao]*.[8]

Mythologically, *wen* seeks to capture the "orderly" cosmos within its own form, and that form is literature. One might even say that *wen* is itself the cosmos, not a sign in place of something else, but a sign that is the very thing to which it refers. Stephen Owen has referred to the Chinese text as an "omen of the world"—a manifestation of reality, diminished and metonymic, but wholly as significant as the world itself.[9] And this sign/script is not just literature in a general sense, but also in the individual, specific, even minor writings of the literate person.

Of the terms that evolved to mean "literature" in Chinese, after *wen*, the next most common and most persistent is the disyllabic compound *wenxue*, which James J. Y. Liu glosses as "literary learning."[10] While the term *xue* commonly means "to learn," originally it meant "to study," or better "to emulate/imitate" *[xiao]*. This last meaning is particularly pertinent to our purposes here, for from it we can understand *wenxue* as a transformation of the *xue wen* ("to study/emulate/imitate *wen*"), yielding "studies of *wen*" or "*wen* emulations/imitations."[11] In this way *wenxue* would be emulations of "significant traces," traces of nature or of another person (i.e., his writing), which ultimately lead back to those natural patterns. This is foreshadowed by another part of the myth that surrounds the origins of writing, which says:

> Heaven creates divine things; the holy sage takes them as models *[ze]*. Heaven and earth change and transform; the holy sage imitates *[xiao]* them. In the heavens hang images that reveal good fortune and misfortune; the holy sage reproduces these. The Yellow River brought forth a map and the Lo River brought forth a writing *[shu]*; the holy men took these as models.[12]

Just as the sage of antiquity imitated models for his *wen*, including those primal texts (the Yellow River map and the Lo River writing), the traditional poet would turn to *wen* for his model to imitate, giving us *wenxue*. The models available to mere mortals are not those of the cosmos but those of literature, *wenxue*; thus, in China literature is essentially a type of textual imitation.

The Chinese literati did not wander the countryside observing the *wen* of the sky and earth as they prepared for their exams. In their day-to-day lives, literature was a much more mundane affair; they were always reading. In the best of times this was a rich and rewarding life, as literature in its broadest sweep became the object of their affection as well as their ambition. Yet, in its extreme forms, when the world seemed to be an uninterrupted series of texts to be memorized, preparation for those careers could ruin the candidates physically, economically, and mentally. Learning then became a burden.

The Script in History

The task of the degree candidate in traditional China was intensified by the continuity of the written record with which he was expected to become familiar. The only major hiatus in the history of this inscripted continuity was during the transitional but formative period of Qin and early Han rule. While the Qin unified the script, and the Han standardized it into the form still used today, this period and these actions also mark a moment of substantial textual disruption. The infamous Qin "book burning" of 213 B.C., which destroyed a substantial amount of the historiographic and literary manuscripts of the time, merely exacerbated the already difficult transition and translation of pre-Qin texts into the unified, then standardized, script. The subsequent burning and looting of the Qin capital by Xiang Yu (d. 202 B.C.) at the end of the dynasty worsened the situation by damaging the imperial library holdings themselves. This all led to the loss of several major texts and the rise of the "old text" *(guwen)* vs. "new text" *(jinwen)* controversy, a controversy that plagued the intellectual and political community of Han China, and remained an active literary debate up until modern times. Yet even that hiatus is a only a matter of few decades; there was still a fundamental continuity through the script reform.[13]

The four centuries that separate the Han from the Tang were a time when the Central Plain was filled with conflict and strife, resulting in the north-south division of China and much disruption to its literary heritage. Of the changes in the intellectual world of this time, most important was the full establishment of Buddhism in China proper. The coming of Buddhism not only gave the Chinese world a new set of philosophic assumptions, it also introduced the new perspective of Sanskrit language and linguistics, which allowed the Chinese a deeper cognizance of the nature of their own language and its role in literature. Yet, in the end, Sanskrit would be accommodated to literary Chinese in the great translation projects of the Tang.

The introduction of Buddhism into China accompanied the loss of political control of the northern plain to non-Chinese peoples during the Six Dynasties period. In A.D. 311, Central Asian Toba armies lay siege to the capital of the Jin dynasty in Luoyang. The sacking of the city and the ensuing flight of Chinese nobility to southern China not only left the northern plain in the hands of the "mutton-stinking barbarians" but also spelled doom for major imperial and private art collections. This resulted in massive losses of cultural objects, including manuscripts. Once ensconced in the southern city of Jiankang (modern Nanking), the Chinese retreated into an elitist culture, which sustained and was sustained by a rich and refined literary milieu. Holding the non-Chinese armies tenuously at bay, the southern nobility rebuilt and greatly expanded their bibliographic collections. In the middle of the sixth century, the then-empowered southern Liang dynasty boasted huge imperial and private libraries, around which influential literary salons revolved. Then came devastation with the fall of Jiankang.

In a desperate struggle against Hou Jing, northern rebel turned southern invader, ineffectual and factional forces under Prince Xiao Gang (502–557) (soon to be Emperor Jianwen of the Liang) were forced to torch the huge library of the late Crown Prince Zhaoming (Xiao Tong, 501–531). John Marney summarizes and reflects on the official account of Xiao Gang's actions in the Liang capital on that day:

The barbarity of the campaign [by rebel Hou Jing] was best impressed upon the historian's literati audience by the report that a man of Xiao Gang's sensibilities could be driven to incinerate the East Palace library. When he first moved into the East Palace some twenty years previously, Xiao Gang inherited Crown Prince Zhaoming's library of thirty thousand folios. On December 10, 548, Hou Jing invested the East Palace, which gave him a clear field of fire into the imperial palace. That night, while Hou Jing and his men were drinking and carousing with the palace women they had captured, Xiao Gang sent a task force to burn down the palace. The *Tai dian* (Dais Hall) and the entire library of several hundred cases were destroyed. One source compares this calamity to the notorious "burning of the books" by the first emperor of the Qin (Qin Shi Huangdi, r. 221–210 B.C.): "Previously Jianwen [Xiao Gang] dreamed that someone painted a portrait of the first emperor of the Qin, saying, 'This one will again burn the books.' This came to pass." [14]

Here is recounted the loss of the very library upon which compilation of the most important anthology in Chinese literature, the *Wen xuan*, was based. In a tradition marked by flourishing art patronage, the irony of one of the greatest Chinese bibliophiles ordering what has been compared to the Qin book burning and more recently called "the fifth and last great 'bibliothecal catastrophe'" in China is chilling.[15] Yet the resilience of the literary heritage that this collection represented is attested to by the recollection and cataloging of the Sui imperial library one hundred years later. Even though the entry notes in that bibliography of 5,178 titles suggest the loss incurred from Xiao Gang's decision, in the face of such destructive forces the continuity of this literary tradition is all the more telling.[16]

The literary activity of the South obviously maintained, in fact entrenched and intensified, the literary language. Yet even in the North, Chinese language was the mainstay of official and literary activities; non-Chinese languages remained largely unscripted. Thus while there was a great deal of social upheaval between the Han and Tang periods, that upheaval did not disrupt the basic linguistic and literary continuity of China. Indeed, even more than the way Latin in the European Middle Ages bound the diverse communities to each other and to Rome, the

Chinese literary language tied the most divergent, even non-Chinese, states to each other and to the Han by its shared written language and literary culture.

Where the analogy between the European and the Chinese Middle Ages most clearly breaks down is that China had no late medieval Dante to offer a new linguistic alternative for literature: China had its "Latin" but not its equivalent to Italian. Consequently there was no "anxiety of linguistic mutability," which might result from a new language challenging the permanence of literary culture; there was no linguistic intrusion to shake the foundations of the late medieval continuity in China.[17] Instead, when China entered its Renaissance in the Tang, it wholeheartedly reaffirmed the classical language, in the end turning to a conservative neo-classicism (i.e., *fugu* and its *guwen* movement).

Certainly the lexicographic and hermeneutic activities that fill the Han-Tang period suggest some sense of change in the linguistic tradition, but that change was not as intense as that which confronted the early Renaissance poets in Europe, such as Petrarch. In Europe the new science of philology brought increased awareness of the mutability of language and the problem of historical knowledge, causing particular problems for the humanistic trends of the age. As Thomas Greene suggests for the European experience: "If a remote text is composed in a language for which the present supplies only a treacherous glossary, and if it is grounded in a lost concrete specificity never fully recoverable, then the tasks of reading, editing, commenting, translating, and imitating become intricately problematized—and these were the tasks that preoccupied the [European Renaissance] humanists."[18] The concern of the Chinese lexicographers of the late medieval period lay more in the phonetic mutability of the language rather than its loss of meaning. The Chinese lexicographer, and even more so the Chinese literary encyclopedist, was a collector of cumulative meaning rather than an arbitrator of an exclusive, "true" meaning; their work suggested that meaning did not change but rather expanded. New meanings did not replace older ones, but rather formed polysemiotic layers.[19]

In China there is a sense of "straying" from the original language, but there is not a sense of "fall" or "loss" as there was in the European Renaissance with its Judeo-Christian underpinnings. The Chinese tower of language is not one of Babelian confusion. Thus, the intensity of feeling behind the need to reaffirm the past is qualitatively different in these two traditions. In China we see a need for affirmation, corrective adjustments, a "return" to the past, rather than the leaps upward of the post-lapsarian West, or the literary excavations needed in archaeologically minded Europe. For the Chinese Renaissance poet there was a relative ease in establishing connections with the classical past. This was seen in the simple appropriation, often through the medium of such texts as the *Wen xuan* and the literary encyclopedias *(lei shu)*, of literary material from the Han and earlier. The poet in the Tang was much enriched and complicated by these Middle Ages, but he was still fundamentally, consciously and unconsciously, connected to the Han. The Tang literati referred to themselves as "men of Han," and they did so in a written language completely shared by the actual men of the Han, and one that led them directly to classical Zhou China and to their mythological past.

Imitative Poetics in the *Wen xuan*

The sixth-century anthology the *Wen xuan* represents the most important intertextual moment in the pre-Tang literary world of China.[20] This collection of 731 poetic and prose works defines and concretizes the entire early medieval tradition, such that those writers of the Tang regarded this collection as the "textbook" for their degrees in literary scholarship. They wrote both consciously and unconsciously in reconfigurations of those texts; it was and is the canon of *belles lettres* of early China, which paralleled the orthodox Confucian canon of pre-Han poetic, philosophic, and historiographic writing. The *Wen xuan* was composed under the auspices of Xiao Tong (Prince Zhaoming of the Liang), and represents gleanings from the massive imperial library that Xiao Gang put to the torch in 548. The *Wen xuan* casts a heavy but unthreatening shadow over the earlier part of the tradition. While pre-modern poets would turn to their encyclopedia and rhyme tables to work out the details of their poetics, they would turn to the *Wen xuan* to study/emulate the larger workings of their literary art/patterns. This is especially so for the rhapsody *(fu)* and lyric *(shi)* selections.

Among the different types of lyric poems collected in the *Wen xuan* there is a large group that operates by a marked praxis of textual imitation, specifically the sixty-three *zani* (Miscellaneous Imitations) in chapters 30 and 31. Moreover, this group is surrounded by other types of poems that operate in similar imitative ways. A description of these imitative types will help put our discussion of *yuefu* intratextuality into better perspective. These types are usually identified by the use of a key term in the title indicating the exact type of textual relationship in which they are engaged.

1. Reply *(da)*: The "reply" poem is written in response to, or as what is sometimes called an echo of *(chou)*, another poet's work, often a specific poem. There are a number collected in the anthology, especially in the "Presentation and Response" *(zeng da)* subcategory (seventy-two poems in chapters 23–26) We often read these poems in isolation, but the original "presentation-response" context is certainly a better environment in which to appreciate them. In the *Wen xuan* we have that opportunity in two poems by the Xie cousins, Xie Huilian (394–430) and Xie Lingyun (385–433), that illustrate this type of poetic "correspondence." The following sections (first of five in each poem) suggest this relationship.

Ill Winds on Xiling Lake, Offered to Kangle

I planned to sail in the first month of spring
But in the second month I still haven't left
On the road I have a distant appointment to keep
My thoughts on parting bring uncontrollable longing
Bags packed, I wait for a favorable morning
On the bobbing boat I enjoy the auspicious moon
Gazing at the road ahead brings little comfort
But to turn back will bring unfulfilled longing

In Reply to Cousin Huilian

Sick in bed, I withdrew from the world
Without a trace into the cloudy peaks
Crags and gorges dazed my eyes and ears
Separated from the face and voice I hold dear
Forever severed from my heart's delight
Always worrying that I had no friends
At road's end I met my fine cousin
With a joyful face and full heart[21]

The interrelationship between such poems is relatively loose and topical—much in the vein of an exchange of letters. While each poem stands well by itself, read together they suggest deeper relationships.

2. Contra *(fan)*: The contra poem is a minor, but striking, "imitative" type, in which the response poem acts not as a reply to, but rather an argument against, its model. The one example in the *Wen xuan*, "Contra Recluse" by the obscure poet Wang Kangju (fl. 300), actually forms a "Contra" subcategory unto itself, closely associated with other "reclusive" subtypes. Our interest is not in the actual thematics here, but rather with its textual relationship with a "model." The "Recluse" poems, of which there are two in the *Wen xuan*, argue that it is better to retire into reclusion rather than to sacrifice one's moral principles (and often one's life) in the service to the state, but Wang's "contra" poem urges the recluse to "Come back home to times of peace / With all things forever equalized" (*WX* 22.1030–31). The most famous "contra" poem in the early tradition is Yang Xiong's (53–18 B.C.) "Contra-sao," which argues against the solution (suicide) that Qu Yuan found to his moral dilemma in the "Li sao." Qu Yuan's poem is collected in the *Wen xuan*, but Yang's controversial poetic response is not.

3. Matching *(he)*: This praxis, also called *tong*, is one in which a person writes a poem that matches the rhymes (and perhaps theme) of another. This interrelationship, actually a phonetic mirroring, is one that is lost in translation and partially lost in the diachronic phonetic

changes that occurred in the spoken language. Rhyme was ever-present in Chinese poetry and a great deal of energy was spent in the pursuit of it, including the compilation of extensive rhyme tables. While there is not a "Matching" category *per se* in the anthology, there are a number of poems designated as such in their titles, including four within the "Miscellaneous Imitations" by Xie Tiao (464–499), kin of the Xie cousins (*WX* 30.1410–18). Obviously the modeling in these cases, in which the specific poem is mentioned, is more determinative than in the "reply" poems, but it is not generally a thematic modeling.

4. Emulation *(xue . . . ti)*: Here we have an excellent example of how the term *xue* is used as "emulation" in the literary context. We find it in a title by Bao Zhao (405–466) among the "miscellaneous imitations" called "In Emulation of the Style of Liu Gonghan" ("Xue Liu Gonghan ti" [*WX* 31.1449]). The object of imitation here is, however, the *ti*, "style" (not a specific text), which also is found in the title to Jiang Yan's set of thirty "Poems in Miscellaneous Styles" ("Zati shi sanshi shou" [*WX* 31.1452–86]), all of which have a model poet/persona designated in the title to the individual poem. David Knechtges notes that "almost every poet who occupies a prominent place in the *Wen xuan* is represented in Jiang's imitations."[22]

5. Imitation *(ni* and *xiao)*: In the *Wen xuan* and elsewhere, *ni/xiao* is by far the most common type of "imitation," which is thematic, and either model or text-type specific. The two terms are both used and seem to have similar, if not identical, meanings. A common form of this usage in lyric poetry is with the *ni/xiao gu* designation, "imitation of an old theme,"[23] which might be a quite generalized imitation, as in Bao Zhao's three poems (*WX* 31.1446–49), or to be more specific, as in the two by Liu Shuo (431–453) (*WX* 31.1144–45)—we shall look at Lu Ji's examples of this later type in Chapter 4. Within this collection there are also specific imitations of other literati poems, such as Zhang Dai's (fl. 285) close paraphrase of Zhang Heng's (79–139) "Four Melancholies" ("Si chou"). First the model poem, which draws heavily on Han and pre-Han literary sources:

> Oh, the one I long to be with is on Tai Mountain
> I too would like to go along the Liangfu slopes
> Craning I gaze eastward, tears soak my writing brush
> The fair one presents me with a gold jade-carving knife
> How will I requite her with a precious piece of jade
> The road is long, no one will be able to make it so far
> So why do I cling to such sorrow, my tormented heart

WX 29.1357

This poem is the first in a set of four very similar ones, all of which pursue similar themes and use the identical prosody and structure. The Zhang Dai imitation included in the *Wen xuan* is also one of four (the last), and is thematically and structurally identical with both its models and its set.

Imitating the Four Melancholies

> Oh, the one I long to be with is in Rong Zhou
> I too would like to go along the dangerous road
> Climbing the cliff I gaze afar, sobbing tears flow
> The longing I feel causes wounds in my heart
> The fine one leaves for me a green-silken lute
> How will I requite her with two gold pieces
> I would follow the flowing waves, to vault the depths
> But in the end no one will be able to sing forever

WX 30.1431

This *ni/xiao* designation does not appear to extend beyond text models to the emulation of personal styles, however—at least not without the *ti* designation.

6. Substituting *(dai)*: This is a designation that appears only once in the *Wen xuan* but is more prevalent in other contemporaneous sources. It occurs in the formula "Substituting for [title]" and seems to

be entirely text-specific. Thus, it shares territory with *ni/xiao*, but *dai* is restricted to anonymous titles, at least in its early usage. The example in the *Wen xuan* is Bao Zhao's "Substitution" for the title "The Lord is Longing for Someone" ("Dai Junzi you suosi" [*WX* 31.1450]), which now occurs earliest as a title by Lu Ji (*WX* 28.1302), but there is assumed a lost model for both of them. This type of "substitution" is particularly interesting to us because it often occurs with those titles now identified as *yuefu* poems, as it does with this poem by Bao Zhao. This association of the *dai* designation and *yuefu* poetry may be related to the supposed musicality of the poetry, which is one topic of discussion in the next chapter. Perhaps *dai* originally meant "in the melody of. . . ," but, as we shall see, it might be better understood as "in the voice of . . . ." In other sources we see the extensive use of this term with the *yuefu* titles, and its usage seems to alternate with the following imitative type.[24]

7. Entitled: There are many poems in the *Wen xuan* that participate in imitative relationships without clearly indicating that relationship, but there is one type of designation that is either entirely transparent or totally obscured, depending on the reader's working knowledge of the tradition. This occurs when one poem takes the title, or a derivation of it, from an earlier one. In the *Wen xuan* these are found under the *yuefu* heading where are collected three anonymous poems, and thirty-seven literati poems with titles that are largely identifiable as derived from other sources. In the following chapters we shall consider the complexities of the textual relationships manifested in those poems, which are sometimes strictly imitative, but are, in any event, always intratextual.

Influence and Anxiety in Post-Tang Poetry

In the pervasive literariness of life in early medieval China, any literary effort, from the schoolroom poetry contests to the imperially commissioned rhapsody, depended on an actual and potential interrelationship with previous and future literature. The *Wen xuan* imitative types reviewed above are concrete examples of that interrelationship. While the basic literary canon was described by a restricted numbers of books, the further the literati moved up the ladder of bureaucratic-literary success, the wider their range was expected to be. The growing presence of the literary encyclopedia during the Tang-Song period was a manifestation of that expected range. The possible conflict here between imitation and inspiration, especially as the writer moved into maturity in search of a poetic voice, is obvious. While the demand for imitative and intertextual writing in classical China was paramount, there also was, especially after the Tang, another need to free oneself of the influence of the tradition. Viewed in the context of world literature, this drive for inspiration may strike us as relatively weak in the pre-modern Chinese literary tradition, but in its own context that drive takes on relative strength in the post-Tang period. This manifests itself in a number of ways, including statements by major poets themselves. When the late Tang poet Li Shangyin (813?–838) claims his freedom from such interdependency, we recognize the burden of the tradition in his disclaimer:

> At first, when I heard my elders say that in learning the Dao one must seek it from the ancients and in composing literature one must follow rules, I felt greatly unhappy. Then I withdrew and thought to myself: How can what we call the Dao be something that only the ancients called the Duke of Zhou and Confucius were really capable of? For, inferior as I am, I can personally partake in it together with the Duke of Zhou and Confucius. Therefore I have tried to practice the Dao without depending on the moderns or the ancients, and in writing I have directly wielded my brush, being loathe to plagiarize the Scriptures or the histories, or to avoid what may cause offense to the contemporary world.[25]

The self-reflective anxiety that informs this statement might be seen as a sign of the passing of the Chinese Renaissance and the coming of a new self-consciousness and self-doubt that characterize the latter half of the Chinese poetic tradition. At the risk of blatant reductivity, one could suggest that Chinese classical poetry *(shi)* divides itself into two basic periods, falling on either side of the great High Tang poet Du Fu (712–770), whose position and influence is preeminent in the literary tradition.[26]

The millennium of Chinese poetry that preceded Du Fu took its point of reference from the Zhou and Han literary legacy, centered especially on the poetry and persona of Qu Yuan. This pre–Du Fu literary relationship to the past was generally anxiety-free, similar to the relationship seen in pre-Romantic Europe, and I would suggest that it was anxiety-free for quite the same reasons. In the West, the poets of the Middle Ages affirmed their continuity with the classical culture, while Renaissance poets, recognizing their isolation from the past, turned their art to the task of bridging that gap and integrating classical culture into their work. In its general pattern, this description also works well for Chinese poets and their relationships with the literary heritage of China. Because of the uniformity in the Chinese linguistic tradition, the nature of that continuity with and isolation from the past during the Six Dynasties and Tang was qualitatively different from that in Europe. But in a larger sense, the social disruptions of the Six Dynasties did isolate the Tang from their avowed cultural model, the Han, and there was a similar robust reaching back to that period by the Tang Renaissance poets.

Du Fu was the epitome of this warm embrace of the past by the Tang, and the convergence of the tradition in the work of Du Fu changed the perspective on the literary past for those who followed. From that point on, one could not simply look directly to the classical heritage; instead, one also had to view it through the filter of Du Fu's poetry— poets after Du Fu lived in the shadow of his famous line "I have read to tatters ten thousand books."[27] In this way Du Fu holds a position in the literary tradition of China similar to that held by Shakespeare or Milton in the English. W. Jackson Bate has described a post-Restoration anxiety, the burden of the Elizabethan-Jacobean past that could paralyze the Romantic poet, such that Keats felt that "there was nothing original to be written in poetry; that its riches were already exhausted."[28] Goethe, on the other hand, shunned Shakespeare, who had "already exhausted the whole depth of human nature," taking refuge in his German heritage: "But had I been born an Englishman, and had those manifold masterworks [of Shakespeare] pressed in upon me with all their power from my first youthful awakening, it would have overwhelmed me, and I would not have known what I wanted to do!"[29] In his essay on the anxiety of influence, Harold Bloom argues, however, that in the English tradition it is Milton, not Shakespeare, who was the focus of the belated poet's obsessive attention. This is because Shakespeare is too strong for the later poet to engage; he is universal in vision and scope. Milton is, on the other hand, more threatening because he is humanly closer to the aspiring poet. Bloom says: "If one examines the dozen or so major poetic influences before this century, one discovers quickly who among them ranks as the great Inhibitor, the Sphinx who strangles even strong imaginations in their cradles: Milton. The motto to English poetry since Milton was stated by Keats, 'Life to him would be death to me.'"[30]

Whether Du Fu was a Shakespeare or a Milton is difficult to say, and one suspects that he lies somewhere between them, especially given the simultaneous universality and provinciality of the early Chinese literary tradition. It was both all and the only literature known—where would Du Fu's Goethe be? In any event, the post–Du Fu poet in China gradually became conscious of the problem of being compared to Du Fu, much more than were pre-Du Fu poets anxious of a similar comparison with their models. The anxiety of those writers who felt not so much isolated as belated, an anxiety that grew to immense proportions in the movement from Romanticism to Modernism in the West, also fills the later stages of the development of Chinese poetry. Stuart Sargent's essay on the sense of poetic belatedness in Northern Song poets designates Du Fu as the source of this feeling: he calls Du Fu the "First Poet," whose language approached an "original language" *(wen)* toward which the belated poets must strive.[31] Huang Tingjian, who embraced textual imitation as poetic praxis, clearly delineates the length and cumulative heaviness of Du Fu's poetic shadow:

> When Du Fu wrote poetry and Han Yu wrote prose, there was not a single word that did not have an origin in some place; now later men have not done much reading and so say Han and Du made up these phrases themselves. Those who wrote in the old days were truly able to mold ten thousand things; even though they selected stale words of the ancients, once they applied brush and ink, it was just like a grain of elixir of immortality changing iron into gold.[32]

Huang's alchemical metaphor is one of the most common ways in Chinese critical writing of describing that mysterious regenerative process that the master hand has with the worn language—in the West we find an analogous apian metaphor, where the bee gathers nectar from the various flowers (models) and blends it into honey (creative imitation).

In both the West and China the "anxiety" caused by these new, post-classical models is in part due to the proximity of the model, both chronologically and culturally. As Bate suggests for the early Romantic poets of Europe:

> For us now, looking back on the last four centuries as a whole, the central interest on the eighteenth century is that it is the first period in modern history to face the problem of what it means to come *immediately* after a great creative achievement. It was first to face what it means to have already achieved some of the ends to which the modern (that is, the Renaissance) spirit had at the beginning aspired.[33]

The poets of the Song dynasty certainly felt a similar proximity of the Tang achievement in all their *shi* poetry (which may partially account for the popularity of the new, relatively shadow-free *ci* poetry), which leads Sargent to note: "This means that a poet who comes after Du Fu is faced with the task of approximating an original language which is not lost, not an abstract concept, but present in a corpus of real poems. How can one approach the same level of universality without simply repeating the lines of the Universal poet?"[34] This is not to say that this is the first moment of such an anxiety of influence in the Chinese tradition, nor that the Song was paralyzed by the Tang achievement. Jonathan Chaves has argued well for a more balanced assessment of Song poetics, one that acknowledges the "fusion of the two sources of influence: the world, and previous poetry," and he dismisses the presence of Bloomian anxiety in Song poetics.[35] Yet much of the evidence that Chaves cites, in which poets *insist* on the inspiration of the world, actually betrays the beginning of a true anxiety over the "self" and "creation." In these poet-critics' warnings against the poetic praxis of textual imitation we find the most basic Bloomian swerve. Thus, Wang Ruoxu (1174–1243), claimed that "each plagiarizes from the preceding [poet]; this is the major flaw in their poetry!"[36] Yang Wanli's (1127–1206) insistence on nontextual inspiration was more reasoned, yet it was nonetheless a similar swerve:

> As for "echoing," what contact [with the world] is there? Who is moved [by this contact]? Who writes on the theme? It is entirely a matter of someone else [i.e., the impetus to write comes entirely from the work of another poet]. When the poem comes from heaven [or naturalness] one respects the commentaries of heaven [what is natural]. When it is concentrated in oneself, one respects the "restraining bowstring" of the self. But in the present case [of echoing another's poem] one is in the control of another person pure and simple.[37]

This statement is certainly filled with anxiety of influence, and must be seen as a retreat into the self, where the poet asserts poetic separateness from the tradition, especially through radical use of the language. A similar defensive posture can be detected in the unusual lines by Shi Yannian (994–1041), "Grassblades bend their golden hooks, / The green not yet returned," which Chaves has offered as evidence of "inspired experience." Certainly Chaves is correct in this identification (assuming the background anecdote is accurate), but his suggestion that there is no anxiety here because "at no point in this process [of composition] is Shi said to agonize over previous poets' treatment of grassblades" is somewhat misleading.[38] If Chaves has himself considered the lines against "previous poets' treatments of grassblades," certainly we should assume Shi did the same, even if unconsciously. That the anecdote does not mention this agonizing is hardly evidence that the process did not include it.

Thus, the mere insistence on at least equal time for experiential inspiration is in itself an affirmation, rather than a denial, of anxiety. Stephen Owen has suggested that "the Song was no less emotional and intense than the Tang, but the Song writers felt ill at ease with their intensities. They were no less impelled by forces which are the common fate of the species, but they were conscious of being impelled and yearned desperately for an attitude through which they could rise above those forces."[39] Preeminent among those forces was the shadow of the literary tradition, and one way they tried to rise above its influence was to insist on inspiration from personal experience, not textual imitation. Chaves' conclusion that this poetic stance is a return to the pre-Tang poetics (as first seen in *The Mao Preface* and the *Wenxin diaolong)* is further confirmation that their anxiety was identified with the immediate Tang past, and not with the classical heritage. Through the subsequent centuries this focus slowly changes as the poets become more separated from the Tang achievement, such that the neoclassical *(fugu)* movement of the fifteenth and sixteenth centuries took the High Tang, especially Du Fu, as its model.[40]

The continuity that binds the Chinese literary tradition leads easily to intertextual and imitative poetics. In the earlier part of that tradition those relationships were less anxiety-ridden than those practiced by the post–Du Fu poets. While there is an assumed self-consciousness in textual imitation but little or none in intertextuality, intratextuality can be either unconscious (nearly inadvertent) or filled with device and self-reflection. The more extreme, more studied of these relationships are what we find in the High Tang and Song periods, but their origins lie earlier in the Middle Ages of Chinese literary history, where true intratextuality began. Below I shall argue that the *yuefu* genre was generated out of a relative anxiety-free intratextuality of the pre-Tang period, but that the anthology that defined the genre was a retroactive formation that was informed by the more complex and anxious intertextual relationships of the Song period.

2

Materials: The Genre Defined and Redefined

The origins and organization of the Music Bureau *(yuefu)*, a Han imperial institution, are relatively clear and have been the concern of a number of literary studies. The poetry that shares this name, *yuefu shi*, or Music Bureau poetry, is a particularly complex genre whose nature, on the other hand, has been usually dismissed with conventional taxonomies. These taxonomies have themselves become more the focus of attention than the poetry, which has been neglected or been read outside its generic context. This has been true at least since the eleventh century and continues in most modern studies.[1] This endemic distraction from the central issues of the genre in studies of *yuefu* poetry has arisen because those issues have been obscured by historical accident and tautological arguments. Before discussing the problems with the common interpretations of this genre, let me first outline how it is conventionally understood in both China and the West. Hans Frankel's essay "Yüeh-fu Poetry" most succinctly summarizes this type of study of the genre, but in this he follows several Chinese sources, especially Luo Genze's *Yuefu wenxue shi (History of Yuefu Literature)*. Here and elsewhere I draw heavily from both Frankel and Luo.

By all historical accounts the Music Bureau was an important Han institution, by almost all accounts it was a Han invention, and by most accounts it was the brainchild of Emperor Wu of the Han (ca. 115 B.C.). Whether or not Emperor Wu actually established the Bureau has been the topic of lengthy discussion in conventional, especially Chinese, studies. That issue revolves around two conflicting passages in the historical records.[2] This textual problem, coupled with the flamboyant personality of Emperor Wu, has kept many literary studies centered on that issue. These discussions might be useful to the institutional historian, but they are hardly pressing for the literary critic, or even the literary historian. Let us just say here (following Luo Genze, Yu Guanying, and Jean-Pierre Diény) that Emperor Wu was instrumental in expanding the scope of the Music Bureau, if not responsible for its inception, and that his name has been consistently associated with the Bureau and its activities, which, not incidentally, has lent considerable weight to all considerations of the institution. It is probably safe to say that the Music Bureau as we now conceive of it was a product of Emperor Wu's personal initiative.

Once we have deferred the question of origins of the Music Bureau to others, we can move on to the question of the functions of the Bureau, and more specifically how they relate to the literary history of the genre. Here we have a general agreement of the historical sources and their studies. As commonly described, the activities of Music Bureau in the Han were twofold: (1) to collect and compose music by imperial command; and (2) to perform that music at certain court functions, both ritual and social. Emperor Wu's contribution to the development of these activities is generally acknowledged to have been considerable. This is assumed to be especially so in regard to the collection of music, which is highlighted in several passages from contemporaneous or near-contemporaneous sources.[3] During the Han period, Chinese music had undergone severe disruption in the transition to an imperial state. This disruption was compounded by the apparent lack of musical scores —unlike its literature, China's early music was transmitted outside of the scripted culture and its inherent ephemerality was easy victim to the passage of time. Historical sources indicate there was a concerted effort during the Han to recover the lost music, or to find a viable substitute. Under these conditions there arose the "new music" *(xin sheng)*, which was imported from the West (i.e., Central Asia) as a byproduct of Han expansionist policies.[4] Diény has been especially perceptive in explaining Wu's role in the promotion of this new music, with all its unorthodox associations. Thus, while there was a strict ritual aspect to the Bureau, from its conceptual origins it also had certain popular connotations. These connotations were strong enough to cause the abolishment of the Bureau in 7 B.C. by a particularly conservative Emperor, who declared upon taking the throne: "The music of the state of Zheng was licentious and destroyed the proper music, thus the sage kings shunned it. I shall therefore abolish the Music Bureau."[5] Whether because of these associations or for more mundane reasons, the texts that we have from the period of the Music Bureau's actual existence are all of the ritual type.[6] Even though that is true, the Bureau's popular associations are still more often the focus of attention in the secondary literature.

Thus, the history and textual legacy of the Music Bureau in the Han is relatively short, if not unexciting, and seemingly not the candidate for lengthy literary discussions. Yet the nominal legacy of the Han Music Bureau extends for at least a millennium after its abolishment, and it is that legacy that represents the bulk of material under consideration here. Down through the centuries a large corpus of poems became associated with the name of the Music Bureau. That corpus and its patterns of association with the Bureau reached a definitive shape in the eleventh century anthology *Yuefu shiji (Collected Music Bureau Poems)* by Guo Maoqian (fl. 1085).[7] We shall return to consider in more detail the nature and inherent problems of Guo's work, but for the time being let us take it, as do nearly all studies of *yuefu* poetry, as the authoritative voice on the configurations of the genre.

Guo Maoqian organizes his corpus of some fifty-five hundred poems under twelve categories—listed here with a simple translation/gloss and, as an indication of the size of the group, the chapters that they occupy in the *Yuefu shiji*:

1. *Jiaomiao ge ci*, lyrics for ritual songs, 1–12
2. *Yanshe ge ci*, lyrics for banquet songs, 13–15
3. *Guchui qu ci*, lyrics to tunes for drum and winds, 16–20
4. *Hengchui qu ci*, lyrics to tunes for horizontal flute, 21–25

5. *Xianghe ge ci*, lyrics for songs with strings and bamboo winds, 26–43
6. *Qingshang qu ci*, lyrics for tunes in the *qingshang* key, 44–51
7. *Wuqu ge ci*, lyrics for songs with dance tunes, 52–56
8. *Qinqu ge ci*, lyrics for songs with lute tunes, 57–60
9. *Zaqu ge ci*, lyrics for songs with miscellaneous tunes, 61–78
10. *Jindai qu ci*, lyrics for recent tunes, 79–82
11. *Zageyao ci*, lyrics for miscellaneous songs and ditties, 83–89
12. *Xin yuefu ci*, lyrics for new Music Bureau poems, 90–100

Under each of these categories Guo has collected the appropriate poems, often using subcategories, both labeled and implicit. The twelve categories themselves have a long textual history starting in the Han, with various changes, expansions, and simplifications in the subsequent millennium. Most studies of the genre have focused on this classification system.[8] I shall have occasion to return to certain aspects of Guo's system below, but let me first note that the definitions of many of these types are confused by unclear terms and contexts. True, Guo introduces each section with extensive notes and citations, but his introductions are more cumulative than decisive, with conflicting or unrelated information given equal and uncriticized weight. One might be able to describe quite accurately the parameters of one of these designations at any given time, but to assume that that designation was diachronically stable is problematic, and to further assume that such an understanding unified the poems collected under its heading is patently fallacious. As a simple example, consider the *xianghe* category (certainly the most important in Guo Maoqian's typology). In his notes Guo suggests that the poems of this type were so designated because they (1) were put to the music of strings and pipes, bells and chimes *(xian guan jin shi)*, or silk strings and bamboo winds *(si zhu)*; (2) were ritual tunes *(diao)* that were the legacy of the Zhou, combined with tunes from the state of Chu; and (3) they were "popular songs of the streets and lanes of Han."[9] Obviously this is neither a structural nor a functional definition for the category as a whole, but rather an undiscriminated collection of momentary associations. The deficiencies of Guo Maoqian's typology have induced later critics to try to improve on it. Hans Frankel has, for example, extrapolated a listing that attempts to circumvent the inherent problems in Guo Maoqian's list, but still maintain the integrity of the *Yuefu shiji* collection:

First, *yuefu* referred to hymns (texts and tunes) composed at the [Han] Music Bureau for ritual purposes.

Second, the term included texts selected by the Music Bureau from works of known authors and provided with music at the Bureau, also used at state ceremonies.

Third, it meant anonymous songs collected by the Music Bureau from various parts of China (the Chu region was the richest source) and from abroad. Most of these already had tunes; for those that did not, music was composed at the Bureau.

Fourth, after the abolition of the Music Bureau in 6 B.C. (most of its functions were taken over by other government offices), the name *yuefu* continued to be applied to hymns and popular songs of the three categories just listed. The new song words were either fitted to existing tunes or created with new music; their titles were sometimes traditional, sometimes new. Hence there are four kinds in this category: (1) old titles, old tunes, new words; (2) old titles, new tunes, new words; (3) new titles, old tunes, new words; (4) new titles, new tunes, new words.

Fifth, numerous men of letters from the late Han times down to the modern period wrote poems in the style of anonymous *yuefu* poems. These imitations, which were not necessarily set to music, often bore the same titles as their anonymous models but were apt to differ considerably from their models in meter and content. Some literati rather than using traditional *yuefu* titles, created new titles for their *yuefu* poems. Such new titles were often taken from old *yuefu* texts.

Sixth, some Tang poets of the eighth and ninth century, such as Yuan Jie, Bo Juyi, and Yuan Zhen, used the term *xin yuefu* ("new *yuefu* poems") for their poems of social criticism. These were written, like some of the oldest *yuefu* poems, in lines of uneven length; otherwise they were rather different from earlier *yuefu* poetry in their titles, content, and style. They were not set to music.

Seventh, the term *yuefu* is sometimes used in a very broad sense to include all poetic genres that were originally accompanied by music, notably *changduan ju (ci)* and *qu*.[10]

Although these types are not the organizational categories used by Guo Maoqian, this listing, and there are similar ones in the Chinese sources, reflects the genre as collected in his anthology—type 7 is generally not associated with Guo, and Frankel does not account for a group of pre-Han poems in Guo's category 11. There are a number of issues that are glossed over by both of these listings, not the least being the general heterogeneity of the groupings, but Guo has a long tradition of typologies behind him, and Frankel certainly is in good company with such a revised description.

Before exploring further Guo Maoqian's collection, let us note some points of Frankel's list that are perhaps not immediately obvious, but are extremely pertinent to this discussion.

1. As he notes at the beginning of his list, Frankel is using the term *yuefu* to stand for *yuefu shi*, which is a common practice in many studies; thus the name of a genre becomes synonymous with a governmental office.

2. While the first three types are directly related to the Han Music Bureau, the actual number of extant texts of these types is minimal and some of those are fraught with problems of provenance.

3. Conversely, types 5 and 6, while appearing peripheral to central concerns of the genre, actually constitute the bulk of the materials available. I should note that this de-emphasis of the literati poems is found throughout the various studies of the genre.

4. At several points in Frankel's description there seems to be an odd emphasis on the titles of the poems, at least equal to their form and content.

5. Finally, while music seems to be a critical issue to the genre, as one would suppose from the name, it is not immediately evident how that association works across the genre.

Each of these points, implying certain literary and extraliterary assumptions, derives from particular manifestations in the configurations of the genre.

Now that we have an idea of the general shape of the genre as conventionally described, we can turn our attention to the assumptions that lie behind that description and its subsequent interpretations. Behind those assumptions lurk the critical but largely unexplored issues of *yuefu* poetry. Below I shall consider afresh the evidence that can actually be brought to bear on four assumptions that yield the common conceptions of the genre. I want to reconsider those assumptions in the light of the functional aspects of the genre. That is to say, I want to ask if these are the conventions that are most essential to the contract between poet and reader (including us, as modern readers) as they/we converse through the medium of the genre. By scrutinizing each of those basic assumptions we can perhaps transform the discussion of *yuefu* poetry from tautological typology into an appreciation of the defining conventions of the genre. If so, then we return the genre to the dynamics of literary dialogue and away from the stasis of description.

First Assumption: Musicality

We should first address the very important question of the implied musicality of *yuefu* poetry, since it is at the heart of the various problems and heretofore suggested solutions to the definition of the genre. To pursue this line of inquiry we must first look more closely at the organizational principles of the *Yuefu shiji*, for in them we find the quintessential peculiarity of the genre. However, let us not forget that the history of music during the millennium encompassed by Guo Maoqian's corpus was, quite unlike that of language during the same period, filled with disruption and hiatus. While many of Guo Maoqian's musical categories contain texts from across the centuries, it should not be assumed that the preservation of categories or texts includes preservation of the accompanying music. Modern studies may indeed provide insights into music of a particular historical moment, but it would be erroneous to assume that those insights apply to music similarly designated but from a different period. The conservative nature of nomenclature should not be confused with continuity in the music named. This is true for large classifications, such as instrumentation and mode, and for smaller designations, such as melody and tune. No one would suggest that music is not important to the bulk of materials collected in Guo's anthology, but we should keep in mind that musicality is more a synchronic characteristic, rather than a diachronic continuity, despite the persistence of categories and names. Moreover, even with this awareness of the synchronic nature of the poetry's musicality, exactly how that musicality is involved in the definition of the genre *as a whole* is still difficult to ascertain. Frankel, for example, comments that the usefulness of Guo's twelve categories is limited, "since nearly all his terms have to do with the musical settings rather than the literary aspects of the *yuefu* songs. As the music has long been lost, the situation is about the same as if we had a collection of paintings, preserved only in black and white copies but classified on the basis of the original color schemes."[11] Yet the disparity in the relationship each group finds with its "musical setting" is even more unsettling than Frankel's clever analogy allows. First we should note that in many cases Guo Maoqian had no more information about the original "color schemes" than we do; this is especially true with any pre-Tang material. His access to the musicality was more conceptual than actual, more textual than aural. The lure of theoretical musicality even induces Guo to include poems that predate the Music Bureau entirely, including a number of poems that are associated with the early mythological and legendary periods.[12] Moreover, if by some miracle of science we were able to restore "color" to the black and white copies, it still would be less than clear what those "color schemes" have to do with generic conventions, for the musical settings to which Frankel refers are not nearly as uniform as the color schemes of his analogy. There are several different, often logically incompatible, types of musical relationships in Guo's twelve categories. We have:

1. Those based on occasion—the ritual, banquet, and dance settings of categories 1, 2, and 7;
2. Those based on instrumentation—drums, winds, and strings in various configurations of 3, 4, 5, and 8;
3. Those based on modality or key—the *qingshang* songs of category 6;
4. Those with no specific musical setting—the miscellaneous songs of 9 and 11;
5. Those based on the extramusical criteria of chronology—the modern lyrics, 10;

6. Finally, one group that is defined by *nonmusicality*—12, the "new *yuefu*," of which Guo says "since their lyrics are fully *yuefu* but they are not usually put to music, they therefore are called 'new *yuefu*.'"[13]

This categorization suggests that restoration of these musical settings, where there were any in the first place, is not only inherently impossible, but would do little to bring cohesion to the genre. We would have not a group of paintings organized according to color scheme, but rather a gallery of different groups of paintings organized by criteria as diverse as color, compositional materials, provenance, chronology, and lack of paint!

Not only does the criterion of music fail to unify adequately the corpus of *yuefu* poetry, it also fails to distinguish it clearly from other poetry in China, which had musical associations from its earliest times. This is most obvious in regard to "songs" *(ge)* in both pre-Tang and Tang anthologies, but may be assumed for the early history of the *shi* genre.[14] Thus, the assumed primary association of music is not a criterion that can be easily used to define the *yuefu* genre. This is in part because of the ephemeral nature of the music itself, but also because musicality does not appear to have distinguished the genre historically. Yet the genre's musicality, which was not defining but nonetheless conceptually and actually part of its poetics (especially since it seemed embedded in the genre's very name), was in part responsible for the diachronic expansion of the genre. The analogies that might be drawn here with the Western lyric are obvious. While the musical associations of the two genres are very different from each other, the general configurations of the development of each genre and its "musicality" are similar. Music was certainly important to Western lyric poetry early in its generic history, but that association was lost or obscured by other conventions that rose out of it, and in the end destroyed it as a functional part of the generic contract. Those derived conventions—and we have analogous ones in *yuefu* poetry—then allowed the genre to expand far beyond its original parameters. Music might have been contributed to the production of the lyric poems by both Sappho and Pound, but that music is not what makes them so essential to the genre and so mutually informing.

The inaccessibility of the assumed musicality of the *yuefu* poetry has induced critics to discuss the poetry in terms of "secondary" musical features. This is especially so with modern critics, but even traditional critics participate in such discussions. Indeed the belated critic had little else to talk about when it came to the musicality of the genre. For example, in the introductory notes to "Lyrics for Horizontal Flute," Guo Maoqian, following an early Han reference, describes the music as "military music . . . played on horseback."[15] While he does include information on instrumentation in this introduction, that information is generally less substantial than his comments on the music's Barbarian and martial associations. And we have already seen that the *xianghe* poems, generally regarded as the oldest *yuefu* poems, are described by the *Song shu* (ca. 500) as "popular songs of the lanes and streets of the Han period."[16] The reclassifications of the *yuefu* corpus by modern critics such as Luo Genze, James Robert Hightower, and Hans Frankel tend to focus on similar "secondary features" that are more accessible even though they lie behind the assumed primary musicality. In each of these there is an effort to accommodate the diverging diachronic/synchronic nature of the genre, which does so much to fragment the corpus. Hightower suggests the basic nature of the genre is twofold, hymns and ballads, with the latter divided between those (1) early, Han (?) ballads; (2) imitations of those; and (3) new songs in the ballad tradition.[17] Hans Frankel elaborates this basic dichotomy slightly to derive a new typology of five, which is offered parallel to the seven-fold descriptive categorization cited above.

1. Ritual hymns of the Han period
2. A special class of ritual hymns from the Southern Dynasties
3. Anonymous ballads of the Han period
4. Anonymous ballads of the Southern and Northern Dynasties
5. Ballads in the *yuefu* style by men of letters[18]

The dichotomies of hymn and ballad, folk and literati, Han and post-Han that we see in Frankel's typology are common in such descriptions of the genre, but of course these dichotomies themselves seem to describe quite different, if not mutually exclusive, types of literature. This is not to say that Frankel's description somehow misrepresents the genre; it is, in fact, a quite accurate account, using this type of descriptive system, of the corpus as seen in Guo Maoqian's anthology. But these distinctions represent a retroactive, and in some cases cross-cultural, literary evaluation that does not reflect the distinctions that the indigenous (not only Chinese, but also medieval) critic or poet would have made. Some of these criteria in fact would have been nearly invisible to Guo Maoqian, to say nothing of the *yuefu* poet—such as the distinction of literary vs. folk that is so common in modern discussions of the genre. Therein lies the real problem. Since musicality as a generic convention is not only invisible to us, but perhaps not even defining through most of the genre's history, we turn to other criteria that are both useful and available to us. Yet we must wonder if such criteria are merely convenient *post facto* descriptions, or whether they have a functional value as well. We must even begin to question whether *yuefu* poetry is a genre at all in the contractual sense of the term; perhaps we have only an anthology masquerading as a genre. To go beyond these descriptive typologies, we must look more closely at the history of the genre, and in doing so we must turn away from Guo Maoqian's collection.

Second Assumption: *Yuefu* Poetry Originates in the Han

Each major period of Chinese dynastic history is commonly associated with one literary genre. The reductive quality of this way of thinking is obviously dangerous, but it is nonetheless exceedingly common. Thus, if you are studying *xiaoshuo* (fiction) it is usually Ming-Qing *xiaoshuo*; *zaju* (drama) is assumed to be Yuan *zaju*; *shi* (lyric poetry) will most likely be Tang *shi*; and if one mentions *yuefu* poetry it will be assumed you mean what is commonly called "Han *yuefu*." Descriptions of the genre that we have noted above all give due weight to the Han associations of the genre. The textual evidence in the Han materials for the activities of the Music Bureau, along with the extant ritual hymns, would certainly suggest that this is well founded, even if there are none of the often-mentioned "ballads" in those materials. Of course, we must be careful not to assume that the existence of the Music Bureau as an institution assures the existence of Music Bureau *poetry*. That is, we must remember that the term *yuefu* is not the same as *yuefu shi*. Masuda Kiyohide has approached the question of *yuefu (shi)* as a generic literary term with innovation and thoroughness, and much of the argument below derives from his materials and thoughts.[19] Again, nomenclature becomes a critical issue. Everything is in the name, and "Music Bureau poetry" is certainly a most peculiar name of a literary genre.

The earliest sources for genre designation in China are bibliographies and general anthologies; for our purposes, the latter are particularly useful. Our earliest bibliography is Ban Gu's (32–92) *Han shu* "Yiwen zhi," but its section on poetry contains only *fu* (rhapsody) and *geshi* (lyric song/poems).[20] Within the latter are listed groups of regional (folk?) poems that might very well have been associated with Music Bureau activities, but they are not so designated. The ritual poems associated with the Music Bureau are not included in the bibliography, but are fully discussed and recorded in the history's monograph on ritual and music.

In the centuries immediately following the collapse of the Han we have the beginning of literary criticism and the general anthology.[21] In criticism, the earliest we have is Cao Pi's (187–226) "Lun wen" ("Discussion of Literature") and Lu Ji's (261–301) celebrated "Wen fu" ("Rhapsody on Literature"). Under poetry headings, Cao again only has the *fu* and *shi* categories, while Lu expands slightly with a *song* (eulogy) listing—despite the fact that both Cao and Lu are now well-known *yuefu* poets with healthy collections in Guo Maoqian's anthology. During this time we also have the first general anthology of Chinese literature, the *Wenzhang liubie lun (Collection of Different Types of Literature)* by Lu Ji's contemporary, Zhi Yu (ob. 311). The anthology itself is lost but most of the introductory "discussions" *(lun)* for the genres remain. While Zhi does not have a section on *yuefu* poetry, he does mention the term under the *shi* section, but it is only a glancing reference and is referred to at the same level as other "minor" forms such as "comic verse and entertainment songs" *(paixie changyue)*.[22] This is apparently the first reference we have for *yuefu* as a genre, and context *does* suggest that the reference is to the "ballad" type of literature, not the "hymn" type. A little over a century later we also have the first known, and actually one of few, references to *yuefu shi* by a practicing poet. This occurs in Bao Zhao's (414–466) preface to his "Song bo pian," where he says he came upon "the *yuefu* poem 'Guihe pian'" [by Jin poet Fu Xuan], which he imitated *(ni)*.[23]

Two centuries after the theoretical statements by Cao Pi and Zhi Yu we have three monuments in early Chinese literary criticism and anthology making, the *Shi pin* by Zhong Hong (ob. 518), the *Wenxin diaolong* by Liu Xie (465–522), and the *Wen xuan* edited by Xiao Tong (501–531). Zhong Hong does not even mention the genre, despite the fact that he discusses several poets who are now well known for their *yuefu* poetry and mentions several poems now considered central to the genre. Liu Xie and Xiao Tong, however, both include sections on the Music Bureau (poetry). Liu presents a general discussion of *yuefu* and music, while Xiao collects forty *yuefu* poems under ten headings. Liu's discussion of *yuefu*, which is on a par with (in fact falls between) his discussion of *shi* and *fu*, is wide-ranging and abstract. It dwells on the general spiritual and moral importance of music—at one point even suggesting poems by the mythological Yellow Emperor also are *yuefu* poems, which may have encouraged Guo Maoqian to include pre-Han songs in his collection. Yet when Liu does get down to specifics he does mention events, categories, and poems that we recognize from Guo's collection. The *yuefu* poems collected in the *Wen xuan* are also very much part of the corpus we now know, including three well-known anonymous "old *yuefu*" poems, along with the authored poems. Here again the *yuefu* poems are subsumed under the *shi* category, on a par with such subcategories as travel, military, and funeral poems. Closely following Xiao Tong's general anthology we have Xu Ling's (507–583) anthology of *shi* poetry, which contains a number of *yuefu* poems, both anonymous and authored. The designated *yuefu* poems are all found in Guo Maoqian's corpus, but we do notice a number of undesignated poems that are now considered *yuefu*.[24] This treatment of *yuefu* poetry as a subcategory of *shi* is carried on by the next great general anthology, *Wenyuan yinghua*, compiled by Li Fang (925–996) as an intended continuation of Xiao's *Wen xuan*.

The assumed association of *yuefu* poetry as a literary genre with the Han dynasty is not supported by these early references, which begin noticeably late and generally refer to poetry not from the Han. Even the *Wen xuan*'s three "old *yuefu*" are not claimed to be Han, although we now assume they are. The most reliable source for Han *yuefu* of this anonymous, folk type is generally agreed to be Shen Yue's (441–513) *Song shu*, in which sixteen are collected. Yet we should note that they are *not* called *yuefu* by Shen, only "songs from the lanes and streets of Han times."[25] That they now form the core of the Han *yuefu* poems is the result of retroactive incorporation into the genre. Thus, while there was a Music Bureau in the Han, there is little evidence that there was a recognized genre, with known literary conventions, associated with it at this early date. *Yuefu* poetry as a genre seems to be a relatively late phenomenon; every indication so far is that it began to emerge between the fourth and sixth centuries, fully four hundred years after the end of the Music Bureau in the Han.

The common Han connotation of the *yuefu* poetry is, of course, clearly present in the ritual poems associated with it from very early on, and which form the opening fifteen chapters of Guo's collection. Yet every early source that mentions the *yuefu* genre excludes, either implicitly or specifically, those ritual songs from the group.[26] Zhi Yu mentions the ritual *jiaomiao* category on separate but equal terms with *yuefu*, and Xiao Tong lists his one *jiaomiao* separately from the *yuefu* poems. Liu Xie is more expansive in his treatment but does not explicitly mention this type of poem in his discussion. Thus, not only did the concept of an identifiable *yuefu* genre develop late relative to its now common Han associations, but that early concept does not appear to have included the Han ritual poems. There is evidence, in fact, that Guo Maoqian's inclusion of these ritual poems in the *yuefu* genre is his own innovation.

Shortly after the compilation of the *Wen xuan* there begins a series of collections and studies of *yuefu* poetry. Of those extant or of which we know the original contents, *none* includes these ritual poems in the genre. The corpus of *yuefu* poetry defined by these pre-Song anthologies is limited to those poems collected in Guo Maoqian's chapters 16–90, excluding the ritual and banquet poems, as well as the Tang "new *yuefu*."[27] The listing of the Han ritual poems in Zheng Qiao's (1104–1162) discussion of *yuefu* in his encyclopedia, *Tong zhi*, suggests that their inclusion was a Song convention. Yet a coincidence in Chinese literary history indicates that the inclusion may just have well have been a more personal, innovative decision by Guo Maoqian, followed by Zheng. At about the time Guo's collection was coming into circulation in the South (ca. 1340), Zuo Keming in the north (Yuan) was compiling his own anthology of *yuefu* poetry, the *Gu yuefu (Ancient Music Bureau Poetry)*.[28] This extant but neglected volume also does not include the ritual poems, even though it concentrates on pre-Tang texts. Thus the inclusion of the Han and later ritual poems in the *yuefu* genre, the poems we often consider "pure" *yuefu*, seems to reflect a very late and perhaps personal concept of the genre by Guo Maoqian.

The long and varied history of the *yuefu* genre has contributed to its complexity at every level. That complexity is best seen in the confusion that surrounds the different attempts, both traditional and modern, to construct a consistent typology of the genre. We see very disparate manifestations of the same problem in the inclusiveness of Zheng Qiao's list of fifty-three categories and in the reductivity of Hightower's simple dichotomy of hymn and ballad. This is not to suggest that there is some other typology of the genre that is "right," either because it is antique or innovative, but rather that the history of the *yuefu* poetry, as reflected in Guo Maoqian's corpus, has included any number of literary forms. It certainly would be erroneous to think that the various poets who wrote in the genre, from Cao Zhi to Bo Juyi, had a consistent understanding of the *yuefu* poem as a set of structural conventions. To try to devise a description based on common poetic distinctions that would account for those changes necessarily introduces conflicting or illogical categories. Our task is to discover what features might be most consistent in the ongoing definition and redefinition of the genre, features that allow the widest range of inclusiveness, but at the same time are exclusive enough to give the genre a separate identity in its literary context. In that vision of the genre we must search for the most effective way to participate in the genre as readers, to allow the poets their *generic* voice. While Guo Maoqian's inclusion of the ritual poems in his anthology seems at first to be a major aberration in the genre, on closer inspection it suggests what I believe is the core identity of the genre. Despite what Guo himself probably thought, that identity has little do with its musicality or Han associations.

Third Assumption: Literati Poems Are Derivative

The assumption that literati poems are chronologically second in Guo Maoqian's corpus of *yuefu* poems certainly can hardly be disputed. Even if we doubt the genre's Han identity, we still must admit that there *were* early anonymous poems that provided the models for certain literati imitations. While this is not evident in Guo Maoqian's twelve categories, whose synchronicity obscures these derivations, it is evident at a lower level of his organization of the genre. At the subcategory, usually subchapter level, poems with shared (or derived) titles are listed chronologically, with any "old version" *(gu ci)* listed first, clearly indicating Guo's understanding of this sequence of derivation. Moreover, Guo and earlier commentators have explicitly discussed the derivations. For example, after quoting a number of sources referring to "Mulberry along the Lane" ("Moshang sang"), Guo concludes the introduction to the "old version":

> Lu Ji's [poem by the derived title "Sun Rises in the Southeast Corner to Shine" with the line] "Brushing the Mulberry tree it rises to shine" sings about how good and cordial the beautiful woman was. It starts out like the "old version" but ends differently. There are also the poems titled "Picking Mulberry Leaves" that are derived from this [poem]. (*YFSJ* 28.410)[29]

In addition to the folk poems found as "old versions" scattered throughout the central part of Guo Maoqian's collection, such as the one referred to here, we also see large numbers of "anonymous" *(wuming)* poems, especially associated with the Southern Dynasties, in chapters 47–49.[30]

The assumed primacy of the folk poems is seen throughout modern descriptions of the genre, including those by Hightower and Frankel cited above. Not only is the dichotomy of folk and literati poetry consistent, but so is the supposed secondary nature of the literati poems. While there is often an effort by the critics to include a balance of folk and literati in their theoretical descriptions of the genre, the assumed importance of the folk is clearly betrayed in the actual poems selected and studied. This assumption often coincides with pro-Han prejudices. For example, Yu Guanying's standard *Yuefu shi xuan (Selected Music Bureau Poems)* includes only poems up to (but not including) the Tang, and in that selection, 147 poems are the non-authored "folk" type, while there are only thirty-four literati poems from eighteen authors. In Wang Yunxi's book of essays, *Yuefu shi luncong (Discussions of Music Bureau Poetry)* there are none that deal with literati poetry specifically, and there is only an occasional incidental reference to it in the others. Of the fifty essays by various authors in the *Yuefu shi yanjiu lunwen ji (Collected Essays on the Study of Music Bureau Poetry)* there are only two that specifically deal with the literati poets. This folk orientation is only partly the effect of the literary disposition of critics from the People's Republic of China. Collections and studies from the early Republican period, from contemporary Taiwan studies, and from Japan show a similar, if not as consistent, prejudice. Wang Zhong's *Yuefu shi xuan zhu (Annotated Selected Music Bureau Poems)*, the standard textbook in Taiwan, is composed of over fifty percent anonymous poems, even though it includes Tang poets; the selection by Sawaguchi Takeo contains no literati poems.[31] There is no similar bulk of material to compare in the West, but my estimation is that our orientations are similar to those of the Chinese: Hans Frankel's essay, for example, includes discussion of some twenty poems, and only two of those are literati, and only one from the Tang. His recent "High Literary Genre," is, however, devoted to the study of literati *yuefu* poetry, but it is restricted to the earliest poets now associated with the genre (i.e., of the Han and Wei periods). This certainly is a reflection of his ongoing assumption of the primacy of the earliest strata of the genre. Anne Birrell's book cannot be faulted since it is explicitly devoted to Han poems, but one might argue that her choice of that subcategory of *yuefu* poems as a topic of study is because of similar assumptions.

   A quantitative evaluation of the genre reveals a much different impression of the relative importance of the folk and literati poems. This evaluation has parallels in the perceived importance of Han versus post-Han materials. For example, there are only sixteen "old versions" in the most reliable source (Shen Yue's *Song shu)*, and the total listed by Guo Maoqian is less than seventy-five. While the later, mostly Southern Dynasties, "anonymous" poems are more numerous, they do not come anywhere near the number of literati poems. Of the five and a half thousand poems in the Guo Maoqian corpus, no more than five percent are designated either "old" or "anonymous," while eighty percent are literati, with the remainder in odd categories, such as ritual poems and pre-Han songs. It is difficult to estimate exactly how those literati poems are distributed throughout the millennium covered by the collection in the *Yuefu shiji,* but there is definitely a shifting of material towards the Tang end of the spectrum, despite such statements as "The most important period for *yuefu* poetry was during the Han, Wei, Jin, and Northern and Southern Dynasties."[32] Of the eight poets who have more than forty poems listed in Guo Maoqian's corpus, four are from the Tang, two from the Liang, one from the Northern Chou, and one from the Jin.[33] All these numbers point to the Tang literati poems as the most important in the genre. Of course, it could be argued that quantity is not quality, that the best *yuefu* poetry is still the small number of folk poems, around which the literati ones are just so much literary flotsam. Such a contention is difficult to counter, but the unquestioning presentation of that argument suggests that a closer look at those literati poems might be informative. The common, and certainly logical, assumption is that without the folk poems the literati imitations would not exist.

The nature of Luo Genze's study of *yuefu* poetry, as a chronological literary history up through the Tang, gives more balance to his review of the different manifestations of the genre, including Tang material. In Luo's relatively detailed discussion we begin to see more clearly the relationship of imitation to model that is often mentioned but little discussed in the studies of the genre—little discussed because the tendency is to look solely at the model and never at the poems for which it serves as model.[34]

In the diagram a number of relationships are pertinent to our discussion. First, of course, is Luo's separation of musical and nonmusical poems, with the musical receiving the greatest detail—we have already noted the difficulty of entering into a discussion of that musicality, and in fact in his accompanying essays Luo himself has little to

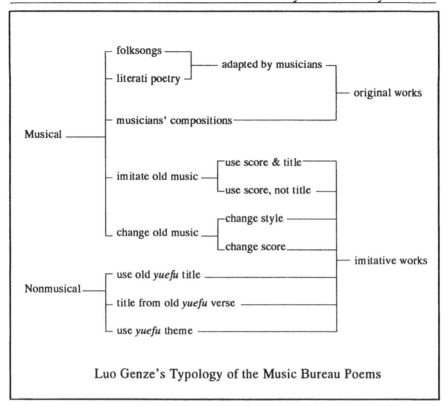

Luo Genze's Typology of the Music Bureau Poems

say about it. At the other end of his chart we find the distinction between original and imitative compositions, with the latter spanning both musical and nonmusical divisions. The patterns of imitation Luo lists here are wide-ranging and can ultimately lead us deeper into the central issues of the genre. They are, for example, often the principle by which Guo Maoqian organizes his corpus below his twelve categories of musicality.

We have little information on that musical imitation (as did Luo)—mostly only gleanings from some secondary comments in historical sources, usually involving ritual music.[35] Such is the case, for example, with a number of comments about and by Wei minister Miao Xi: "When Wei had received the mandate to rule, they changed the twelve ['Duan xiao naoge'] tunes. [Emperor Wu of Wei] had Miao Xi create lyrics for them in order to praise the virtue of replacing the Han."[36] At another point Miao petitioned the emperor, saying: "The 'Songs of Peace' were originally Han songs, but the texts *[wen]* of the poem-songs that we use now are not those of former days, therefore it is appropriate to change them."[37] Shortly after this, in the Jin period, we have Fu Xuan (217–278) involved in similar work. Referring to the *jiaomiao* ritual poems, the emperor "had only the lyrics to the music changed, ordering Fu Xuan to compose new words."[38] Such references support the maintenance of Luo's categories of musical imitation, but they do not give those categories any real substance (especially for us) or any real sense of continuity through the diachronic length of the genre. Again, without the music they are merely names. While patterns of musical imitation are invisible in the *Yuefu shiji* corpus, nonmusical patterns are often very visible. Though critics have often scoured the poems and secondary materials trying to glean possible musical continuity in a category or subset of *yuefu* poems, they have been seemingly blind to the patterns of nonmusical imitation. This is despite the fact that nonmusical imitation is as pervasive in the genre as the details of Luo's listing suggest, and those patterns are neither random nor necessarily limited to the modeling on "old versions" or other folk compositions. In the latter part of this study we shall look closely at different types of relationships found in these patterns of intratextuality, but here we might describe briefly two sets of poems as illustrations of possible configurations of those subsets in Guo Maoqian's corpus.

The first set is one that begins with an "old version" from the *Song shu* entitled "Bai hu" ("White Swans"), collected in Guo Maoqian's anthology under its tune name, "Yan ge he chang xing," in four verses *(jie)* (38.576). The poem describes how a pair of swans became separated when the female fell ill, which serves as an explicit metaphor for the separation of human lovers that is lamented in the closing stanzas. There follows immediately a poem with the same title by Cao Pi in five verses, but with a drastically altered thematic thrust (here more of a *carpe diem* theme). This is a common pattern of Wei imitations—shared titles, but not theme—and we assume that this is indirect evidence of shared musical patterns. These two poems are both labeled "Performed to Jin Music," which is a designation of a number of early post-Han poems. These are followed by four poems (Liu Song through Tang) that are thematically related to the "old version" but have new titles derived from the first line of that poem. Here we assume that the musical continuity has been disrupted, and the interrelationships are thematic and visible.

This pattern of supposed musical imitation followed by thematic imitation and intratextual derivation is often seen in subsets containing very early poems. Yet there are many subsets (the majority) that do not contain such early poems, but in which similar intratextual relationships are present. In the second set of poems, Chen *yuefu* poet Zhang Zhengjian (fl. 550) began a series when he wrote his "Bronze Sparrow Pavilion" ("Tong que tai"), whose theme derives from historical information about Cao Cao—his commissioning of a pavilion by this name as a residence for his women-in-waiting after his death, all of which is recorded in Guo Maoqian's introductory notes. Following Zhang's poem we have nine imitations with this same title, mostly from the Tang, that develop in various ways the theme of the lonely, isolated woman. In addition, Guo lists a series of sixteen poems with the derived title "Bronze Sparrow Ladies" ("Tong que ji") and two poems called the "Sparrow Pavilion Lament" ("Que tai yuan"). Each of these sets, spanning through the Tang, is also thematically interrelated with the others.

Subsets of this type, whose sequences begin with a literati, not folk, poem, are scattered throughout Guo Maoqian's corpus. Some of them even begin with Tang poets, but the majority begin in the late Six Dynasties period, especially with well-known poets (e.g., Xiao Gang, Yu Xin, and Bao Zhao).

To return to our original question of the primacy of folk versus literati *yuefu* poems, we now can suggest a new understanding of that textual relationship. The emergence of the *genre, yuefu* poetry, which we have documented above to the fourth through sixth centuries, occurs at a time of a heightened praxis of thematic imitation by literati poets, not only of folk but also literati models. We see this specifically in Guo Maoqian's corpus, as well as in the various forms of "imitation," especially the *ni* type, found in the *Wen xuan* and *Yutai xinyong*. We could argue that the conscious modeling of a poem on previous *yuefu* text draws that imitative poem into the genre, marking it too as a *yuefu* poem. But when does the model, especially the literati model, become part of the genre? Why, for example, does Zhang Zhengjian's "Bo wei jin ming yue" ("Shining Mirror Moon on Thin Curtains") not enter the genre when his thematically and prosodically similar "Bronze Sparrow Pavilion" does?[39] I would say it is because the "Mirror Moon" poem was never imitated as was the "Bronze Sparrow;" that is to say, the *model* also becomes a *yuefu* poem only when it is imitated, when it is drawn into the intratextual convention. Thus, it would appear the model and its imitation enter the genre simultaneously; they enter because of the process of imitation, not because of any prior prosodic, thematic, or contextual property. Yet we might even suggest that the imitative poem enters the genre *first*; as soon as the process of imitation begins, it engages the intratextual conventions of the genre, but a model only enters the genre later, when the imitation is complete and the relationship of model to copy is established. This line of argument would lead us to conclude that Zhang's poem became a *yuefu* after the poems that imitated it.

The obvious, if somewhat unexpected, conclusion to the above line of thought is to suppose that the folk poems that served as models for the literati imitations are also dependent on those intratextual relationships for their inclusion in the genre. While that argument may encounter some difficulty when applied to specific cases, in general it is tenable. At the very least I would suggest that without that intratextuality the *yuefu* genre would never have existed—mere numbers suggest that. Without their imitation, early "folk" poems would have been simply absorbed into the broader category of *shi* poetry, where they are found in the earliest anthologies. In this way, early "folk" *yuefu* poems, like literati models, belong to the genre only because of later imitations, either specifically or generally. Thus, they became *yuefu* poems after their literati imitations already had engaged the genre.

The literati poems are therefore not secondary, but rather primary in defining and sustaining the genre. The "original" *yuefu* poems owe their existence *as members of the genre* to those later imitations and intratexts they create. The intratextual relationship is central to the genre; so central, in fact, it induced Guo Maoqian to include in his corpus those dynastic ritual poems. In all accounts of the production of those ritual poems there was a conscious effort to imitate, if not restore, the proper models. That imitative base led to their inclusion in the genre. We first suppose that their Han origins and/or musicality accounted for their inclusion, but upon further consideration, and in the face of their historic isolation from the genre, we discover that the intratextual relationship of imitation and model best accounts for the inclusion of the ritual poems in the corpus.

The Song dynasty's sensitivity to the poetics of imitation/emulation, which were part of the larger neoclassical *(fugu)* aesthetics of the time, certainly must have influenced Guo Maoqian's inclusion of the ritual poems in his corpus, and, in fact, must have influenced the compilation of the entire anthology. On one hand Guo was constructing an anthology based on supposed musicality, but imitative/intratextual poetics was probably the unconscious inducement for the whole project, especially in its unprecedented comprehensiveness.

Fourth Assumption: Thematic Imitation Is Secondary

Those who discuss the imitative aspects of *yuefu* poetry generally suggest that thematic imitation is a small part of that praxis. Luo Genze, for example, lists thematic imitation as only one of seven possible types, with the others mostly related to music.[40] Guo Maoqian's inclusion of the ritual poems into his *Yuefu shiji* also rests on their assumed musical imitation. Outside of those poems, there is only a small group that appear to imitate exclusively on musical grounds; this is assumed since they have no thematic relationship with their designated models. The poems that imitate solely on musical grounds are almost entirely associated with the earliest, Wei-Jin, poetry, especially that by the three Cao poets. Thus, Cao Cao and Cao Pi write "wandering immortal" poems to the title of an "old version" whose titular theme is about a chaste wife (every poem after Cao Pi's in that lengthy intratextual series displays at least glancing reference to the original chaste wife theme).[41] There clearly is, however, thematic imitation early in the history of the genre, especially in the works of the Jin poet, Fu Xuan.[42] And I would argue that here is the actual beginning of the genre; after Fu, thematic imitation becomes increasingly important throughout the genre. When and whether it is accompanied by musical imitation is a difficult question, difficult mostly because so much of the evidence of musical-ity is missing.

If one wishes to study the praxis of musical imitation in *yuefu* poetry, perhaps the most obvious way to circumvent the lost musicality would be to deal directly with the visible prosody of the poems. In terms of generic identity, however, discussion of *yuefu* prosody is actually quite unrevealing. While irregular line length is associated with a number of the early poems, this is not entirely distinctive, and in any case most *yuefu* poems are prosodically identical with other genres. Nor does visible prosody bind poems of any given set together, as it does in the later *ci* poetry and as one might expect if music lies behind their shared identity. In any titular set of *yuefu* poems we may find a wide range of prosodies. Thus, instead of specific prosodic patterns, most discussion of the formal aspects of this poetry must focus on its general style, especially on what is deemed its "folk" orientations, including the very problematic issue of orality.[43] We should note that discussions of the "folk style" commonly associated with *yuefu* poetry are not only problematic, though certainly not entirely without basis, they also are *not* discussions of musicality, but rather of language, texts, and ulti-mately thematics. When all is said and done, it is solely theme that is available to us for any lengthy, meaningful discussion. Denied access to the poetry's music, modern critics feel they must settle for these relatively unimportant thematic issues—second-class citizens of *yuefu* hermeneutics. What is truly startling about these discussions is that, once "detoured" to the content of the poems, almost no critic has engaged the most obvious and ubiquitous of the thematic issues, that is, the interrelationship of poems within Guo Maoqian's subsets of poems (i.e., intratextuality).[44] I believe that focus on thematic intratex-tuality is not a distraction from the genre, but actually will help us read *yuefu* poetry in a more vital setting, allowing us to enter into the poet-reader contract of the genre.

Guo Maoqian was certainly aware of the thematic relationships within his subsets of poems with shared or derived titled poems. While he introduces the general sections with an accumulation of citations and thoughts on the musicality of those categories, in discussing the poems and subsets themselves he necessarily confines his own remarks to themes and other textually visible characteristics. Guo Maoqian may very well have wished to discuss musical imitation, especially as he was surrounded by living examples of it in the new *ci* poetry, but his isolation from most of the *yuefu* music led him inevitably to these textual matters. But Guo Maoqian is not alone in his interest in thematics of the genre. Other critics before him, whom he often cites, also have had much to say about the contents of these poems. As an illustration of these concerns, I here translate Guo's introductory remarks to the series that begins with the "old version" of "Bai tou yin":[45]

The *Gujin yuelu (Musical Record Old and New)* [ca. 568] says "Wang Sengqian's *Ji lu (Skilled Record)* [ca. 450] says 'The song "Bai tou yin xing" is the old "Qi ru shan shang xue" piece.'" The *Xijing zaji (Various Records of the Western Capital)* [ca. 350] says, "Sima Xiangru had made arrangements to have a woman of Maoling as his wife. Zhuo Wenjun composed 'Bai tou yin' in order to break off with him, thereupon Xiangru desisted in his plan." The *Explanations of Music Bureau Titles* [ca. 700] says, "The old lyrics read 'Glistening like snow on a mountain / White as a moon among the clouds'; they also read 'I wish to get a man who has thoughts only for me / To stay with him until our hair is white.' It starts out mentioning that the husband has designs on someone else, therefore she comes to break off the marriage with him. Next it mentions taking her leave near the waters of the canal. This describes the original feelings. In the end it mentions that if the man valued his own ambitions, what would be the need for money. Similarly we have the line by Bao Zhao of the Song, 'Straight like red silk [lute] strings'; or that by Zhang Zhengjian of the Chen, 'Throughout life she clung to the straight way'; or that by Yu Shinan of the Tang, 'Her spirit was like orchids on a deserted path.' All of these show how she was hurt when her husband withdrew his favor because of the slander that defamed her purity and virtue. Thus they are very close here to the old text." There is also one source that says that "Bai tou yin'" is about how anxious he was to know her, thus he pushed the old aside for the new. Since she was unable to reach an age of white hair, therefore the title. There is also the poem by Yuan Zhen of the Tang, "Lyrics on Breaking Up," that is derived from this. (*YFSJ* 41.599–600)

Because of the distinctive content of the early "Bai tou yin" poems, as well as the associated tale of Sima Xiangru and Zhuo Wenjun, the thematic citations in this passage are particularly rich; yet it is not atypical in this emphasis. Guo Maoqian consistently comments on thematic continuity and variation, or even lack of continuity, in his subsets.

Guo's concern for thematic continuity even goes beyond the intratextual subsets to include the interrelationship between the subsets themselves. While not consistently, Guo does tend to group subsets and unrelated single poems together on the basis of theme. Thus, chapter 23 has sets of poems that deal with the twin capital cities of Chang'an and Loyang, chapter 39 concentrates on poems related to birds and women, chapter 64 is entirely wandering immortal poems, and most of the poems in 66 and 67 are related to knight errant themes. How widely these thematic patterns might range is an interesting question (our last example suggests that there are at least occasionally supra-chapter principles involved). Thematic organization of literary materials is an extremely old activity in Chinese intellectual history, and one that was perhaps most vital during the Song with its interest in encyclopedia compilation and antiquarian studies. Guo Maoqian's desire to give his corpus a structure below the category of nominal musicality yields several ad-hoc organizational schemes, but none as widespread or as convincing as that of theme.

Guo Maoqian's interest in the thematic configurations of the *yuefu* series, especially in the ubiquitous literati poems, is fully foreshadowed by Wu Jing's (670–749) text, *Yuefu [gu] ti [yao] jie ([Essential] Explanations of [Old] Music Bureau Titles)*. This text is composed of comments ranging from a title to a short essay on thematic associations of various *yuefu* poems. A major portion of Guo Maoqian's introductory remarks, as we saw in those for "Bai tou yin," are composed of citations from Wu Jing's comments. Wu's preface to his book indicates how problems of thematic continuity had overshadowed those of musicality already by his time.

The rise of *yuefu* can be traced in origins to the Han-Wei period. Through the ages the [imitative] compositions of the literati have been very abundant. Sometimes they had not seen the original text, but took the theme *[yi]* from the remaining title. For example, to wish a man *bon voyage* they would extrapolate from "Sir Don't Cross the River"; for the birthday celebration of someone, they would use "Raven Gives Birth to Eight or Nine Children"; they would recite a "Pheasant's Colors" poem just to praise the beauty of embroidered collars and brocade bodices; or they would sing a "Heavenly Horse" poem merely to describe galloping and wild kicking. Examples like this are too numerous to count.

In its evolution, one replaced the other as this type of imitation was practiced; through repeated usage [new interpretations] became common. Wanting to make sure the [old themes] continued in the future, I thought about what could be done to secure the correct [interpretations]. Thus, occasionally when reading through some traditional records or using the collected writings of various authors, whenever I came upon something of use, I casually recorded it. Over the months and years these notes piled up to form a whole scroll. Recently I put them in order and entitled them the *Essential Explanations of Old Titles.*[46]

The very name of Wu's volume suggests that in the end these shared or derived *titles* are significant signatures of the genre, for they provide the potential for intratextual relationships between poems. Riffaterre says about the general intertextual nature of poetic titles:

> Titles . . . can function as dual signs. They then introduce the poem they crown, and at the same time refer to a text outside of it. Since the interpretant [the sign that leads from meaning to significance] stands for a text, it confirms that the unit of significance in poetry is always textual. By referring to another text the dual title points to where the significance of its own poem is explained.[47]

How much more so for the *yuefu* title, which leads the reader back to a very concrete, often complex, intratext composed of all the poems in the titular series. If the *yuefu* title signals a theme, shared or derived titles should signal shared or derived themes, but Wu Jing protests that the relationship between title and theme has diverged too far. He wants to restore that relationship in order to allow the thematic series to continue more consistently. This is the first example we have of someone reflecting on the tendency of the intratextual relationship to dissolve into general intertextuality.

I have suggested above that at the earliest stages of the genre (or proto-genre) musical imitation seems to have been the common practice. Yet we do have evidence that even at that early stage thematic intratextuality was known. This is seen with two types of poems that Guo Maoqian has linked with "old versions": these are the so-called *ben ci* (original lyrics) and *Jin yue suozou* (performed for Jin music). Sometimes the Jin music version is identical with the "old version," or sometimes, as with the "original lyrics," the texts are only closely related.[48] In either case it is obvious that it is the theme, even the same lyrics, that link the poems, not just music. In the case of a different Jin music version we know that musicality actually *separates* the associated poems. Theme, title, and shared language bind them together. This type of "imitation" may have been the impetus for conscious literati imitation of *yuefu* themes, especially as identified with the Jin poet Fu Xuan.

The repeated mention of *yuefu* "titles" in modern descriptions of the genre by such critics as Luo Genze and Hans Frankel is therefore not incidental, but rather leads directly to the intratextual identity of the genre. While we would expect modern descriptions to emphasize this textually visible element in the genre, the comments by traditional critics cited above indicate that this emphasis was also important to the historical workings of the genre. When *yuefu* poets chose such titles, they chose to have their poems read as part of a series of poems, that is, as *yuefu* poems. They chose to write not only in their own particular voices, but also in the borrowed voice of the intratext, which was the integrated voice of all those who had written before. Titles are the signature of that intratextual relationship, and therefore of the genre.

Conclusion

Yuefu poetry, according to the above description, should be understood as a genre that begins around the fourth to sixth century and is centered on poems of thematic imitation or intratextuality. Conventional wisdom tells us that in several ways this definition is not entirely accurate. We can find numerous exceptions to it in the poems of Guo Maoqian's *Yuefu shiji*. Some of those can be dismissed as the result of Guo's extravagant inclusiveness, but some, such as isolated literati poems of the late Six Dynasties and Early Tang period, or imitative poems that predate the conception of the genre, cannot be so easily dismissed. In those cases we must decide whether the poems are not part of the genre, or whether they *are* within the genre as defined, but meet the criteria in more subtle ways. Our understanding of the genre does not account for every poem in Guo Maoqian's corpus, but it does account for the majority of the core poems, especially when we move from "imitation" to "intratextuality" as a defining criteria. More importantly it accounts for them in *textual* ways, ways that are visible and meaningful to the reader. Other descriptions that rely on theoretical or invisible criteria, such as musicality, do us no good; we have no way to test, no way to appreciate, no way to read the genre.

Thus our new definition is "correct" in that it is functional; it lets us participate in the genre in ways poets expected us to participate; it lets us read as they wrote, textually and intratextually. Historically there may have been other ways to produce and appreciate the genre (such as in its musical environment), but for us (and I suspect that it has been so for centuries) this is the best, most meaningful way to read *yuefu* poetry.

Intratextual Reading Reconsidered

When we read any *yuefu* poem as part of a titular set, we need to pay attention to the affinities it shares with the other poems in the set and to the ways in which it diverges from them. That is to say, the negation and mutation, as well as the affirmation and continuity, of those themes are a significant part of the intratextual relationship, significant because they give the poem textures that would be invisible outside of the relationship. Thus, when literati "imitations" of the Luofu theme [a faithful wife's spirited rejection of improper advances] feature an acquiescent "palace lady" typical of late Six Dynasties verse in Luofu's stead, we are shocked by this "negation" of the heroine.[49] Without the context of the Luofu poetic series, however, there would be no sense of loss; we would accept the woman merely as a type seen throughout the poetry of that period, instead of as a transformation of the early Luofu. This is one way the defining convention of the *yuefu* genre moves beyond imitation into intratextuality.

The potentiality of any given *yuefu* intratext varies both diachronically and synchronically. With the diachronic extension of the series from a single model into numerous imitations, its thematic threads grow in length and complexity as each poem adds new dimensions to the set. As we have suggested with the Luofu poems, even the discontinuity of certain themes, broken threads as it were, gives new texture to the relationship. Each additional poem identified with the set demands that the set as a whole and the individual poems as members of it be reread in light of that addition. This retroactive reading of the series can also bring to light thematic material in the earlier poems that would have gone unnoticed without its later exploration. The seemingly bland or glancing reference gathers weight as it is developed and expanded in the later poems, and that weight, by the nature of intratextual reading, keeps redistributing itself over the entire set. As mentioned above, this type of retroactive reading has parallels at a higher level when a poem's inclusion in the genre results from such belated revision; when that happens the poem, the set, and the genre are all affected.

The intratextual relationships within a set of poems can vary synchronically as much as they can diachronically; that is, the configuration of those relationships is as much a question of *who* is writing and reading the poem as *when* it is written or read. This is obvious, as we shall see, in the case of *yuefu* poets exercising their own poetic voices as they write in, but at the same time restructuring the parameters of, a given intratextual set. While this is true, we must acknowledge the difficulty of establishing the intent of the author of a given text, or even the author's familiarity with the intratext within which the poem is written. Yet, as our discussion in Chapter 1 suggests, literati culture during this period was characterized by a pervasive textuality that allows us to assume the poet's knowledge of the general outlines of the intratext, even if we do not have evidence of exposure to a specific poem. This was especially so for the poetics of the literary salon that became so important during this period, such as those of Xiao Gang and

Shen Yue.[50] That assumption is also supported by the tradition of anthologizing of *yuefu* poetry that is accounted for by the listings in the *Suishu* bibliography—see the Bibliographic Note.

In any event, the identity of the intratext is established as much by the reader's ability to read as it is by the writer's intent in writing; that is, the intratext exists only as much as it is recognized by the reader. Thus, the scope of the intratextual potentiality depends very much on the literacy of the readers—how much material they can fit into the potentiality of that intratext, thereby defining its parameters. When anthologists, or any other readers, expand the intratext, their literacy overrides the author's by creating intratextual relationships unknown or unavailable to the writer—in *yuefu* poetry the most obvious case of this power is Guo Maoqian's inclusion of poems theretofore not designated as *yuefu* poems, such as the Han ritual poems. The complexity of the intratext is most enhanced when readers of superior literacy turn to participate in the genre themselves. They *write* poems of heightened intratextuality, which are in turn read by readers who can expand *their* scope. Thus the potentiality of the intratext expands diachronically but is especially enriched at particular moments of fertile reading, represented by the literatus as reader and writer.

We should note that not only is the *yuefu* intratextual relationship different from that found in textual imitation and intertextuality, but it is also not the same as the textual relationships of a poetic sequence, either that of a poet or of an anthologist. When individual poets create their own poetic sequence or series, the relationship between the poems in the group can be most easily understood as a product of their personal creation, either as part of their intention or by unconscious forces working on them. On the other hand, the textual relationship within poetic sequences created by the anthologist cannot be viewed in the same light. In those cases the will of the compiler, most clearly seen in the Japanese *Shinkokinshū*, establishes those relationships, quite divorced from the authors' intention or knowledge.[51] The intratextual poetics of the *yuefu* genre is somewhere between these two relationships; it is like both, but not quite either one of them. We assume that there is authorial intent to participate in the relationships as defined by a given set of *yuefu* poems at the moment of creation—the poet chooses to write in the voice of others. Yet the compilation of the *yuefu* anthologies, especially that of Guo Maoqian, undoubtedly suggests relationships that were never the intent of the poet. In this way the anthologist is a "supra-reader" who expands the scope of the intratext. As modern readers we enjoy the freedom to modify further that potentiality of the intratext, either by stretching or reducing its parameters. Our reading cannot be restricted by known authorial intent, nor should we assume that the anthologist is in every case a better arbiter than we are. Yet we must acknowledge the power of the self-conscious poet, such as Li Bo, and the later anthologist, especially Guo Maoqian. In Li's *yuefu* poetry we find the best intratextual writing, and in Guo's anthology we find the greatest undertaking in intratextual reading.

3

Threads: Thematic Lines

The set of *yuefu* poems that share the title "Yin ma chang cheng ku" ("Watering Horses at the Long Wall Spring") begins with a celebrated *gu ci* ("old version")—one of the three collected in the *Wen xuan*—and continues with sixteen less well-known literati imitations dating from the Wei through the Tang dynasties.[1] There are several thematic threads that run through this series of poems, threads that sometimes cross and merge to form dense systems of meaning, but that at other times are found only as strands barely visible except against the intratextual light of the set as a whole. Here I shall be concerned primarily with three thematic lines: separation, the border, and water. In my discussion, I shall focus on twelve of the seventeen "Yin ma" poems, and generally I shall work chronologically through the material.[2]

Before tracing these three specific themes through the "Yin ma" set, I first want to introduce all seventeen of the poems, thereby allowing readers to view for themselves the general configurations of one complete titular *yuefu* set—for a short description of each poem see Reading Notes to the Poems appended to this chapter.

Watering Horses at the Long Wall Spring

1
Gu ci, Han (?)

Growing green the grass along the river bank
Long, linking thoughts of a distant road
I can't bear to think of that distant road
When in the night he comes in a dream
I dream he is right here beside me
But suddenly I know he is in another land
In another land, each in a different district
Life going on without ever seeing each other
The barren mulberry feels the'heaven's wind
Ocean water feels the heaven's cold
Others return home to enjoy themselves
Why would they want to talk with me?
A traveler comes from a distant region
Presenting me with a pair of carp
When the boy prepares them for dinner
Inside we find a long letter on silk
I kneel quietly to read it
What does the letter say?
At the top it says "Make sure you eat well"
Below it says "Forever thinking of you"[3]

YFSJ 38.556

2
Cao Pi (187–226)

The ships float across the Yangtze River
Seeking bandits, punishing the enemy
Martial generals array the shields in lines
Assault troops attack with the metal drums

Long lances in a hundred thousand squadrons
Dark feathers in hundred-pound crossbows[4]
The chariots strike out like thunder, like lightning
One strikes out, then four or five follow

YFSJ 38.556

3
Chen Lin (ob. 217)

Watering horses at the Long Wall spring
The cold water cuts them to the bone
The men call to their supervisor on the Wall
"Don't keep the Taiyuan troops here too long"
"Each tour of duty has its allotted time
The Wall will progress as does your song"
"Men should die glorious in battle
Why should we suffer building this Wall?"
How the Long Wall goes on and on
Goes on and on for three thousand miles
Many young men are in the border towns
Many abandoned women in their homes
He writes a letter to her at home
"You should marry again, don't wait for me
Take good care of your new in-laws
But think of me often, your old husband"
A letter came in reply to the border
"How crude are your words these days
There you are in the midst of hardship
How could you ask me to be another's wife?
'Giving birth to a son, don't fuss over him
Giving birth to a daughter, wean her on dry meat'
Can you alone not see near the Wall
'Skeletons of the dead all tangled together?'
Doing up my hair I became your wife
My heart's desire was denied me

Now I know how bitter border life is for you
And how could I ever go on all by myself?"

4
Fu Xuan (217–278)

Growing green the grass beside the river
Sad and lonely the road of ten thousand miles
Grass comes to life in this spring season
And it is the time to retrace that distant road
Spring has come, but the grass does not come to life
The time to return is gone in silent sighs
The world fills my heart with longing
Dreams bring forth thoughts of love
Dreaming we are like Mandarin ducks
Wing to wing, we soar among the clouds
But I awake to no sight of you
Separated like the stars Orion and Lucifer
While the Yellow and the Luo have their constancy[5]
They are not like the stability of the Central Hills
The flowing currents never return
Floating clouds come and go freely by
Mournful winds move my heart with longing
Who could know my loneliness?
The afternoon sun cannot stop to rest
Moving on like galloping horses
Tilting my head to catch an echoing murmur
Turning eyes away, tears fall in streams
Since there is no time to meet in this life
I shall see you below in the Yellow Springs

5
Lu Ji (261–303)

Driving their horses they climb the Yin Mountains
Mountains so high the horses refuse to go on
From the commander of Yin Mountains
They learn the powerful enemy is at Yanran
The war carts roll ceaselessly along the rutted road
Banners and pinions move constantly back and forth
Raising their eyes to face the snow piled peaks
Lowering them to wade through frozen streams
Arriving in winter, the next fall they're still there

Separated from their families by an endless distance
Indeed the Xianyun barbarians are not yet pacified
How could the assault troops come back in vain
The suicide squadrons rush forward screaming
The evil tools of war leave both sides maimed
If the soldiers win, the rewards are meager,
If they lose, their worthless bodies are left behind
But to honor the legacy of Gan and Chen
They win merit capturing the Khan's flag
He reviews the troops, rewarding their leaders
With official positions in the diplomatic quarters

YFSJ 38.557

6
Shen Yue (441–513)

The border horses cross the Dragon Wastes
The road winds and they turn round and round
They ask ahead about the outpost at Changhai
There are various rebel forces already at Luntai

Our banners curl in the evening fog and rain
We can only go on through the freezing mists

7
Chen Shubao (550–604)

The assault horse enters another land
Mountain flowers glow in the evening light
Separated from the herd it neighs to its shadow
In the wind their fragrance is stirred again
The moon's beauty envelops the wall darkly
Voices of autumn mingle in the border long
How will I return my lord's favor?
With horsehide coffins on the battle ground[6]

8
Zhang Zhengjian (fl. 560)

The autumn grasses are startled by the Ordos winds
Watering their horses they leave the Long Wall
Startled, the herd is still too timid to drink
The area is dangerous, better to keep moving
The cutting ice gathers around the frozen hooves
The terrifying cold sharpens the chilled voices
With no way to cross to the southern Wu slopes
They have entered the Tibetan fortress again

9
Wang Bao (fl. 575)

Northward we hurry along the Chang'an Road
The assault cavalry always traveling this way
Battle walls overlook troops in Formation Eight
The bannered gate faces the two Military Portals[7]
Garrisoned soldiers guard north of the Corridor
Watering their horses at the corner of the Long Wall
In the deep snow there's no road back home
Ice forms over the river stilling the waves
Flying dust collects in the unending columns
The sand is flat, the cavalry hoofprints are many
Dark and dusky the moon on Corridor slopes
Silver and shining the river in the mist
The imperial troops still wrestle for sport
The generals still enjoy the fine music
Entering the fray, we have often drawn our swords
Repeatedly faced with danger we have grasped the lances
Now autumnal winds moan in our horses' ears
The day ends—what should we do?

YFSJ 38.558

10
Shang Fashi

The assault horses cross over the Long Wall
Stretching over the landscape, they work to stay together
They enter the ice, passing through the freezing water
They drink from the waves, gathered in the rippling currents
Their saddles glisten as if stained with moonlight
Their reflections move like floating clouds
In our separation let us have the endurance of pines
I must leave now to go join our General

YFSJ 28.558

11
Sui Yangdi (580–618)

Mournfully the autumn wind stirs
Marching a thousand miles into the distance
A thousand miles, and where do we march
Spread out across the desert, building the Long Wall
But how could this be my own idea
It was built by the wise rulers of the past
They established a policy for ten thousand generations
So millions could go on living in peace
How could we shirk our duty
And live the high life in the capital
Our martial standards fly high over the northern river
Our war banners unfurl for a thousand miles
Mountain streams emerge and disappear
The wild plains stretch on without end
The banging gongs halt the march
The beating drums raise the troops
A thousand wagons, ten thousand cavalry move
They water their horses at the Long Wall spring
In the autumn dusk, clouds beyond the border
Fog darkens the moon above Pass Mountain
Along the cliffs the post horses climb
Through the air the beacon fires glow
Asking for the lords of Chang'an
The Khan enters our court to submit
The turbid aura clears over the Heavenly Mountains
Morning light shines on our noble gates
The soldiers are discharged and return peacefully
Our work in the wastes is now done
When the drinks arrive we declare our return
Our merit will come to the ancestral temple[8]

YFSJ 28.559

12
Li Shimin (597–649)

Beyond the border the mournful wind stabs
At Jiaohe the ice is already frozen
On the Gobi waves pile in hundreds of folds
The Yin Mountains are a thousand miles deep in snow
On the remote forts stir the beacon fires
Ridge after ridge display signal flags
Sad and lonely the furling banners
Watering their horses they leave the Long Wall
Cold sand enchains the cavalry tracks
The Ordos wind severs the border voices
The Hun dust finally clears near Jade Pass
Tibetan flutes harmonize with military gongs
Throughout the desert shields and pikes are retired
Wagons and troops shake the plains
The Chief Commander returns to Corridor hills
Generals turn back toward Horse City
Standards raised, the air and mists are still
The steles inscribed, merit and fame established
Along the vast border there is only one uniform
To the Cloud Pavilion victory songs return

YFSJ 38.559

13
Yu Shinan (558–638)

Galloping horses ford the river banks
They struggle across the deep currents
Up ahead they meet the ambassador's carriage
The Chief Commander is in place at Loulan
The mounts of the light cavalry are still muzzled

The horses of decoy troops remain unsaddled
Into warm pools fall the cascading brooks
The plank catwalks connect dangerous ridges
No rewards yet for opening of the hinterlands
How could losing the city be forgiven
There is a moon, but the pass is still dark
Although it's springtime, the Corridor remains cold
The clouds are dark again casting no shadows
Ice has formed so we can't hear the rapids
Forever separated, I shall long for you
With this meal I would keep you awhile

YFSJ 38.559

14
Yuan Lang (fl. 620)

The Ordos wind blows the autumn grasses
The Chang'an roads are cleared for the imperial carriage
The Long Wall goes on and on without end
And protects us from our enemy's armies
Its construction was the act of a sage
The difficult labor was clearly a great deed
The coastal tribes are part of the fold
The dragon wastes are open to us again
The dust devils at Jade Pass are settled
The road through Gold Mountain has been opened
Tang, avenging insult, made the northern assault
Shun's praises influenced the southern areas
The work of taming the wilds was first done
And then pacifications of the border were numerous
In our court robes we trample their Wolf Mountain
Our victory songs float through Horse City
The mountains resound with the phoenix's call
Frost patterns decorate the precious lances
Our tributary states return home, standards held high
The Khan comes now only after knocking at the pass

The setting sun brings forth the cold clouds
The startling river covers the parched plain
The falling leaves are already cold
The river's current is clear and swift
The corvée labor is completed for all seasons
Shields and spears are stored for a thousand years
We are now in such a time of peace
The sweating horses never will be sent out
And so we turn to our writing brush and inkstone
Drafting the imperial thanksgiving to heaven and earth

YFSJ 38.560

15
Wang Han (fl. 710)

The young men of Chang'an have no grand plans
Their lifelong desire is to carry the imperial banners
The unicorn bows to the Son of Heaven in the reception hall
The galloping horses strike westward for him against
    the Huns
The Hun winds blow sand like arrows in our troops' faces
The Han soldiers and enemy can't see each other when
    they meet
In the distance we hear the war drums shaking the earth
It is said the Khan will do battle even at night
How could we value more our safety than your favor?
For you we should destroy ten thousand in one march
The warriors' spears dance holding back the setting sun
The spattered blood of the Khan stains the wheels red
Returning we water our horses at the Long Wall spring
Beside the Wall road there are many whitened bones
Asking the old timers where these people came from
They say they were construction troops of the Qin
No cooking smoke in the yellow dusk north of the border
The cries of ghosts wailing rise up into the heavens
The innocent were executed, the successful unrewarded

Lonely souls of the dead wander along this Wall
Back then the Qin emperor rose with sword in hand
The feudal lords crawled away not daring to look up
That rich empire ruled with powerful armies for twenty years
Corvée laborers suffered nine thousand miles of construction
How foolish it was for the Qin emperor to build that Wall
Heaven in the end destroyed him, not the northern Huns
One day, calamity arose within his lonely palace walls
Xianyang along the Wei was never to be the capital again

YFSJ 38.560

16
Wang Jian (fl. 755)

The Long Wall spring
Many are the horse bones beside the Long Wall spring
In ancient times there was no well, there was no stream
It came only with the Qin troops who built the Wall
Assault troops water their horses, sad they can't return
The Wall has become but a heap for homeward gazes
The hoofprints not yet dried, the men near the spring
But after the horses, the stagnant water is depleted
With bows for pillows they sleep waiting for the spring
        to refill
One can't see the Yin Mountains at the forward columns
And when a horse throws a shoe, it's hung around its neck
If all the young men die in battle who will be enfeoffed?

YFSJ 38.560–61

17
Seng Zilan

When the traveler approaches the Long Wall
He waters his horse at the Long Wall spring
The horse neighs at the stench of the water

In which the bones of the assault troops soak
Even though it might be a flowing spring
Gushing on without ever stopping
It can wash away the dirt on the bones
But not the wronged souls inside them
The bones are like flowing water itself
Their returning spirits travel the four seas
Wailing, their voices flow through the air
Perhaps speaking these very words

YFSJ 38.561

Lines of Separation: Dreams and Letters

The most consistent theme that threads its way through the first part of the "Yin ma" series, but not into every poem, is that of separation, and specifically the separation of a young couple when the man is forced into government service on the northern border of China. Separation is a theme found throughout early Chinese poetry, with this specific configuration particularly important in times of Chinese imperialist expansion. Thus, we can understand the theme in this series as a microcosm of such thematic lines in a great deal of that early poetry, which means this intratext connects easily with the greater intertextual world of Chinese poetry.

The portrayal of this separation fills poem 1 (the *gu ci*), from the opening "distant road" to the closing of the husband's letter. The point of view is that of the woman, and her voice will echo down through the centuries in the laments of hundreds of lonely wives. The beginning of those laments (the "abandoned wife" *(qi fu)* poems) is generally identified with the Han "Nineteen Old Poems," with which this poem shares definite affinities and probably a similar provenance. The similar thematic line is carried by language, images, and motifs shared with the "Old Poems." For example, the first line of the *yuefu* poem is found verbatim as the opening line of the second "Old Poem." Moreover, the important "letter motif" that concludes the *yuefu* poem is found couched in language and usage like that of another of the "Old Poems" (no. 17), which in several ways mirrors the *gu ci* of the "Yin ma" set:

> First month of winter brings on the cold
> With its biting north wind
> I am more melancholy as the nights grow long
> Gazing at the stars arrayed above
> On the fifteenth the bright moon is full
> On the twentieth it begins to wane
> A traveler comes from a distant region
> Presenting me with your letter
> At the top it said, "Forever thinking of you"
> Below it said, "How long is our separation"
> I put the letter inside my robe
> For three years the ink never fades
> My heart is always filled with thoughts of you
> But I fear you do not know of my concern

WX 29.1349–50

While the final lines of this poem are somewhat reorganized and include an additional denouement, the affinities between the two letter scenes, including shared verbatim passages, are striking. In another "Old Poem" (no. 16), which also portrays an abandoned wife, we find a dream sequence similar to the one in the middle of the "Yin ma" poem. Here are the pertinent lines from that "Old Poem":

> Sleeping alone, the long nights grow heavy
> I dreamt of his fine, bright features
> My good man thinks only of me, his old love
> So he comes calling, offering me his carriage

WX 29.1349

Finally, the unusual closing verse of the *yuefu* poem, where the husband's letter urges her to "Make sure you eat well," can be found as part of a projected conversation in the closing of the first "Old Poem":

On and on, again on and on
I am separated from you for life
More than ten thousand miles apart
Each one at the edges of the world
The road is long and impassable
Who knows when we will see each other
The Hun horse leans into the north wind
The Viet bird nests on the southern bough
Day by day we are further apart
Day by day my sash is more slack
Floating clouds block the shining sun
The wanderer doesn't turn back to look
I have grown old just thinking of you
The years have passed so suddenly
Abandoned, but forget it now
Just make sure you eat well[9]

WX 29.1343

I do not believe that these affinities between the "Old Poems" and the "Yin ma" *gu ci* are the product of influence or borrowings, but rather are derived from the literary system to which they belong. While we must assume a shared sociolect, that does not mean they had actual textual contact. We would note that the language throughout the "Old Poems" is somewhat more generalized and elevated than that of the *gu ci*, especially in its use of parallel couplets, as seen in the middle part of the last poem cited.[10]

When viewed against these "Old Poems" and the "Yin ma" *gu ci*, the rest of the series suggests other complications of the separation theme. For example, not only do the warm and forgiving words of the woman in the first "Old Poem," "Just make sure you eat well," find their direction nearly reversed in the first "Yin ma" poem, where they are spoken by the man to her, but also when we find a glancing reference to it six centuries later in Yu Shinan's poem (no. 13) we seize upon its implications.[11] There, in the context of imperial militarism, we find the concluding couplet spoken suddenly and unexpectedly by, we must assume, the woman again: "Forever separated, I shall long for you / With this meal I would keep you awhile."[12] This abrupt entry of the woman's voice into the closing couplet of poem 13 asks that we reconcile it with the surface-level meaning of rest of the poem. In light of the earlier contexts in which we have seen that voice, we might assume a fragment of an earlier dialogue, such as that seen in the end of the second "Old Poem," or perhaps the exchange of letters. Nothing there or in Yu's poem allows us that letter—we must simply appropriate it from the related poems, "Old Poem" 17, the "Yin ma" *gu ci*, or, better, poem 3 by Chen Lin. By reading the last two lines of Yu Shinan's poem as a letter, we put the poem in much closer contact with the mainstream of the early part of the "Yin ma" series, thereby enriching the series, while the series explicates it.[13]

Assuming a letter in the closing of Yu's poem is especially possible because of Chen Lin's use of the letter in his development of the theme of separation (no. 3). Chen expands the letter into correspondence, extrapolating the man's concern into exaggerated altruism, and the woman's resignation into intense devotion. The concluding lines of the dialogue are, however, closer in tone to the resigned despair that we find throughout the "Yin ma" series. Abandoned at home she asks rhetorically, "And how could I ever go on all by myself?" Chen doesn't reply, but three hundred years later Wang Bao (no. 9), describing the "bitter border life" that Chen Lin's heroine hears about, is still wondering "The day ends—what should we do?" Fu Xuan's (no. 4) answer to that question meanwhile gathers dust as the answer that no one wants: "Since there is no time to meet in this life / I shall see you below in the Yellow Springs."

Thus, the thread of this bittersweet theme of the separated lovers finds itself slowly unraveling as the "Yin ma" series grows. We seize every opportunity we can to revive it intratextually, such as finding antecedents for the "wandering traveler" *(you ke)* of poem 17 in the "Nineteen Old Poems" and in the *gu ci*. But in the end we must abandon "separation" for another theme, that of the "border life." In the early part of the series these are not themes that run counter to each other, rather the "border life" is the story of separation told in the male voice. When the man contemplates that separation he naturally turns to the pain he suffers (either actually or conventionally) on the border of China, and especially to the Wall that defines that border.

Border Lines: The Tripartite Title

The title "Watering Horses at the Long Wall Spring" is itself replete with signs that connect it with the complex system of border images. While the first two poems in the series (along with no. 4) do not include any reference to the tripartite image of horse/wall/spring, we do find it scattered, in varying degrees of identity with the title, throughout most of the later poems. In fact, already in the third poem, which probably predates poem 2, the title appears verbatim in the first couplet of the poem, "Watering horses at the Long Wall spring / The cold water cuts them to the bone." This simple appropriation of title for verse occurs two other times in the series (in nos. 11 and 17). In five other poems (nos. 8, 9, 12, 15, and 16) we find verses that can be easily identified as variations of the title, and in most of the rest we find traces of the tripartite image. In Wang Bao's poem (no. 9) he offers a simple substitution of one character in the title—"corner" replaces "spring"— as his verse variation, which allows the line to enter in the rhyme scheme that unites the poem. In Wang Han's poem (no. 15) a variation is built by adding two words, *hui lai,* "returning," to the beginning of the title to increase it to the requisite seven-syllable prosody he is using. With this addition the watering of horses becomes part of the relief felt by the soldiers *returning from,* rather than going to, battle.

Poems 8 and 12 share a slightly more complicated variation that rearranges and substitutes words of the title, yielding "Watering their horses they leave the Long Wall." Since this line is shared by the two poems it suggests that we might look more closely at the relationship between these otherwise rather divergent poems. Zhang Zhengjian's poem (no. 8) is an effective description of the Chinese soldier trapped in a "Tibetan fortress"; Emperor Li Shimin's poem (no. 12), on the other hand, celebrates the victorious return from a border war, which ends as

"Tibetan flutes harmonize with military gongs." Here we have the extremes of potentiality of that Wall, symbol of the place where China ends and China begins. For the soldier it is a land "with no means to cross," but for the emperor it is a place from which to return victorious, thereby securing the heartland of China (a sentiment shared by the other emperor's poem in this series, no. 11 by Sui Yangdi). While such a contrast was always present between the visions of the defenders of borders and those who have them defended, the two poems read against each other, pivoting on the shared line, bring that contrast into sharper focus. This is especially so when we draw in Wang Han's poem (no. 15), which embraces the two visions. Wang Han's "returning" variation, mentioned above, also leads the reader away from battle toward an imperial celebration, but Wang suddenly turns his poem into an indictment against such a celebration. His transformation of imperial victory into defeat (epitomized by the fall of the *too* imperial Qin) occurs exactly between this "returning" line and the next, which reads "Beside the Wall road there are many whitened bones."

The last verse variation on the title, found in poem 16 by Wang Jian, diverges even further from the original and sharpens this contrast of suffering and of military victory; at the same time it leads us into another whole line of intratextual relationships. Wang Jian's poem is filled with the tripartite image, introduced by a variation that extends over the first two lines: "The Long Wall spring / Many are the horse bones beside the Long Wall spring." Here the nutritive "watering" is undermined by references to the skeletons of horses for which that water is intended. We have echoes of the "whitened bones" that transformed poem 15, and Wang Jian follows suit with a poem of deprivation and despair. The bones and the water (or the lack of it) are the very things that spell danger for the border soldier, but which are hidden, either actually or metaphorically, from imperial view. We shall return to the poems' concern with water, but first we need to see whence come these bones.

The bones, it turns out, come with the Wall, and their association is found in some of the earliest intertextual references. In his introductory notes Guo Maoqian says:

In Li Daoyuan's [ob. 527] *Shui jing zhu (Commentary to the Classic of Waters)*, he says "In the twenty-fourth year of the First Emperor's rule [223 B.C.] he had the Crown Prince Fusu and General Meng Tian supervise construction of the Long Wall, which began in Lintao and extended to Jieshi. In the east it touched the Liao sea, in the west it ran parallel to the Yin Mountains, altogether being somewhat over ten thousand miles long. Thus Yang Quan's [fl. 525] *Wu li lun (Discussion of Phenomena)* says 'When Qin constructed the Long Wall, the dead lay on top of each other.' A folk song says "If it's a boy, don't bother to fuss over him / If it's a girl wean her on dried meat / Don't you see near the Long Wall / Corpses tangled up with each other." *(YFSJ 38.555)*

The Wall is everywhere throughout the middle and later part of the "Yin ma" series (and peculiarly absent in the beginning), with specific references to the Qin construction most numerous in the later poems. To this day the suffering associated with the building of the Long Wall is a commonplace in Chinese thought, often symbolized by the bodies of the conscripts that were thrown into the wall as they died. The best-known legend of the Wall, that of Meng Jiangnü, centers on this unnerving practice—a legend that leads to and from the theme of the separation of lovers.[14]

The folk song quoted by Guo Maoqian, assumed to date from the Qin or early Han, is found nearly verbatim (and I have marked it as a quotation) in the plea by the husband in Chen Lin's poem (no. 3), where the corpses have ossified into "skeletons tangled together." To the Chinese mind unburied human bones portend the most unhappy of ghosts, thus when the bones reemerge in the Wang Han's poem (no. 15), they are accompanied by the expected ghostly wailing. In the last poem in the series (no. 17) those ghosts and that wailing become nearly the sole topic of concern, as the whole question of the border fades into the background. In Wang Jian's poem (no. 16), however, the human bones are transformed into equine ones, a most peculiar metamorphosis it would seem at first, but logical enough if viewed within the emerging militarism of the series, where the horse becomes more the focus of attention than the man.

For the Chinese during and after the Han the horse represented the border and war. They learned to use the mounted horse from the border people; they discovered and imported Arabian horses (which were at times nearly worshipped) from the border; and they used such horses almost exclusively in battles along those borders in the North and Northwest. Thus the symbol of the "Huns" *(hu)*, the horse, became the symbol of those who fought against them, the Chinese border troops. When a horse was watered at a spring near the Long Wall, there can be no doubt what it was there for—to *zheng*, to punish, to avenge, to attack, thereby protecting the heartland of China. This common military term first appears in this series in Cao Pi's early, somewhat peripheral poem, but soon the concept and term *zheng* comes to pervade the whole intratext, especially in the binomes *zheng ren* (assault troops), *zheng ma* (assault horses), and *zheng qi* (assault cavalry).

We have seen that there was an attempt by some poets to move this basic militarism into an imperially appreciated heroism, but those efforts were consistently threatened by the intratext in which they wrote. The "bones," human and equine, kept showing up, until finally in poem 17 we have bones, exposed and rank, littered throughout— "The horse neighs at the stench of the water / In which the bones of the assault troops soak." Thus, the suffering moves from the conscripted laborer to the conscripted warrior, and beyond to his lonely ghost wandering the world. The Wall is not the end of his travel, but the point from which he moves out, following the imperialist drive of the state, into a land that is not China. His separation becomes that of a man isolated by the "distant road" in "another land" that is a totally non-Chinese world.

The description of that non-Chinese world beyond the Wall occupies much of the poetry in the later part of the "Yin ma" series. While those descriptions share much with a larger corpus identified as the "border poetry" of the Tang and earlier, they find a more delimited identity within and between themselves. If any part of the title can be identified with the generation of those descriptions it is the "spring" and its aqueous associations. Intratextual associations of water, or the lack of it, form the last of our thematic lines to be explored.

Water Lines: Fire and Ice

In the early Chinese concept of the world, the north and west border regions were defined almost exclusively by cold and aridity. This thinking was well established even before the great Han expeditions during the reign of Emperor Wu (140–87 B.C.), which brought the Chinese into contact with the far regions of the Pamirs and India. The following passage from the "Zhao hun," a text that dates at least from the early Han, gives an indication of the connotations that those regions held for the Chinese at that time:

> Oh soul, come back! For the west holds many perils.
> The Moving Sands stretch on for a hundred leagues.
> You will be swept into the Thunder's Chasm, and dashed in
>   pieces, unable to help yourself;
> And even should you chance to escape that, beyond is the
>   empty desert,
> And red ants as huge as elephants and wasps as big as
>   gourds.
> The five grains do not grow there; dry stalks are the only
>   food;
> And the earth there scorches men up; there is nowhere to
>   look for water.
> And you will drift there for ever, with nowhere to go in that
>   vastness.
> Oh soul, come back! lest you bring on yourself perdition.
>
> Oh soul, come back! In the north you may not stay.
> There the layered ice rises high, and the snowflakes fly for
>   a hundred leagues and more.
> Oh soul, come back! You cannot long stay here.[15]

The western border areas also had favorable connotations by virtue of their early association with the mythical Kunlun Mountain, but this "west" was the west contiguous with the Sichuan basin, that is, the eastern, Chamdo, region of the Tibetan plateau. The Chamdo region, in which are found the headwaters of the three great river systems of East and Southeast Asia, was known for its well-watered, densely forested mountains. Due to the extremely articulated landscape and heavy forest, the area remained almost completely untouched by Chinese western expansion, which traveled instead through the Gansu Corridor out along the so-called "silk routes" of the central Asian desert. The Gansu Corridor, referred to as the area of *Long* (translated as "Corridor") in the "Yin ma" poems, lies in a northwestern direction from the Chinese central plain, protected by the western arm of the Long Wall just to its north. Thus there was always a "northern" feel to these western regions in the Chinese mind.

The depiction in literature of the north and northwest border region as cold and dry is obviously accurate: the Mongolian steppes in the north are very cold, and the western region of the Taklamakan desert is one of the driest areas in the world. Yet there is also a great deal of stereotyping involved in the tradition that assumes everything outside the central plain was uniformly inhospitable. The vague geographical references for these regions in the "Yin ma" poems, usually merely called the "border," encourages the commingling of these two images of cold and aridity. From this commingling is generated a whole complex of images associated with the border, images that have a strong intertextual life since they were seldom challenged by actual mundane experience with the border regions. Border poems were continuously generated intertextually out of the language of aridity and coldness of other poems.

But, of course, the "Yin ma" series *does* center on the image of "watering," thus introducing an anomalous aqueous element into the equation. Annotators of the poems did not let that element pass unnoticed. Guo Maoqian notes: "The *Guang ti (Broad Titles)* says, 'South of the Wall there is a wet slope, in which is a hole in the ground. From that hole a spring flows. In Han times when the commanders led assaults to the north of the border, they all watered their horses there.'" Which brings Li Daoyuan to the conclusion: "Today at the entrance of the southern gorge near Baidao we find the Long Wall. North from the wall there is a steep slope, along the side of which there is a spring that flows from a hole in the ground. You can scoop out water without ever exhausting it. When the song mentions 'Watering horses at the Long Wall spring,' these are not just fanciful words" (*YFSJ* 38.555). This disclaimer does betray a basic suspicion of the association of water and the Wall. Nonetheless, the poems, especially in the later part of the series, exploit this aqueous association well, even when the rest of their imagery, conventional as it may be, is forcing them out into the "Moving Sands" of the Taklamakan Desert.

The references to water in the earliest poems of the "Yin ma" series are surely to water of the central plain, not of the border—the first poem's river bank surrounded by verdant growth (echoed in no. 4) and Cao Pi's mention of the Yangtze River. These poems actually have very little to do with the border at all; the geographical terms of the first poem, "another land" *(tuo xiang)* and "different district" *(yi xian)* (which it shares with the "Old Poems") are not only vague, but also likely to have been within China proper. Guo Maoqian's statement that the *gu ci* poem is about "a soldier in the assault forces who stop at the Long Wall to water their horses, and about his wife who reflects on his travails" is obviously a retrospective explanation (*YFSJ* 38.555). The poem by Chen Lin (no. 3) is the first to employ the aqueous image in the context of the border area. Wu Jing's *Explanations* highlights this change of emphasis: "The old version is about how the wandering husband can't return home; some say the text is by Cai Yong. Chen Lin's text, which reads 'Watering horses at the Long Wall spring / The cold water cuts them to the bone,' then refers to the bitter corvée labor that the Qin people suffered building the Wall."[16] In Chen's poem the northern cold turns the nourishing spring into a destructive "chill" in the bones of the horses, which are proxies for the soldiers, both soon to be transformed into skeletons. Repeatedly through this series the water's natural benefice is turned into something harmful; following Chen Lin's lead, this transformation is usually performed by coldness that is so easily associated with the border.

The most obvious derivation of Chen's image is in poem 8, where the cold water, having turned to ice (already mentioned in poems 5 and 6), becomes in the process more "cutting" *(shang)*: "The cutting ice gathers around the frozen hooves." Poem 10 continues these developments, in spirit and in word, with the line "[assault horses] enter the ice, passing through the freezing water." This coldness and its ensuing ice soon begin to negate the water itself—ice in this sense is not water because it cannot be drunk. Coldness also pervades much of Yu Shinan's poem (no. 13) until the closing where the "ice has formed so we can't hear the rapids," as if the sound of flowing water were nourishment itself or news from home. In Wang Bao's poem (no. 9) the negation of the water is parallel to the negation of the road home; rain turns to snow and waves to ice, both foreboding effects of the wild North. Once the water is negated, we move into aridity and the landscape of the "Moving Sands"—"Flying dust collects in the unending columns / The sand is flat, the cavalry hoofprints are many." The merging of coldness, water, and aridity suggested by Wang Bao's poem is continued by Emperor Li Shimin's poem (no. 12) where not only are the water frozen and the Yin Mountains deep in snow, but the Gobi replaces the ocean—"On the Gobi waves pile in hundreds of folds." The "cavalry hoofprints" of Wang's poem now blend even closer with the images of cold and dryness: "Cold sand enchains the cavalry tracks." The horses' hooves are freezing, not in the cold water of the spring, but in the frozen sands of the far West.

After the positive military stance found in the poems of Li Shimin, Yu Shinan, and especially Yuan Lang (no. 14), the last three poems of the set return more to the imagery of the title, especially that of the spring. Poems 15 and 16 both continue the negation of that water, but in ways quite different from that of cold and simple aridity, and here the militarism is more subdued and less conventionalized. Poem 16 mixes the human and equine to undermine the nourishing water, but it does so with an assumed frailty of the spring, in addition to contamination. First explaining the presence of the spring as unnatural and tainted by its association with the Qin construction project—"In ancient times there was no well, there was no stream / It came only with the Qin troops that built the Wall"—Wang Jian then describes how man and horse must now share the "stagnant water." This contamination is even worse since the men come second, after the water has been depleted by the thirsty horses. Again the hoofprints appear, but they are not in the cold, dry sand; rather they are in the mud of the stagnant water; the thirsty men look down into a spring empty except for those muddy tracks. For a drink they must wait overnight, "with bows for pillows," as the spring refills. Like the Wall, which is "but a heap for homeward gazes," the spring is a shadow of its earlier, nourishing self.

The last poem, as we have noted above, is particularly concerned with the contamination of the spring water by the bones that soak in it, which yields a stench that even the horses cannot stand. Here the bones of all the suffering conscripts who fill the poems render the water unfit for the horses. As the series draws to an end, the tripartite image of horse/wall/spring is fully present, but in a configuration that is innovating and startling.

Loose Ends

In his notes and in his organization of chapter 38, Guo Maoqian delineates two smaller groups of poems that have ties to the main body of the seventeen "Yin ma" poems. These sets have titles derived from the first two "Yin ma" poems. The power of Guo's remarks asks that we consider those poems as an extension of the intratextual relationships that help define the set. I would also suggest that these associations can be drawn even further out of the intratext.

The smaller of these sets is composed of two poems, which are "derived" from Cao Pi's (no. 2) imitation—their titles are taken verbatim from the first line of his poem. In case we miss the connection Guo Maoqian's note to the first poem makes it clear: "Wei Wendi's [Cao Pi] 'Watering Horses at the Long Wall Spring' has the line 'The ships float across the Yangtze.' Here that is used as title" (*YFSJ* 38.562). There is little in the poems themselves, however, that suggests the military theme of Cao's poem. In fact they have more thematic affinity with the early "separation" poems of the "Yin ma" set, from which Cao's poem so obviously diverges. This is particularly true with the first of these, by Xiao Gang (Emperor Jianwen of the Liang):

The Ships Float across the Yangtze

With the bright sun shining on blue waves
The wanderer sets out from the royal domain
He gazes at layered hills curving along the shore

> But sees only a few sails up ahead in the distance
> Over the broad water blows a floating cloud
> The wind on the River stirs his night robes
> The migrating geese share the night on the isle
> But in the cold a duck flies off between the moorages
> When he is upset, what traveler
> Does not think of returning home early

YFSJ 38.562

This poem is related in a general way to the "Yin ma" poems through the common themes of separation and travel. Yet we cannot identify any specific link, and it is distinctly unrelated to the "border poetry" of that set. We have here much more a "central plain" poem related to a huge corpus of separation and farewell poems in the early Chinese poetic tradition. Of the poems we have mentioned above Xiao Gang's poem is most related to the first "Yin ma" poem and to a number of the "Nineteen Old Poems." Even there the connections are, however, tenuous, and it is really only Guo Maoqian's alignment that suggests their intratextuality.

Guo Maoqian does not have any introductory note to the second set of derived poems, but their position in the anthology directly following the "Yin ma" poems and before the "Across the Yangtze" poems makes their assumed derivation clear. This set of five poems takes its title verbatim from the opening line of the first poem of the "Yin ma" set, which, as noted above, is shared with the second poem of the "Nineteen Old Poems." The poems' general theme of the "abandoned wife" again finds affinities with the "Yin ma" and "Nineteen Old Poems," but in this instance we have more specific relationships in shared imagery and language. We also have more connections between the five poems themselves, indicating the functional intratextuality of that set.

Of these five poems the most intratextual is the longest and last, by Xun Chang (fl. 420), which even includes reference to the "border" poems. In order to illustrate that intratextuality I shall interject remarks and related passages between sections of this translation of Xun's poem (*YFSJ* 38.562).

Growing Green the Grass along the River

Blazing are the fires on the mountains,
Distantly cut off from east of the Corridor,
East of the Corridor is out of reach.

This reference to *Long*, the Gansu Corridor, places this poem immediately in the context of the border poems of the later part of the "Yin ma" series. This context clearly establishes, and is established by, the (beacon) "fires" of the first line, which are part of almost all border poems, acting as signs for all the purpose and danger of the border war. While most poems with such an opening would continue with similar border imagery, this poem "reorients" its focus by twice referring to "east [literally 'right'] of the Corridor" that is, China proper. Thus the "border poem" quickly transforms itself into a "central plain poem," whereupon Xun picks up the woman's voice:

Then his bright spirit comes to wake me from sleep
Awakened we are together between coverlet and curtain
But suddenly I know he is in another country
In another country, each in a different city
Always seeking but never reaching each other

These lines obviously derive directly from the first poem of the "Yin ma" series where the woman also dreams of his visit from "another land" (lines 5–8). The simple language of the "Yin ma" poem is nicely enriched with coverlet and curtain, while at other points it is repeated verbatim or nearly so. Xun continues in a similar vein:

Lost ruins in the gazed-through mists
Leaves fall and feel the ice harden
With rising dawn each enters his own home
Who would want to bring me along with him

Here again we see the direct imprint of the "Yin ma" *gu ci* (lines 9–12), which Xun has elaborated with new and more difficult language. His variation on the verb *zhi* (to feel/know/sense) and its related imagery is especially effective. Attention is also drawn to the strained syntax of his first line and the forced derivation of this closing, where the simple verb *yan* (to talk) is transformed into the complex and forceful *panqian* (to pull up or along).

> A traveler comes from the northern area
> Presenting me with a bolt of heavy silk
> I tell the servant to open the silk
> Inside is hidden a jade tablet
> I kneel quietly to read the hidden tablet
> The words are bitter, and the tone sad
> At the top it says "Each should work hard"
> Below it says, "Forever longing for you"

The immediate source for these lines is again obviously the closing of "Yin ma" poem 1 (lines 13–19), which Xun follows closely but also works to enhance, as silk replaces fish and jade tablets replace letters. While there seems to be no connection in Xun's closing with the "letter passage" in Chen Lin's poem (no. 3), we do hear the distinct echo of the "Nineteen Old Poems," not only from the letter passage of "Old Poem" 17, but also obliquely from the opening lines of "Old Poem" 18—"A traveler comes from a distant place / Presenting me with a bolt of fine silk." Thus we can best understand Xun's poem not as a creation in isolation, but as a conscious and specific effort to participate with the "Yin ma" intratext that he knew.

While the "Across the Yangtze" poems devolve into thematic concerns quite unrelated to the central "Yin ma" poems, Xun Chang's "Growing Green the Grass along the River" is intratextually bound to the first "Yin ma" poem. In these two poems we therefore see the very edges of the intratextual range, on the outer border dissolving into intertextuality and on the inner condensing into imitation. Between these two opposite movements lie the "Yin ma" poems, which, with all their variation, generally hold to the center of intratextuality and give the peripheral poems their point of reference.

Conclusion

The other four poems that precede Xun Chang's poem in this set are as much related to the "Nineteen Old Poems" as they are to the "Yin ma" poems; this includes language and images that they share with the "Old Poems" and among themselves. Shen Yue's poem is perhaps the best, but not atypical, example of the complexity of that interrelationship.

> Soft and silent the dust lies on my bed
> My heart stirs with memories of a friend
> But that friend does not come to mind
> I sigh alone in the deep of the night
> Sighing I think of his fine face
> Do not talk of our distant separation
> The separation slowly grows longer
> From my empty bed I offer him a cup of wine

YFSJ 38.561

Read intratextually, Shen's sixth line can be seen as the woman's response to the letter that "she" received in "Old Poem" 17, with echoes also in Xun Chang's poem and in several "Yin ma" poems. At the close of that letter the man speaks of "how long is our separation," but Shen, with a slight modification of language, has the woman pleading with her lover not to talk about their "distant separation," which "slowly grows longer." If we read Shen's sixth line only within the context of the poem itself it seems awkward and unattached; that is because its proper context is far beyond the poem, in this intratext.

While the last line of Shen Yue's poem seems perfectly comfortable in its immediate context, a similar intratextual reading may also be possible there. The "empty bed" of the last line, which gathers dust in the first line, brings us easily back to the closing of the second "Old Poem," which reads, "My wanderer is gone and doesn't return / This empty bed is hard to keep alone." Thus, the toast that Shen's woman offers is from that "difficult" bed, and it is a toast meant to relieve some of her loneliness. But whom does she toast? Her separated lover, or someone there with her? Perhaps the bed was just too hard to keep alone, and she has taken another lover as she was urged by "her" husband in his letter to her in Chen Lin's poem (no. 3)—"You should marry again, don't wait for me"—but she still *does* remember her "old husband," as he hoped.

Throughout this chapter we have seen the "Yin ma" poems, especially the early ones, continually interact with the "Nineteen Old Poems." This interrelationship is even more pronounced in these derived poems; in fact, we can argue that here the "Old Poems" are more part of the intratext than the "Yin ma" poems from which these poems are said to be derived. Since the "Old Poems" are part of a *yuefu* intratext we might suggest that *they* too are a type of *yuefu* poetry, despite their exclusion from all the standard *yuefu* anthologies. We should remember that the title for this second derived set of poems, "Growing Green the Grass along the River," is also the title of the second "Old Poem," which seems to be as much the model for the "imitations" here as it was for other imitations in the *Wen xuan*.[17] As have others before him, Jean-Pierre Diény has argued for the affinity between the "Old Poems" and *yuefu* poetry, but he has emphasized the literati adaptation of those poems. He says: "The *yuefu* artists and their successors created—and in my view this is their principal accomplishment—a new poetic language, in which the early authors of the *gushi* poetry found literary materials whose elements they arranged into orderly forms. Most of the 'Nineteen Old Poems' are merely skillful rewritings of formulas derived from the repertoire of court entertainers."[18] Guo Maoqian's exclusion of the "Nineteen Old Poems" from his anthology is certainly an acknowledgment of their separate listing in the canonical *Wen xuan*. Yet by the definition of intratextuality, these poems might be considered as much a part of the *yuefu* genre as many others in Guo Maoqian's corpus, and more so than some. Thus, that is where I would place them, belatedly in the *yuefu* genre, increasing the corpus by nineteen.

Reading Notes to the "Yin ma" Poems

1

The "old version" is a standard anthology piece of the "Han *yuefu*" type, regarded as a folk poem of that early period by most readers.[19] Its main theme, the separation of lovers, its prosody (five-syllable lines), and some of its language are shared with the "Nineteen Old Poems," which are believed to date from the same period.[20] The poem's most distinctive features—the dream sequence, the closing letter, and the woman's voice throughout—have significantly contributed to development of the intratextual relationships of the set.

2

The poem by the Wei Emperor Cao Pi celebrates a naval assault, perhaps that by the Wei against the kingdom of Wu, across the Yangtze. Cao's poem is only vaguely related to the *gu ci* or to its title, and we assume music is the significant but invisible connection. Prosodically the poem is highly wrought, with pervasive parallel couplets and unified end rhyme, distinguishing it from many of the more freely formed poems in the series.

3

This poem is the only other well-known member of the series, and is one of only four extant poems by Chen Lin, who was associated with Cao Pi's father, Cao Cao. The poem is seminal in the conflation and projection of the several thematic lines discussed and in this way overshadows the *gu ci* poem while it accepts important motifs, such as the exchange of letters, from it.

4

The opening of Fu Xuan's poem, as well as its general thematic lines, borrows much from the *gu ci*, but the general abstraction of the theme of separation and the pervasive parallelism mark the poem as particularly Fu's, who was a major court figure during the Jin. The ending is an especially noteworthy variation on the original and may be derived from Chen Lin's (no. 3) closure.

5

While it pays little attention to the *gu ci* or other preceding poems, Lu Ji's elaborately constructed poem is noted for its mixing of images of war and those of imperial splendor, all complicated by far-ranging literary references. This poem is discussed at length in Chapter 4.

6
This nicely wrought poem by the major poet Shen Yue is quite divorced from the central lines of the "Yin ma" intratext, connecting with it only in the general exploration of the border imagery. The final couplet is especially effective, and later poems in the set give its aqueous imagery more weight when viewed retroactively.

7
The elegant poem by Chen Shubao (Chen Houzhu, last ruler of the southern state of Chen) has prosodic affinities with that by Cao Pi (no. 2); yet it also includes subtle nods to the *gu ci* poem (e.g., "another land"). The general theme of militarism, which can also be traced to Cao's poem, is here complicated by the startling and vaguely disturbing imagery in which it is embedded. The intratextual connections of this poem are perhaps the most subtle in the series.

8
Zhang Zhengjian's poem is filled with timidity and hesitation, rather than martial bravura. In this way, it is one of the first in the set to question the theme of military heroism that builds through the later part of the series. The images and language this poem shares with the previous (but later) poem by Chen Shubao suggest that Chen wrote his poem with this one specifically in mind.

9
This elaborate poem by Wang Bao, a well-known poet of the Northern Zhou, continues the military themes of earlier poems but undermines their heroism with the bleak imagery similar to that in Zhang Zhengjian's poem and to that in "border poetry" of the Tang period in general.

10
The poem by the monk Shang Fashi is a relatively straightforward treatment of the general border motif—the unusual lunar imagery in line 5 may be a scribal error; I suspect the line should read "clear moon" *(qing yue)* rather than "stained moon" *(zi yue)*. There is, however, an effective exploitation of

the water imagery in the middle couplet, while the focus on the horse as a surrogate for the soldier is weakened somewhat in the closing lines, when the man suddenly speaks out.

11
The poem by Emperor Yang of the Sui dynasty is the first of four in the set that celebrate the imperialist significance of the Wall. This is a border poem of the most, perhaps blindly, optimistic kind. Even the connotations of the titular verse in the center of the poem are changed by its surrounding text; the watering of the horses is an easy act on the way to easy glory.

12
The poem by the founding Emperor of the Tang, Li Shimin, shares much with the preceding imperial poem by Sui Yangdi, but diverges even more from the series in a number of ways, the most significant being in its closing, where military victory is celebrated in an imperial setting. The title's signature is there surrounded by a pastiche of conventional "border poetry" images, which seem to jar against Li's intended heroism. More than any other example in this series, intratextual reading undoes the naive surface of the poem, producing another, presumably unintended, meaning.

13
Yu Shinan's poem shares a number of affinities with that of his emperor (no. 12), with whom he was politically and personally close. But the general tenor of "incompletion" in Yu's poem (almost every line contains an adverb meaning "not yet") contrasts with the sense of "accomplishment" celebrated in the closing of Li's poem. Moreover, Yu's closure diverges radically by reintroducing images that suggest the sadness of separation, including what may be an indirect reference to the closing of the *gu ci* poem.

14
The poem by Yuan Lang is consistently more optimistic than the rest of the poems in the set. Every image that would conventionally be construed in an unfavorable light, from frost and swift currents to the Wall and corvée labor, is rewritten into praise for the state. It is more "imperial" even than the two poems by the emperors quoted above. All the conventions of the intratext are there, but they have been oddly revised by Yuan's patriotic zeal, and thus remove the poem from the mainline of the intratext.

15

Wang Han's long and somewhat clumsy poem turns the militarism and heroism of the earlier Tang poems into a diatribe against that militarism, as epitomized in the easy, perhaps allegorical, target of the first Qin emperor (who was the "hero" of the preceding imperialist poems). Buried in all this is the signature title, "Returning we water our horses at the Long Wall spring" (line 13), with its white bones in the next line marking the thematic turn of the poem from military heroism to regrettable despair.

16

Wang Jian's poem is built around an extended exploitation of the water images that have been building through the later part of the series. The folly of the Qin is implied, and we are in the suffering of the "border poetry" variety; yet Wang has enriched the common border imagery with a vivid conflation of water, man, and beast.

17

The last poem, also by a monk (Seng Zilan), has an unearthly air as it dwells on the corpses and souls of the dead soldiers. It participates fully in the set by including the various intratextual signs (including the title as verse) in its relatively straightforward language, but it does take a somewhat more abstract, philosophic stance on the death commonly associated with this intratext.

4

Knots: Intersections of Persona and Text

The focus of this chapter is the *yuefu* poetry of four literati in the early history of the genre: Cao Zhi (192–232), Lu Ji (261–303), Bao Zhao (414–466), and Xiao Gang (Liang Jianwen di) (502–557). These poets are not only dispersed chronologically throughout the formative period of the genre, but also separated by circumstances and personality. Their lives are relatively well documented, and their personalities easily, if often reductively, described and recognized. I have chosen to focus on their *yuefu* poetry to explore not only what those poems can tell us about the poets' voices, but also what it can tell us about the genre. Of the four, Cao Zhi and Bao Zhao are generally recognized as more central to the tradition, but I shall reverse this common approach and concentrate on Lu Ji and Xiao Gang, using Cao and Bao more as foils for discussion. My comments here are in several ways a preface to Chapter 6, which is a consideration of the most important of the *yuefu* literati, Li Bo (701–762); at that time we shall again have occasion to discuss the *yuefu* poetry of Bao Zhao.

By viewing these literati poets as heightened moments in the history of the *yuefu* genre—"knots" that tangle the threads of its intratextual poetics—we can better discern what allows the genre to exist, even to thrive, in the hands of these poets with their distinct poetic voices. At the same time we can see how the genre's intratextuality is irrevocably changed as it passes through these "knots," sometimes weakening, sometimes strengthening, but always giving the poetry more interesting textures.

Four *Yuefu* Corpora

Consideration of the *yuefu* corpora of Cao Zhi, Lu Ji, Bao Zhao, and Xiao Gang reveals certain features of the genre in its formative stages and these poets' relation to it (see table).

Cao Zhi and Lu Ji, both of whom were members of the Chinese aristocracy and victims of its political vicissitudes, stand in interesting counterpoint to each other. Each of them has thirty-odd *yuefu* poems divided between the *xianghe* (bamboo winds) and *zaqu* (miscellaneous tunes) categories. But fifty percent of Cao's corpus is composed of "miscellaneous" poems, distinguishing his *yuefu* poetry from both Lu Ji's corpus and the core tradition. The large number of "miscellaneous poems" in Cao's corpus attests to the "proto-genre" status of much of his *yuefu* poetry, which was drawn into the genre by later imitation and general retroactive reading. Throughout the history of the genre there is a generally decreasing number of *zaqu* poems in the poets' *yuefu* collections. This is because the strengthening of the identity and variety of the genre's categories through its historical development correspondingly disallowed the "miscellaneous" poems, a noncategory. Thus, Xiao Gang, for example, has only seventeen *zaqu* poems in a sixty-two poem corpus, Li Bo has only eighteen out of 119, and Li He (790–816) five out of forty-four.

The presence of *xianghe* poems in the *yuefu* corpora of Cao Zhi and Lu Ji also attest to those two poets' early position in the genre. This category of poems is the earliest and most intratextually generative of the ones now identified with the genre. As the generic identity of *yuefu* poetry expanded diachronically and synchronically, *xianghe* poems gradually came to share their position with new categories of the genre, but the new categories generally replaced the "miscellaneous poems," leaving the *xianghe* poems relatively undisturbed. Thus, *xianghe* poems account for thirty percent of Bao Zhao's *yuefu* poems and thirty-eight

The *Yuefu* Corpora of Four Poets (by Number of Titles)

Guo Maoqian's 12 Categories	Cao Zhi	Lu Ji	Bao Zhao	Xiao Gang
1. *Jiaomiao*				
2. *Yanshe*				
3. *Guchui*				3
4. *Hengchui*			1	4
5. *Xianghe*	14	32	11	24
6. *Qingshang*			3	6
7. *Wuqu*			3	
8. *Qinqu*			3	6
9. *Zaqu*	19	7	17	18
10. *Jindai*				
11. *Zage*			2	2
12. *Xin yuefu*				

percent of Xiao Gang's poems, twenty-three percent of Li Bo's, and twenty-five percent of Li He's.

The relationship that Lu Ji has to the praxis of intratextuality differs significantly from that of Cao Zhi. In Lu's *yuefu* poetry we find one of the earliest attempts to participate consciously in the emerging intratextuality that will define the *yuefu* genre in its maturity. Lu's stance as a practitioner of specific literary imitation, which he shares with his contemporary Fu Xuan, is opposed to Cao's casual patterning on *yuefu* modal and perhaps musical models. Yet Lu's position as an "outsider" to the new Jin court, compounded by his southern origins, contrasts with that of both Fu and Cao, who were both more interior to the highest circles, though in very different ways. The strained, wrought quality that characterizes much of Lu's *yuefu* poetry can in part be explained by his need to establish his literary pedigree with audiences at the royal court, which in the end he does, only to fall victim to their political factionalism. This sets Lu's poetry apart from the *yuefu* of both Cao and Fu; Cao is more rhetorically casual, and Fu more straightforwardly imitative.

The *yuefu* poems of both Bao Zhao and Xiao Gang, on the other hand, delineate categories of *yuefu* poetry as it approached its full identity as a literary genre. Besides the core *xianghe* poems and the ever-present *zaqu* miscellany, we have categories whose claims to musicality are more blatant, if not more conceptual: Xiao has *guchui* (drum and winds) poems, and both have *hengchui* (horizontal flute) poems; they also have poems in the *qingshang* (key) and *qin* (lute) categories as well as in a new "miscellaneous song" *(zage)* category; in addition, Bao has two poems in the more peripheral "dance" *(wu)* category. This array of *yuefu* categories suggests the direction of growth for the genre during the next five hundred years.

While *zaqu* poems often seem to be introduced retroactively into the genre, there are, nonetheless, *zaqu* poems that are important to the genre and to the identity of certain *yuefu* poets. This is the case, for example, with Bao Zhao, whose reputation as a major *yuefu* poet rests primarily on his eighteen "Xing lu nan" ("Hardships of Travel") poems.[1] This is a titular theme that Bao initiated, but which was imitated by Li Bo and many others, thereby bringing it into the center of the genre. This is true for many of his other *yuefu* poems as well. Bao obviously wrote consciously in the genre, as his preface to "Song bo pian" clearly notes (cited in Chapter 2), but not all his "*yuefu*" poems as we now refer to them were actually produced as part of the genre.[2] Not until the High Tang was Bao known primarily as a *yuefu* poet. The often noted close relationship between the *yuefu* poetry of Bao Zhao and Li Bo is evidenced by Li's widespread imitation of Bao's poetry— nearly half of Bao's titles have imitations by Li. Kang-i Sun Chang has suggested that Bao's contemporaries regarded his *shi* poetry more highly than his *yuefu*; we might argue that his reputation as a *yuefu* poet resulted from the Tang (especially Li Bo's) retroactive appreciations and imitations.[3]

The evidence of Xiao Gang's conscious participation in the genre is even clearer. This can be seen in the two anthologies that surround him and his family (the *Wen Xuan* and *Yutai xinyong*), and in Xiao's own poems, which include such obvious title references as "substitution for a *yuefu*" *(dai yuefu)*.

The *yuefu* corpora of both Bao and Xiao are divided nearly equally into poems that draw on earlier titles and those that begin relatively new lines of intratextuality. There are, however, only seven titles shared by the two poets themselves, suggesting very different lines of poetic development. In general, Xiao's *yuefu* poetry is much more at the center of the genre, both contributing to and initiating vigorous lines of intratextuality. Bao's poems, on the other hand, remain rather periph-eral—with the exception of his influential "Xing lu nan" sequence, which has over fifty imitative poems.

Cao Zhi and Lu Ji

Lu Ji's "Yin ma" Poem

As seen in the last chapter, Lu Ji has a "Yin ma chang cheng ku" ("Watering Horses at the Long Wall Spring") poem that is central to the intratextuality of that series. I reintroduce it here as the first of several of his poems that illustrate the particular configuration of his intratextual poetics:

> Driving their horses they climb the Yin Mountains
> Mountains so high the horses refuse to go on
> From the commander of Yin Mountains
> They learn the powerful enemy is at Yanran
> The war carts roll ceaselessly along the rutted road
> Banners and pinions move constantly back and forth
> Raising their eyes to face the snow piled peaks
> Lowering them to wade through frozen streams
> Arriving in winter, the next fall they're still there
> Separated from their families by an endless distance
>
> Indeed the Xianyun barbarians are not yet pacified
> How could the assault troops come back in vain
> The suicide squadrons rush forward screaming

The evil tools of war leave both sides maimed
If the soldiers win, the rewards are meager,
If they lose, their worthless bodies are left behind
But to honor the legacy of Gan and Chen
They win merit capturing the Khan's flag
He reviews the troops, rewarding their leaders
With official positions in the diplomatic quarters

YFSJ 38.557

Several of the points raised in our previous discussion of the "Yin ma" poems are applicable here, especially regarding the conflation of military heroism and the motif of suffering that easily identifies this poem with many other poems in the series, even as it divides itself. The opening ten lines of Lu's poem (from which I have created a stanza) share much of the tenor of the "suffering soldier" poems of the series, while the last ten lines lean toward the heroism of those poems with imperial allegiances. In Lu's well-wrought parallel couplet, "Raising their eyes to face the snow piled peaks / Lowering them to wade through frozen streams" (lines 7–8), we also find an early exploitation of the aqueous images that fill the series.

The second stanza of Lu's "Yin ma" poem introduces a number of images that find their references outside the series. The most obvious is that of the opening line, which uses an archaic (pre-Han) term for the northern barbarians and quite specifically alludes to the verse from the *Shi jing*, "Powerful was Nanzhong / The Xianyun were pacified," thereby urging the troops to emulate this model of Chinese heroism, General Nanzhong of the Zhou dynasty.[4] This inspiration is oddly cooled in the following lines that speak of "*de mo*" and "*xiong qi*"— "suicide squadrons," a reference to the use of military troops as the "end of virtue" *(de zhi mo)* in the *Zhuang zi*; and "evil tools," a reference to military weapons, about which the *Hanfei zi* says, "Weapons are evil tools *(xiong qi)* that must not be used carelessly."[5] In this context even the simple word *zheng* ("rush forward" [contend]) has special significance when it is identified with a reference in the *Wu Yue chunqiu*, which says, "When ladies, lords, and warriors go against virtue, then weapons are evil tools; *contention* is the end of the state."[6] The caution that these references introduce is then itself overturned by the poem's closing, which not only portrays the leaders of the conquering army in a glowing light (in stark contrast to the fate of the soldiers in the first stanza), but also offers other military exemplars, Gan Yanshou and Chen Tang (who were responsible for killing a foreign Khan during the Han dynasty), for emulation.

The imagery in the second stanza of Lu Ji's "Yin ma" poem, a potpourri of intertextual references, often transcends the specific "Yin ma" intratext as we now know it. There is an apparent avoidance of the *gu ci* ("old version") in Lu's poem, more than we see, for example, in the "Yin ma" poem by his contemporary Fu Xuan. Lu wants to place his poem more in the orthodox textual tradition of the *Shi jing* and other pre-Han works even at the expense of coherence. In this, Lu Ji's poem is unique among the set of seventeen, but such allegiances are in keeping with his general poetic stance.

"Long Song"

A number of Lu Ji's poem's have an *ubi sunt/carpe diem* theme, which is not uncharacteristic of the period in which he lived but seems more pervasive and abstracted in Lu's poems. Just as themes of immortality characterize Cao Cao's poems, and themes of loyalty Cao Zhi's, so Lu Ji seems preoccupied with the irrecoverable past and the brevity of life. This is well illustrated in his "Chang ge xing" ("Long Song"), which belongs to a substantial set of similar poems, including three *gu ci* models. A good deal has been said about the meaning of the title, with the consensus being that, whether it originally meant a "lengthy song" or not, it came to refer conventionally to "songs about longevity," or, as often as not, the lack thereof. Wu Jing's comments suggest the continuity of this thematic line:

> The *gu ci* lines, "Green green the mallow in the garden / Morning dew lasts til dried by the sun" refer to the quick passing of the flower of youth, how one should exert oneself to find pleasure and not wait until old age when one will be overcome with grief. In the Wei dynasty this was changed into a musical performance using Cao Pi's composition, "How Tall Are the Western Mountains,"[7]

which considers how unknowable is the vastness of the Way of immortals, how Wang Qiao and Zhi Song were all hollow talk and empty words, and how the distant and strange are difficult to believe. One must actually see the Way of the sages [to understand it]. In Lu Ji's "Indeed it goes on, the sun through the sky / Such grief, it encircles land and stream" he speaks again of the fleeting brevity of human life, and how one should take the time to sing a long song. In this way it is similar to the old text. *(YFSJ* 30.442)

Indeed the theme of Lu's poem, the brevity of human life, is clearly central to the first of the three *gu ci*, with the other two offering thematic variations, including the contemplation of the immortals. Despite their differences, these three songs do share a relatively naive, straightforward style, which Lu Ji writes against. The *gu ci* are:

1

> Green green the mallow in the garden,
> Morning dew lasts til dried by the sun
> Springtime spreads its good nourishment
> The myriad things burst into life
> But always we fear the arrival of autumn
> Withering the flowers and leaves
> The hundred streams flow eastward to the sea
> When will they be able to return to the west
> If one isn't bold when young and strong
> He will be overcome with grief when he is old

2

> On a white deer the immortal rides
> His hair short, but ears so long
> He leads us high up Taihua Mountain
> Grasping mushrooms and red banners[8]
> We come to the host's front gate
> I offer him herbs in a jade case
> If he eats this herbal drug
> Daily his body will grow stronger

Hair turned white will be black again
Extending the years for a longer life

3

High and lofty the pavilion on the mountain
White and shining the stars among the clouds
Gazing afar makes one's heart sink
The wanderer misses those who raised him
Driving the carriage out of the north gate
Looking far toward the walls of Luoyang
How the wind blows the tall jujube trees
Long and lush the leafy branches bend
The orioles fly chasing each other
Chirping they call out in song
Standing there I gaze at West River
Tears fall soaking my silk hatstrings

YFSJ 30.442–43

Certainly Lu Ji's "Chang ge xing" takes its clues, as suggested by Wu Jing, from the first, and probably oldest, of these three poems, but again it is hardly a slavish imitation. The theme remains relatively intact, but the language Lu uses to convey it is quite different; his poem reads:

Indeed it goes on, the sun through the sky
Such grief that encircles land and stream
Precious shadows cannot stop the sun's rays
The high waves swirl on by themselves
The years pass and are quickly lost
Time comes by like frenzied lute strings
Distant future is rarely attained
The full number is seldom completed
The flower of youth falls between morning and night
The body's blessing suddenly departs of its own accord
These things here are difficult to stop
My life span, How can I extend it?

Raising and lowering my head quickly it passes
Suddenly how much longer is there?
Be stalwart, how can I complain
Heaven's Way naturally follows its course
I only regret that there is so little fame
There is nothing to record for posterity[9]
Let's wait out the years' final sunset
With the long song filling our spare time

YFSJ 30.444

Lu Ji's rewriting of the *gu ci* model in this poem is a particularly successful example of his agonized concern with abstract time. Magical mushrooms are replaced by the trappings of the aristocratic lineage; the simple images of the ephemeral dew and relentless river are transformed into abstractions of "time," "distant future," and the "full number." The real flowers of the *gu ci* that fade in the fall are transformed into Lu Ji's metaphorical "flower of youth." And when the images seem easy, for example, the "shadows" of line 3, they are complicated by literary allusion.[10] Just as the degree of abstraction here far exceeds any of the three *gu ci*, the level of rhetoric and difficulty of language is also far beyond them. The message may be the same but the medium is radically altered, all full of what Liu Xie called "exuberant feelings in obscure expressions" *(qing fan er ci yin).*[11]

The "Old Poems"

Of the few well-known poems in Lu's poetic corpus (he is almost exclusively associated with his "Rhapsody on Literature" ["Wen fu"]), his twelve imitations of the "Nineteen Old Poems" are perhaps most important for consideration here, especially since I have already claimed the "Old Poems" for the *yuefu* genre. While these imitations have contributed much to the modern assessment of Lu Ji's poetry as insubstantial and merely imitative, they have traditionally been well-received and I find in them the most satisfying examples of Lu's intratextual poetics.[12] The clearness and certainty of Lu's model here allows a reading that can be more confidently subtle; moreover, the model poems seem to have moderated Lu's thematic abstraction and at the same time his elevated language has enriched their rhetorical thinness. This can be seen in his imitation of the nineteenth "Old Poem," which again deals with his beloved *carpe diem* theme but uses language more derivative of the model, with whose lines I preface Lu's.[13]

In Imitation of "The Bright Moon How Shining and White"

OP
The bright moon how shining and white
Shines on my silken bed curtains

LJ
In peaceful slumber in my north chamber
The bright moon enters over the casement

Here Lu is simply rewriting the model with somewhat more elegant language. He enhances the languor and femininity of the model with the addition of "slumber" and "north chamber," the former being more than merely "to sleep" and the latter a reference to the inner rooms of aristocratic women. The more intrusive verb "to enter" is effective, and soon to become standard poetic language; the "casement" over which it enters is taken from the line of another "Old Poem" (no. 2)—"Shining and white she faces the window casement." The descriptive *jiaojiao* (shining and white) that describes the woman's skin in this line also describes the moonlight in "Old Poem" 19, but Lu shuns it, having already used it in the title.

OP
Sad and melancholy I cannot sleep
Holding up my robe I pace to and fro

LJ
It shines with light overflowing
I take hold but it does not fill my hand

Here is Lu Ji at his best. His verb "to shine" *(zhao)* is standard and from the first couplet of the model, but the sense of "surplus" *(yu)* light is a nice touch ("overflowing" may be an overtranslation). The real finesse comes, however, when he borrows the verb *lan* (to draw toward oneself) from the model "holding up my robe" to describe the futile action of trying to grasp the seemingly abundant moonlight—a quiet, melancholic moment, quite special in early Chinese poetry, that stands in contrast to the plain images of the model.

> *OP*
> Although you find pleasure in your travels
> It would be better to return home early
>
> *LJ*
> A chilly breeze wends through hidden corridors
> A cold cicada calls out from the high willow

In this couplet Lu breaks rank with the "Old Poem" completely in order to extend the autumnal melancholy in images of the declining year, which he finds such a compelling metaphor for the human condition. He stays with the female speaker, and from Han sources draws the image of the cicada, who calls out because he feels the autumn's chill.[14]

> *OP*
> Going outside I walk aimlessly alone
> To whom can I tell my melancholy thoughts
>
> *LJ*
> I hesitate, aware of the seasonal changes
> My eternal wandering has gone on forever[15]

The autumnal scene is now abstracted as Lu avoids the directness of the model lines, choosing to transform the human "melancholy thoughts" *(chou si)*—and this is the melancholy that is phonetically, graphically, and conventionally associated with autumn—into "seasonal [things] changes" *(jie wu)*. His hyperbolic wandering *(wo xing yong yi jiu)* in the second line of the couplet, which would most easily refer to the travels of the man (see the opening of the first "Old Poem"), is an odd variation, if it can be even considered one, on the first line of the model, which obviously refers to the woman—Lu's use of "hesitate" *(chi chu)* in his second line does obliquely connect with her "aimlessness" *(pang huang)* in the "Old Poem."

OP
Turning up my collar I enter the house
Tears fall soaking my gown

LJ
The traveling official met with no success
Parting thoughts are difficult to keep for long

The closure of the "Old Poem" is of a type often seen in early Chinese poetry, where grief overwhelms the speaker and the poem ends in an emotional breakdown—we saw a similar closure above in the third *gu ci* poem of "Chang ge xing." Lu's concluding couplet is, however, an intellectualization of the problem of separation and the point of view seems to be the man's, if it is anyone's in particular. Suddenly we are not weeping for lost love but worrying about worldly, bureaucratic success; the thought that he will have "nothing to record for posterity" continues to haunt Lu. His final line is chilling in itself—Lu can hardly remember the attachment for whose loss the "Old Poem" grieves. It is even more disturbing when read intratextually against what must be its model, that lovely last couplet of the second "Old Poem," which we discussed in Chapter 3: "My wanderer travels on and doesn't return / The empty bed is difficult to keep alone." In his specific imitation of the second "Old Poem" Lu avoids the lady's empty bed, turning it into an "empty room where blows the grievous wind," and here in the imitation of the nineteenth poem he distances himself further from her by suggesting he cannot quite remember his last night there.[16]

Bao Zhao and Xiao Gang

Bao Zhao and Xiao Gang (Liang Jianwen di) did not avoid the empty beds of women, at least not in their writings. This is especially so for Xiao Gang—certainly it is that empty bed that draws the traveler back home in his "The Ships Float across the Yangtze," which we looked at briefly in the conclusion of Chapter 3, but the thematic thrust of Bao's *yuefu* poetry also deserves to be reconsidered.

"A Song in the Night"

Bao Zhao is commonly viewed as the epitome of the suffering gentleman. Of the number of details known of Bao's life, his position as a low-ranking military officer during the final few years of his life is usually foregrounded as the most telling, psychologically and poetically. In standard accounts, Bao's life is usually described as officially unsuccessful and personally difficult, especially in his alleged humble origins and his extensive travel in the military. This association begins with the early assessment by Zhong Rong, who claims Bao's best poems are "guarding the border" *(shu bian)* ones, an assessment that is reflected in the *Wen xuan* collection.[17] That convention is still with us, as his poetry is commonly called "heroic and straightforward," full of social criticism and border imagery, usually written in the "persona of the aging and embittered military man."[18] We can see in these appreciations something approaching that "vicious circle of deducing biographical data from the poet's work and then reading the works in the light of that supposed biography."[19] Certainly nothing has more influenced the critics' appreciation of Bao Zhao the poet than his famous poetic sequence, "Xing lu nan," and I would suggest that once these poems were interpreted biographically, they then were used to understand the spirit of the man as well, which was then used in turn to explicate other poems. We cannot help but note that the very title of the series, "Hardships of Travel," itself contains the key formula for a reductive understanding of Bao's biography, "the humble (military) traveler in difficult circumstances." One wonders what our appreciation of Bao would be like if his most famous literary work were his sequence of "Water Chestnuts" poems (see note 36).

Kang-i Sun Chang's more searching appreciation of Bao Zhao's literary abilities highlights the "lyrical directness" of his *yuefu* poems. She argues that it is his *yuefu* poetry, as opposed to his *shi*, in which Bao finds his personal voice, a voice that shares affinities with the personal voice in Tao Qian's poetry *(shi)* and is characterized by "a preference for flowing syntax, a deliberate use of colloquial diction, a frequent play of rhetorical questions and dialogue."[20] Some of this voice is evident in one of Bao's own, but decidedly not empty, "bed" songs, "Ye zuo yin" ("A Song in the Night"):

> The deep winter night; deep in the night you sit singing
> I already know your desires before you speak
> The frost enters the curtain
> The wind blows through the grove
> The rosy lamp is put out
> And your rosy face is sought
> Following your song
> Pursuing its sound
> Not valuing the voice
> But rather its deep intent[21]

YFSJ 76.1072–73

This poem is certainly not written in the voice of the aging military officer. While the poem's second-person pronoun, *jun* (line 7), suggests the referent is a man, thus the point of view the woman's, Sun Chang is probably correct in claiming the woman as the musician, and the poem the man's (which is the way I have translated it). I am suspicious, however, of the seriousness of the final line's "deep intent," which Sun Chang explicates as "the more one penetrates into the musician's emotional intent, the more one can appreciate the beauty of her musical notes."[22] To me the poem is more superficially lusty and filled with innuendo: in the cold winter night, faces aglow with wine, there is a somewhat clumsy pursuit in the darkened bed where he must rely on *(ti)* sound to find her.

In any case, the lyrical directness of Bao's "Night Song" shows that his poetic voice is hardly limited to that of the "embittered military officer," but neither would I claim that the voice heard here is typical of Bao Zhao's poetry in general. In fact, as Sun Chang implies, examination of Bao's *yuefu* poetry reveals that, while perhaps biased toward the "difficult road," it has a wide range of voices, and those voices come both from the nascent intratextuality of the genre and from his own complex life. This was a life that placed him on the edges of the literary, official, and military worlds, much further from the limelight than either Cao Zhi, Lu Ji, or Xiao Gang, but not, as some would have us believe, a life in quiet or noisy disdain of their aristocratic trappings. There certainly were innumerable cold and lonely nights on those "difficult roads," but there were also some spent drunk in the warmth of a woman's arms, with or without "deep intent."

"The Melancholy of Being Alone"

The evening company Xiao Gang kept has been much the talk of the critics over the centuries. That often disapproving talk has been influenced by poems such as his "The Melancholy of Being Alone" ("Du chu chou"), which Guo Maoqian places in association with Bao's "A Song in the Night," and rightly so:

> The regrets of being alone are many and unending
> I open the curtains to feel the approaching wind
> Playing chess upon the mirror case
> Applying powder in the upper chamber
> Ever since the assault horses left
> No news has yet to get through
> I only fear that behind the gilded screen
> Next year it might still be just as empty[23]

YFSJ 76.1074

Here the "gilded screen" only slightly obscures the so-difficult-to-keep "empty bed." The voice and orientation of this poem, the woman and her boudoir, are typical of Xiao Gang's (and many of his literary companions') poetry; John Marney says of this poetry: "Women were a favorite subject. Their every smile and gesture is recorded; no detail of their dress and cosmetics, bedchamber furnishings and accessories, sighs and resentment is missed. Treatment is uniformly sumptuous, but differs in various ways to suit tears or laughter."[24] Xiao's social position as a famous literatus, powerful prince, and finally emperor suggests that he would have had plenty of access to these bedchambers in his real life as well as in his literary imagination, but he actually seems to have been rather orthodox in his personal behavior. In fact, Xiao's deliberate disassociation of his literary persona from his biographical personality is one of his most significant contributions to Chinese literature. Accepting the concept of "pure literature" (art for art's sake) that is incipient in Lu Ji's "Wen fu," Xiao pushes it further than anyone else, advising his son: "The principles for developing your personal character and for writing literary compositions are not alike. In personal conduct, you first should be cautious and serious. But in literary composition, you should be free and unrestrained."[25] Despite the necessarily fatherly tone of this advice, the spirit of *fang dang*, "the free and unrestrained," or, as Marney translates, the "uninhibited expression of sentiment," that Xiao suggested for literature brought the wrath of conservative critics, both on his art and on what they assumed was his personal life. Xiao has lived with a reputation of licentiousness and decadence ever since his official biography declared his poetry was "not fit for gentlemen."[26] Whether we want to call his art "licentious" or not is debatable (and we certainly refuse to judge his personal behavior from it), but there is a quality of sensuousness and luxuriance that pervades it, as Marney well describes.

Although Xiao Gang was separated from Cao Zhi and Lu Ji by another turbulent century, he shares certain social and literary worlds with them; and yet Xiao's position within those worlds was often quite the opposite of theirs. Like Cao Zhi, Xiao Gang was the scion of the imperial family, but unlike Cao, he was one of the favorites among several siblings, becoming Crown Prince at the untimely death of his older brother, Prince Zhaoming (Xiao Tong). For Cao Zhi, the position of Crown Prince was one that was not to be, but perhaps should have been, his. The denial of that position is one of the most salient points in accounts of Cao's personality and art. Lu Ji, on the other hand, was also very active in the literary scene surrounding the princely courts, but while he was a relative outsider endeavoring to work his way into their favor by virtue of his literary skills, Xiao Gang, as head of one of the most powerful literary salons in the Liang, was center to the literary scene of his time. Xiao Gang may have advocated a separation of personality and persona, but one reason he could do so was the very security of his social position. We could argue that the difficult social and political positions of Cao and Lu, and even more so for Bao Zhao, compelled them to write those positions into their art, but the relative ease of Xiao's social and literary station allowed him to ignore it, to find fictional voices for that "free and unrestrained" spirit.

As a leader of aristocratic literary circles during the southern Six Dynasties, Xiao Gang was immersed in the praxis of "poetic play," most evident in his poetry that uses the formulae we reviewed in poems of the *Wen xuan*, for example "matching" *(he)*, "emulating" *(xue)*, and imitating *(ni)*; or those with formulae that depend on occasional or fictional voices, such as "commissioned" *(yingling)*, "ordered" *(fengming)*, "on behalf of" *(wei)*, "presented" *(fu de)*.[27] In such an environment it is no wonder that *yuefu* poetry became a focal interest of the literati. The lineage of the *yuefu* titles, some of which went back to the Han, gave the poet who was free to explore beyond the poetics of occasion, biography, and didacticism a fecund and ever-growing source of intratextual reference and fictional voices (we must not forget this was also the time when Shen Yue collected his sixteen Han titles, many of which became the famous "Han *yuefu*"). Xiao Gang was just one of many during this time who began to use that source, all anticipated, but little influenced, by Bao Zhao. To be sure, Xiao castigated imitation, declaring that it "more than anything else leads to calamity," but we should understand that this is really a condemnation of clumsy and blind imitation in which the personal voice, fictional or biographical, is not given room for an "uninhibited expression of sentiment."[28] Imitative poetics is assumed; Xiao merely wants to allow it to serve a more purely aesthetic voice than many of his contemporaries.

"The Boatman's Song"

One of the few titles that Bao Zhao and Xiao Gang (along with Lu Ji) do share, "Zhao ge xing" ("The Boatman's Song"), illustrates well both the self-consciousness of their intratextual poetics as well as their individual voices. "The Boatman's Song" is a *xianghe* poem embedded in a set of eleven poems with early but not known "folk" origins. There are elements in Bao's version of the poem that do contribute to the common association of him and the "suffering traveler" motif, and the specificity of the references even suggest a biographical grounding of the poem:[29]

Ever since childhood this constant traveler
Has floated and drifted without a place to stay
Last fall stationed at the edges of the Yangtze
This spring traveling along the banks of the Yellow
I was sent off up with the corvée laborers
Wanting always to talk of my memories of Chu
In the pool chilly and cold the minnows are few
Along the islands sadly honking the geese call
Heavy and hard the steady wind hammers the boat
Heaving and hauling the sails are raised high
The violent waves offer no way of lingering
The sailors on the boat will not dally there

YFSJ 40.594

The possible biographical background for this poem is far from certain, but we can be assured that the "southern" desires, especially in the references to Chu and to the minnows, have an actual as well as literary basis.[30] The generally lucid language and male viewpoint give the travel poem many of the characteristics commonly associated with Bao's poetry, especially its "heroic" directness and implied social criticism. The general tone of this poem is similar to that of "border poetry," of which we saw examples in the "Yin ma" poems and which was to become so popular in the High Tang; those affinities may have contributed to the favorable reassessment of Bao's *yuefu* poetry at that time.

Xiao Gang's version of the "Boatman's Song" develops the latent southern associations of the title into a much different type of poem. While the level of language remains relatively lucid, the point of view is radically altered, producing a woman at the poem's center. Wu Jing, comparing his poem to that by Lu Ji, remarks:

The Jin music performed the text of the poem by Wei Emperor Ming (Cao Rui) with the line "The King spreads great learning," which is entirely about the successful pacification of the Wu state.

But then there is Lu Ji's poem with the lines, "Slowly springtime is about to end," and Liang Jianwen di (Xiao Gang) has "I live on the River Xiang," but these are only about going taking a boat out for a row. (*YFSJ* 40.592–93)

Lu Ji's poem is indeed about boating, but it is a relatively male and public activity.[31] Not so for Xiao; his poem centers on the female and erotic, giving us a woman who is similar to the one in his "Melancholy" poem cited above, but whose circumstances here produce a generally more upbeat song:

> My home is along the River Xiang
> Thus I know the "Water Chestnut Song"
> The wind freshens, bringing up choppy waves
> Where the water is deep, we hold onto the boat
> Leaves are tangled from the trailing lilies
> Silken stems float off the broken lotus
> The spray in my makeup might be delicate sweat
> My damp dress seems intentionally wet
> Clean silks dragged briefly in the muddy water
> Fresh color comes back to the sullied brocade
> Joining together with the beauty Zhao Yenfei
> Asking the Music Master Li Yannian
> Before it was adapted to strings and winds
> Who there sang the "Boatman's Song?"[32]

YFSJ 40.594

We recognize the voice here of Xiao's famous well-kept woman, not in her boudoir but rather out floating along the Xiang river in the heart of the Chu area. This is the same area that Bao Zhao longed for, which to him was a land that represented China, as opposed to the barbarian "north" (i.e., the Yellow River area), but in Xiao's poem the area and river are full of exotic and erotic associations. Here is the site of the famous shamanistic/erotic encounters celebrated in the *Chu ci*; here is also the region of "clouds and rain" where the King of Chu brought that euphemism for sexual intercourse into the language of Chinese poetry.

This woman knows what she does when into its muddy water she casually dips her fine silken sleeve, which, perhaps unlike her virtue, comes out unstained. In contrast to the male and bureaucratic associations of Bao Zhao's poem, each act and image in Xiao's poem blends the feminine and the riparian, the domesticated and the vegetal, never saying but always implying the woman's desires. She flirts with and in the river, like the shamankas who once enticed the river gods in the *Chu ci*. And the lotuses and lilies respond, reaching out to hold her. The description of her makeup, which "might be" damp with perspiration, and clothes, which "seem" intentionally wet, is more appropriate to a love tryst than to the harvesting of water plants. In all this we recognize the voice and vision of Xiao Gang that upset generations of orthodox critics—upset them because it was so good at what it did. And these are the same critics who will in the end turn to Bao Zhao, claiming his *yuefu* voice as the proper one.

The reference in the last line of Xiao Gang's poem to its own title clearly marks its self-conscious participation in the titular set's intratextuality. In this case it also marks its awareness of the larger literary context. Li Yannian, who is mentioned in Xiao's previous couplet, served Emperor Wu of the Han as the head of his newly formulated Music Bureau, which was entrusted with composing music and lyrics for various levels of musical activities, not the least being courtly entertainment. Xiao's reference is acknowledgment of his conscious participation in the *yuefu* genre; and the reference may be even more significant, as this note from the *Gujin yuelu* suggests:

> Monk Wang Yu's "Zhi lu" says, "The 'Boatman's Song' is Wei Ming di's composition 'The King Spreads the Great Learning.'" Some say that there was one by Li Yannian, but it is no longer sung. When Liang Jianwen di resided in the Eastern [heir-apparent's] Palace he created his song; it does not differ greatly from this [by Li?]. *(YFSJ* 40.592)

With this association of Li Yannian and the "Boatman's Song," we can better understand Xiao's closing couplet; he is asking about the song before it entered the court music (pipes and strings), that is, before Li "imitated" it. Here is an early and subtle acknowledgment of Xiao's belief in the folk associations of the genre. Below we shall see that there are very good reasons for that belief, and those have much to do with the general musical and feminine orientation of Xiao's poetry.

The "Jiangnan Nong" Poems

Along with the self-referential last line of Xiao Gang's "Boatman's Song," there is also an intertextual reference to the *yuefu* genre when the woman says (line 2) that she knows the "Water Chestnut Song" ("Cai ling ge").[33] Indeed so did Xiao: the title appears in his *yuefu* corpus as a brief poem with a voice and scene similar to those of his "Boatman" poem:

> Their flowers fallen, water chestnuts tasted again
> The mulberry girls have finished with the new silkworms
> Cassia oars on a sampan like a floating star
> Back and forth through the lotus leaves moving south

> *YFSJ* 51.740

Again the scene is water-borne, feminine, and late spring. The poem is unhampered by difficult language, but enhanced by ellipsis, metaphor, and slightly jumbled syntax. Water chestnut gatherers are joined with the mulberry girls as symbols of spring eroticism, and the leisurely drift of the boat among the lotus offers an image of the carefree, vaguely despondent life.

The origins of this "Water Chestnut Song" by Xiao Gang extend beyond the intratextuality of its titular set out into a tangled web of intertextuality (see chart). Xiao Gang's poem is found among a large group of quite similar poems gathered under the general designation of "Jiangnan nong" ("South of the Yangtze Performances"), which in turn are associated with a complex web of poems called the "Wu sheng" ("Music of Wu") and the "Xi qu" ("Western Tunes"). The *Gujin yuelu* identifies the provenance of the "Jiangnan nong" poems this way: "In the eleventh Tiangai year of the Liang (A.D. 512), Emperor Wu adapted the 'Xi qu' to create the fourteen poems 'Jiangnan shang yun yue' (Music in the Southern Clouds) and seven 'Jiangnan nong' [seven subtitles including nos. 1, 3, 5 listed on the chart]" (*YFSJ* 50.726). The

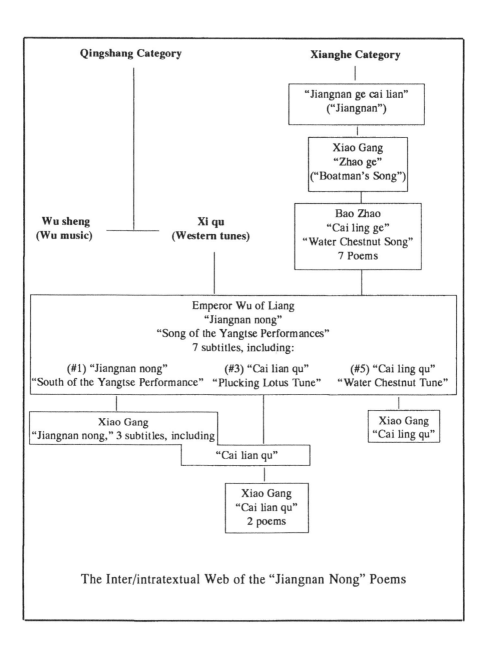

The Inter/intratextual Web of the "Jiangnan Nong" Poems

earliest models for this poetry are associated with southern areas, considered anonymous, and attributed to female singers, as Marsha Wagner describes:

> During this time [Six Dynasties] two groups of popular songs developed in the south: the *Wu sheng ge* or Wu songs were sung around the capital city of Jiankang [present-day Nanking], while the *Xi qu ge* or Western songs flourished farther up the Yangtze River around Jiangling (in modern Hupei) to the west. Both groups of songs tend to follow the four-line or *jueju* form, with four or five characters per line, and both focus on love. The Western songs often have outside settings and deal with the life of the traveling merchant. The Wu songs emphasize the woman's point of view and often describe her boudoir, furnished with "silk curtains, lattice screens, jeweled vanity cases, and embroidered robes."[34]

Thus, these two groups of *yuefu* poems ("Wu sheng" and "Xi qu") and their related "Jiangnan nong" are relatively late arrivals to the genre and have unique origins; yet the many imitations of them by Xiao Gang and his circle quickly propelled them into the literary mainstream, where they were subsequently widely imitated in the early Tang. Kang-i Sun Chang explains the close relationship between these songs and Xiao's poetry:

> From the tender age of six, Xiao Gang was continually moving from one provincial appointment to another, and thus had the opportunity to become familiar with the local popular song milieu. He possessed almost from the beginning an innate sensitivity toward Wu songs *[Wu ge]* and Western melodies *[xi qu]*, and he had a particular gift for rich verbal formulations. . . . He eventually served in Yongzhou, a city not far from Jingzhou, where Western melodies originated. It was during the seven years in Yongzhou that Xiao Gang came to learn from the popular songs the definitive style of sensory realism, and consequently his salon grew dramatically in size and influence.[35]

The three groups of poems, "Jiangnan nong," "Wu sheng," and "Xi qu," thus form a triad of interrelated themes and modes, with titles often occurring in large sequences, sometimes ordered by the seasons or in other ways.[36]

Of the number of imitations derived both from Emperor Wu's original "Jiangnan nong" set and from their subtitles, most interesting are a set of three by Xiao Gang, his son. The individual titles are derived from Emperor Wu's subtitles, to which Xiao Gang has added complicated intertextual subtitles of his own:

1

South of the Yangtze Tune, matching "A Spring Road, As a Lady Crosses"

In the branches and on the water, spring has returned
Long willows brush the ground, peach blossoms take flight
Fresh breezes cool her, the sun shines through her dress
The sun shines through her dress, now it is almost dusk
Tossing yellow gold, she detains the honored guest

2

A Dragon Flute Tune, matching "'South of the Yangtze Performance,' the Soaring Phoenix Lands"

Gilded doors, in jade-inlaid halls near the river I live
First a smile, then a frown, a million times over again
The wanderer left, then returned, would he not go so far
Would he not go so far, but how will I get my wish
A pair of mandarin ducks, both thinking of the other

3

Plucking Lotus Tune, matching "'Home after Plucking Lotus,' Dress Splashed So Soaking Wet"

Cassia oars and sweep of magnolia dapple in the emerald
    water
River blossoms and jade faces are like each other
Lotus scattered, stems broken, a fragrant breeze rises
A fragrant breeze rises, the bright sun is setting
The "Plucking Lotus Tune" causes the gentleman to stray

Again we have the self-referential song title included within the poem itself, in both the subtitle of poem 2, where it refers to "Jiangnan nong," and more importantly in the final line of poem 3, where it mentions its own title. The intended intratextuality of such references is obvious. In fact the last two poems in Xiao Gang's set derive directly from his father's second and third poems, with which they share subtitles. For example, Xiao Gang's third poem had this fine model to follow, including its prosody and the self-referential last line:

> Frolicking in the Five Lakes, returning home after plucking
>   lotus
> Fields burst into blossoms, the petals' perfume seeps into
>   our robes
> For my gentleman I shall sing what is rare and desired in
>   our time
> What is rare and desired in our time: That which is like jade
> The "South of the Yangtze Performances": a "Plucking
>   Lotus Tune"

> YFSJ 50.727

While Xiao Gang may have exploited other intratextual connections in these "Jiangnan nong" poems, the most obvious models were those by his father.

We can now move on to consider the self-referential subtitle that appears in the final lines of both Emperor Wu's and Xiao Gang's poems, "Cai lian qu" ("Plucking Lotus Tune").[37] That subtitle takes on a life of its own, generating not only Xiao's poem here, but other imitations and related titles associated with it (all in YFSJ 50). Xiao Gang himself has two other poems (in a set of twenty-six) with this title, the first of which is an excellent example of the world created by such poetry:

Plucking Lotus Tune No. 1

The afternoon sun shines on the sunken pebbles
Plucking the lotus we feel its afternoon rays

When a breeze rises, the lake becomes difficult to cross
So many lotus picked, but still they're thick
The oars strike, the lotus blossoms fall
The boat moves, the white egrets take flight
The lily pads' slender stems tangle our wrists
The water chestnut's barbs tug at our skirts

YFSJ 50.731

Much of the language, imagery, and ambiance of this poem is familiar, especially from Xiao's "Boatman's Song" discussed above; again the languor, sensual quality, and lush vegetation all sound erotic overtones.[38] Moreover, the often noted puns on "lotus" *(lian/*liän)* and "love" *(lian/*liên)*, and on "threads/stem" and "thoughts" *(si/*si)* suggest the conscious encoding of this relatively plain language. We do not have to push this imagery very far to find other even more erotic images—the difficult passage through the lilies as the seduction with the "oar" brings "deflowering"; the egrets' flight suggesting escape or release; and the ending with the woman again in the clutches of his clinging lotus stems and the barbs of the water chestnut. Obviously this poem is more about erotic play than about the harvesting of lotus.

The "Plucking Songs"

In a more generalized manner this "Plucking Lotus" title is associated with a whole tradition of "plucking" poems with similar feminine and sexual implications. With the exception of herbs for drugs of immortality, almost all "plucking" in early Chinese literature has similar associations, which begin in its earliest text, the *Shi jing*. As an example in Xiao Gang's corpus, we can turn to his "Plucking Chrysanthemums Composition" ("Cai ju pian"). This is an unusual poem since Guo Maoqian did not find an intratextual set in which to place it—it is found nested in a large group of poems that use *pian* ("composition") in their titles. The thematic associations are still there; only the seasonal change moves the woman from vernal expectations to autumnal melancholy:

The moon sparkles lovely on the grass, scattering among
   autumn trees
The young wife of Luoyang is the prettiest of the lovely girls
Chatting as she carries her basket to gather the chrysanthemum
   buds
Up early with the dew still wet, soaking through her silken
   jacket
Off in the east somewhere a thousand cavalry follow his
   black steed
But she will not even come down the hill to meet her old
   husband

YFSJ 64.931

As in other "plucking" poems, the woman here is only in the company of other women, and the male is a haunting absence, who dominates this closure. The eroticism of the spring poems is replaced with the hollowness of autumn, moving us back to those moonlit empty beds with which we began our consideration of Xiao Gang's poetry.

While Xiao's "Chrysanthemum" poem does not occupy part of any marked *yuefu* set, it is connected to many *yuefu* in its general theme, and its language and style anticipate poetry in the coming centuries; this is especially so in its closure, which veers off from the main line of consideration to bring in the absent male. In that closing couplet there are also hidden some very fine intratextual threads that connect with other, very old *yuefu* lines; these connections apparently slipped Guo Maoqian's notice, but certainly are there. Specifically, Xiao's penultimate line, "Off in the east somewhere a thousand cavalry follow his black steed" is an effective conflation of four lines in Luofu's description of her husband found in the closing section of the famous Han "Moshang sang." Those lines (with shared references italicized) are:

In the east somewhere with a thousand cavalry or more
There is my husband positioned at their lead

And how will I recognize my husband?
Their white horses *follow his black steed*

YFSJ 28.411

With this we understand better the implications of Xiao's closing; the woman is being compared to Luofu, an exemplar of marital fidelity, a faithful keeper of empty beds. But we should remember that Luofu was also the most famous "plucker" of the *yuefu* genre, and some of the imitations of her poem took the title "Plucking Mulberry Leaves" ("Cai sang"), including Bao Zhao's and Xiao Gang's. Moreover, in many of these imitations the tenor of Luofu's character had been radically transformed until she was more hesitant about, then even denying, the need to protect her bed and her fidelity.[39] While we are most familiar with the Luofu of the early Han poem, it is this "compromised" woman whom Xiao Gang and his contemporaries had more in mind as their "mulberry girls."

The last line of Xiao's poem leads us toward another early anonymous poem, one located near the edges of the *yuefu* genre. At the same time it adds complicating layers to this young wife's hesitation. The intertextual referent there is a poem not collected in the *Yuefu shiji*, but it is the first poem in the *Yutai xinyong*, and is regarded as a *yuefu* by some critics. Again it is a poem about women out "plucking," this time deer-parsley, that takes its common title from the first line of the opening couplet, which also contains the referent line:

She went up the hill to pluck deer-parsley
She came down the hill and there met her old husband

YTXY 1.1

This conversational poem then narrates the encounter between the woman and her former husband, who has remarried but is not happy with his new wife. He tells his former wife how inferior this new wife is (especially in her ability to produce at the loom), but the "plucker" is not impressed, saying "Well, when you let her in the front door / You let the old one out the back." In Xiao's poem the woman's dismissal of those old marital bonds seems even stronger since she will not even come down the mountain to see this pathetic fellow with his mercantile mind; yet this is apparently because she has a new lover who is off in the east galloping his black steed, not because she has become more independently minded. In fact, the wife in the original "Deer-Parsley" poem strikes us as a particularly strong woman and not a likely model for the typical Xiao woman. Just as Xiao and his fellow literati changed the stance of Luofu in her androcentric world, so he does with this woman. By giving her a new lover, Luofu's husband as it were, he rewrites her rejection of her old husband into an affirmation of other romantic attachments.

Conclusion

Xiao Gang may be mixing his inter/intratextual metaphors here in the last couplet of his "Chrysanthemum" poem, but there is a consistency in the rendering of this young wife and his other more obviously erotic women. While he often writes in the voice of the woman as she melts into sensual poses, these are really fictional poses constructed by a voyeuristic mind. There is something infinitely more sexual about *seeing* a gauzy skirt soaked with water than actually wearing one. And for all the lovely descriptions of the lotus blossoms, it is either the clumpy seed pods or the tough, tangled roots deep in the mud of the lake that the ladies "pluck," not those "fallen petals." Many parts of Xiao's descriptions, from sodden skirts to tangling vines, reflect a hidden desire to keep the woman vulnerable, and thus available to the man.

The gathering of mulberry leaves and chrysanthemum buds is perhaps less difficult and more becoming, but these activities, real or imagined, also functioned to make the woman available to men by prying her out of her domestic surroundings, away from her protective family. Here was the chance to get the "mulberry girl" to oneself. We should remember the effect the original Luofu had on the local men, and when the "governor" arrived on the scene even his horses were stopped in their tracks by her beauty. Xiao's poetry is not sympathetic to Luofu, or even to her husband, but rather to the voyeuristic governor who hopes to seduce her.

More than anyone else early in the genre, Xiao Gang created a fictional voice in *yuefu*; he did so by weaving his own sensual vision with the intratextuality of the poems, creating these women who have thoughts and strike poses that are not theirs, but rather those that a man would hope they would have. These are not women of the early model poems (who tend to be more feminist than feminine), not women he knows (certainly not spouse or kin), and their actions are not part of the world we inhabit, but rather, they are women as artifact, action as fantasy. In writing poems "for her," Xiao has the "mulberry girl" think as she "should" think: to be lonely when the man is away, to sit up late in moonlit rooms fretting over empty beds. Yet this vision says perhaps she should also on occasion be available for a romantic encounter, not to make her life more enjoyable, but to make *his* more interesting. A woman should be faithful to her husband, but somehow also available to the "governors." Luofu's original argument, "How can the Governor be so stupid / You already have your own wife," missed the point.

5

Webs: The Matrix of Convention

In this chapter we return to the consideration of texts rather than poets, to the tracing of the intratextual lines of another titular theme. The set of "Willow" poems that is our topic here exhibits one of the most prevalent forms of intratextuality, albeit an extreme case, in the *yuefu* genre. This is an intratextuality that spreads very thinly through a body of poems, not one built up from the distinct thematic threads that we saw in the "Yin ma" poems, but rather a finer web of modal, thematic, and referential relationships.

The difference between the "Yin ma" intratextuality and this more weblike weave is in part determined by the nature of the titles of the two sets. As we have seen, a *yuefu* title gains thematic force as it is carried along in the development of the genre. A poem with such a theme-laden title as "Watering Horses at the Long Wall Spring" almost writes itself, but a title like the "Long Song" ("Chang ge"), which we saw in the last chapter, gives only vague, and often contradictory, directions to the formation of the poem. The title of the central corpus of poems for consideration here, "Zhe yangliu" ("Breaking Off the Willow"), certainly is less determinative than "Yin ma," but is one that provides more thematic direction than "Chang ge," yielding an intratextuality that is susceptible to wide variation but not to divergent lines of development.

Like that intratextuality, my arguments here are woven together by a large number of poems, giving us an essay that is at times as tenuous as the connections between the poems. There *is* a central set of poems, the twenty-five literati poems that are translated and discussed in the middle of this chapter, but there are also poems that lie on the edges of that central corpus defining the borders of the "Willow" intratext. After introductory remarks on the semiotic nature of the willow in Chinese culture, my discussion begins with sets of anonymous poems that lead progressively toward the central literati intratext. I conclude with consideration of a set of poems found at the far edge of the willow intratext.

The Semiotics of the Willow

The thematic development determined by the "Yangliu" title is closely linked to two cultural associations of the willow tree in ancient China. The first is the rather obvious feminine appearance of the tree, especially with its sartorial image of "swaying skirts," akin to our rather more carnal image of the "willowy blond." The other association is in the more culturally bound linguistic play on the word "willow" (*liu*, Middle/Tang Chinese *liëu*), which was a homophone for the word "to keep, to detain." This homophony led to the practice of using the willow bough as a token gift for someone about to depart on a journey: to give the willow bough was to say, "I wish you could stay, therefore I 'detain' [*liëu*] you with this gift." Because of this latter association, mention of the willow became a convention in all Chinese poems of parting, of which there is a deluge in the literary tradition. Meng Jiao's (751–814) poem from the later part of the central set of "Yangliu" poems spins this cultural-linguistic association into a veritable conceit:

> The weeping willow has many short boughs
> Short boughs that tell of many partings
> Presented faraway, piles of them twisted off
> Pliant tendrils how could they still droop so
> The verdant spring has a set sequence
> But partings have no set season
> They only fear that one leaves in haste

Not caring if one's returning is delayed
Don't talk of boughs and tendrils shortened
Among them are enduring thoughts of you
The blush of your face, the green of willow
Side by side at the moment of parting

YFSJ 22.333

The parting motif that permeates Meng's poem often merges with the other, feminine associations of the willow (as in his penultimate line) to form the central axis of the thematic web of the "Yangliu" poems, generating texts centered on the woman in the context of parting and separation.

A better illustration of the conflation of these two themes (willow and woman) is found in the two earliest poems of the literati "Yangliu" corpus. The set was begun by Xiao Gang (502–557), the poet who was the topic of our discussion in the last chapter, and was followed immediately by his younger brother, Xiao Yi (Liang Yuan di, r. 552– 555). First, Xiao Gang's poem:

Weeping willows, a tangle of silken threads
We twist off boughs in this early spring
Leaves so dense the birds' flight is blocked
In the gentle breeze blossoms still cling
High on the wall short pipes are heard
In the desolate wood the painted horn grieves
In this song there are no thoughts of parting
Here side by side thinking of each other

YFSJ 22.328

And then Xiao Yi's:

The Mountains and Gorges of Wu go on and on
Drooping willows and drooping poplar
Loved ones will break them off together

Old friends longing for old haunts
Mountains as beautiful as lotus
The current like silver moonlight
Throughout the cold night the gibbons howl
The wanderer's tears soak his robes

YFSJ 22.328

While Xiao Gang does not explicitly refer to the themes of feminine grace or the couple's parting in his poem, such associations are ever present, as will be illuminated by further intratextual reading in the corpus. In passing we should note two significant elements in Xiao Gang's poem: first, his reference to music, which in Chapter 4 we saw as a common self-referential mark of his *yuefu* poetry; and second, his elaboration of the titular verb to "break off" *(zhe)* into the "twist off" *(panzhe)*—this verb will become an important signature of the series, as witnessed by Meng Jiao's use of the term in his third line. Xiao Yi's poem is, on the other hand, more explicitly concerned with parting, but the perspective is more that of the "wanderer," who by definition is male; the landscape is, however, entirely female, including the erotic associations of the Wu area and the lotus (with its pun on *lian/*liên*, "to love"). The general melancholy that fills the poem, especially in the "drooping" *(chui)* willow (an adjective commonly used as a descriptive of both the willow and the languorous palace lady), pervades the series, and is coincidentally well conveyed by our term "weeping willow," which I use throughout to translate the term *yangliu*.[1]

The Anonymous Poems

While Xiao Gang's poem is the first in an extensive series of literati "Yangliu" poems from the *hengchui* category, there are several groups of earlier poems upon which he could have drawn. Once again we can turn to Guo Maoqian's introductory notes for a delineation of those sources:

The "Monograph on Music" of the *Tang History* says, "In Liang *yuefu* poetry there is the song to a Hun flute that reads, 'Mounting the horse he does not pick up the whip / Instead she breaks off a weeping willow bough / Dismounting they play the long flute / Such melancholy destroys a traveling man.' The words for this song originate in the Northern states, and these are the *gujiao, hengchui* tune 'Zhe yangliu zhi.'" The "Monograph on the Five Elements" of the *Song History* says, "At the end of the Taigang period in the Jin Dynasty (ca. 290), in the capital of Luoyang there was the 'Zhe yangliu' song which had lyrics that spoke about war's bitter suffering." I would point out that in the old *yuefu* there was a title "Xiao zhe yangliu." In the *xianghe* category there is the title "Zhe yangliu xing"; in the *qingshang* category there are the thirteen *xi qu* poems "Yuejie zhe yangliu ge," which are not the same as these. (*YFSJ* 22.328)

This confusing list of titles suggests a particular tangle of intratextuality, but as indicated by Guo Maoqian's final, somewhat ambiguous statement, not all of these titles seem to be actually part of that intratext. I shall discuss most of the titles mentioned by Guo (as well as others) as an illustration of both the way the "Yangliu" web thins out and detaches along the edges, and at the same time the way our intratextual reading can stretch that web to cover and enrich otherwise peripheral and commonly isolated poems. While the intratextual connections I describe here are not entirely arbitrary, neither are they the only possible ones. The poems are fixed and real, but their potential interrelationships are nearly infinite; we can only materialize a limited number of those relationships in any discussion, and the pursuit of some associations naturally suggests and precludes others.

The Xianghe Poems

I begin with the *xianghe* poems, for in them is the only *gu ci* (old version) associated with the intratextual set, a *gu ci* with a fine pedigree, inasmuch as it also belongs to Shen Yue's group of sixteen Han poems. Yet, even with the most imaginative of readings, this small group of poems (the *gu ci* and four imitations) have little to do with the intratextual relationships of the "Yangliu" poems as we later know them. These *xianghe* poems do offer evidence for the "proto-genre" status of Han *yuefu* poetry. The *gu ci*, a moralistic tract arguing that "everyone gets his due," illustrated by a catalogue of historical examples, has nothing to do with its "Willow" title, which must have been merely a musical designation at this early point in the genre's development, as indicated by Shen Yue's listing.[2] This is also true for the first literati "imitation" by Cao Pi (187–226), whose theme of immortals and immortality is related to neither the *gu ci* nor to the "Yangliu" poems to come, but is typical of poetry from the Cao family generally. Once again the supposed interrelationship here is that of lost musicality. The general thematic lines of Cao's poem may have suggested the subsequent imitation by Lu Ji; but if that is so, Lu has developed it into his own particular concern with the brevity of life.

The final two *xianghe* imitations, by Xie Lingyun (385–433), bring us to the fringes of the "Yangliu" intratext. This is truer for the second poem than for the first. Xie's first imitation, which is somewhat related to the themes of Lu Ji's, shares only a general vegetal coloration with the intratext, but the season, scenery, and theme are still far beyond the scope of the "Yangliu" poems to come. Xie's second poem is, however, explicitly about parting and implicitly about willows:

> Thickly growing the trees by the river's edge
> Green green the grass in the wild fields
> I shall leave my old home behind
> To make a journey of ten thousand miles
> Wife and concubine tug at my sleeves
> Wiping away tears that soak our embrace
> Still I would hold my young son
> But must entrust him to his uncle and aunt
> Parting vows are left unfinished
> The anxious driver is so early to leave
> The tow lines haul my painted boat along
> Hunger and thirst are constantly unquenched
> Who has brought me to such wretchedness?
> Except to sigh and moan, what can I say?[3]

YFSJ 37.548

Here we have certainly moved into the thematic range we saw in the poems by Xiao Gang and Xiao Yi, and away from the earlier *xianghe* "models" for the poem. While the willow is not mentioned as such, the image of "trees by the river's edge" is not only a logical reference to the willow but, along with the second line, is also a specific variation on the opening couplet of the second of the "Nineteen Old Poems"— "Green green the grass by the river's bank / Thickly growing the willow in the garden." The presence of the implied willow is reinforced by the scene of parting that fills the rest of Xie's poem. The domesticity of this scene does, however, distinguish it from that commonly associated with the "Old Poems" and with the "Yangliu" poems, which is more romantic than familial. Xie Lingyun's mention of children (and even of a sister-in-law) is particularly striking. Children seldom make it into Chinese poetry, especially, and perhaps oddly, into poetry that dwells on the lonely woman—abandoned wives and palace ladies are almost universally childless.[4] The opening of this poem may remind us of the "Nineteen Old Poems," but its subsequent description of loneliness is too male and too domesticated to allow that initial resemblance to develop.

The "Monthly Songs"

The next set of "Yangliu" poems to be considered is permeated with a type of loneliness much more akin to that seen in the "Nineteen Old Poems," and thus in this one way is closer to the "Willow" intratext, but this set's use of the *yangliu* term as a prosodic refrain is unique and probably betrays its musical association. These thirteen anonymous poems belong to the Southern *xi qu* (Western Tune) subcategory, which also gave us the similar "Jiangnan nong" poems that were so important to Xiao Gang's poetry. The poems, "Monthly Songs for Breaking Off a Weeping Willow" ("Yue jie zhe yangliu"), compose a sequence of poems that works its way through the seasons and pivots on the themes of love and loneliness, using the vegetation's seasonal change as its central image.[5] As an example, here is the fifth poem of the sequence, which describes the midsummer month:

Wild rice stands shoulder high
For whom will this pure body be a treasure
In the bloom of life how lovely it will be
Break off a willow bough
I shall make sweet round buns
Intended for my love's own hand[6]

YFSJ 49.723

Obviously the "willow refrain" here is primarily prosodic and not integrally thematic, yet its associations of the woman and parting are not totally divorced from the sequence's general themes. While the sequence is anonymous, it certainly is a literati work; this is especially evident in the sophisticated conception and intricate execution of the intrasequential relationships. One feels the heightened presence of the literati mind enjoying the subtle connections and generative nature of the cycle. As I suggested in Chapter 2, poems such as we see in this sequence are better described as "unsigned" rather than anonymous.

Songs for a Hun Flute

From the set of Southern "Monthly" poems we can move on to the two other sets of anonymous poems mentioned by Guo Maoqian, the "Zhe yangliu geci" and "Zhe yangliu zhi ge." While the "Monthly" poems offer only general modal and rhetorical elements to the "Willow" intratext, these two sets provide more specific images that contribute directly to the formation of the "Yangliu" literati poems. These are the poems that Guo Maoqian called the "songs for a Hun flute"; they in fact belong to the *hengchui* (Horizontal Flute) category, which is often associated with poetry of non-Chinese origins, and to which the central set of literati poems also belongs. Of the anonymous poems that contribute to the intratext of "Yangliu" poems, the third poem in the second set is best known in the literary tradition, but this is because of its relationship with the famous "Mulan" poem and not because of its fit into the other "Yangliu" poems.[7] In fact, little consideration is ever given to the other poems of the group; yet certainly each of these poems is enhanced by consideration of it in light of the double nine-poem set.

Song Lyrics for Breaking Off Weeping Willows

1

Mounting the horse he does not pick up the whip
Instead she breaks off a weeping willow bough
Cross-legged they sit playing the long flute
Such melancholy destroys a traveling man

2

Breast filled with melancholy and unhappiness
I want to become my man's horse whip
Going and coming I'd be coiled around his arm
Cross-legged I'd be beside his knee

3

You grazed your horse along the stream
But forgetfully you did not tether her
Now saddle in arms you run after her
How can you catch your horse to ride?

4

Faraway he gazes south toward Meng Ford
Weeping willows with dense and swaying skirts
I am a child in the enemy's family
I don't understand the Chinese song

5

A strong man needs a fast horse
A fast horse needs a strong man
After racing through the yellow dust
Then we'll know the stallion from the mare

Songs for Breaking Off Weeping Willows

1

Mounting the horse he does not pick up the whip
Instead she breaks off a weeping willow bough
Dismounting they play the long flute
Such melancholy destroys a traveling man

2

Before the gate a jujube tree
Year after year it doesn't seem to age
If Grandma doesn't marry the girl off
Then how will she get her grandchildren

3

Click click, clack clack
The girl is at the window weaving
You don't hear the sound of the loom
But only that of the girl sighing

4

Whom is the girl thinking of
Whom is the girl remembering
Grandma agreed to marry the girl off
But this year there is no news

YFSJ 24.369–70

All the major elements that form the main "Yangliu" intratext are found here, albeit in a somewhat immature and underdeveloped form: the "swaying [dancing, *po sa*] skirts," the willow bough as a parting gift, and the general female orientation. There are, however, some elements that will not be accepted by later literati poets, specifically those of the familial associations of grandmother and children. The weaving imagery will be somewhat transformed, but its strong feminine associations keep it within the intratext; this is the imagery that is adopted by the "Mulan" poem. The Northern orientation of these songs gives them their particular equine associations, and while most of the specific imagery—some of it very unusual, as in the third and fifth poems of the first set—is not adopted, we shall see that it does show up in the general "border" orientations of some "Yangliu" poems.

What *is* lost in the transference of these themes to the world of the literati is the general conversational tone and the naivete. These poems seem to be truly anonymous, not merely unsigned. Yet in the more sophisticated poems there are few images to equal the girl's desire to be the whip "coiled around his arm," nor is there any of the gentle humor of the third poem of the first set that chides him for running around trying to catch the horse he carelessly let go.[8]

The Literati Poems

We can now turn to the literati poems that form the central part of the "Willow" intratext (which starts with the poems by Xiao Gang and Xiao Yi quoted in the introduction above). Our movement through these poems will not be chronological but rather intratextual as we follow various and changing clues from one poem to the next. Obviously this is not intended to describe the process of intratextual composition of the poems (although in certain cases that is also possible), but rather to trace a type of intratextual reading. In the first group of poems to be considered the movement from poem to poem generally follows linguistic and semantic signals.

Willows, Words, and Women

The willow tree itself is the most obvious image with which to begin the tracing of this intratext, and I shall have much to say about it, but first we might look for the tree's absence in the series. While every poem in the series is *about* the willow in one or more of its manifestations, there are two poems that do not mention the willow *per se*—one early in the series and one at the very end. Although "willowless," both of these poems are fine examples of literati treatments of the willow themes, revealing the evolution of the "Yangliu" intratext in the hands of the literati through the late Six Dynasties and Tang, and they provide an excellent frame for the series of twenty-five.

The first "willowless" poem is one (of two) by Chen Shubao (550–604), whose refined voice we have already heard in his "Yin ma" poem in Chapter 3. Here again, we have a superb example of that voice in one of the most generative poems of the series:

> Long tendrils yellowed now green again
> Drooping silken threads dense and interlaced
> The blossoms drop on the shy one's path
> Walking in the shadows of the general's camp
> The valley darkens and the gongs echo in the dark
> The wind comes up, flutes clamor through the night
> Would these boughs twisted keep you a while longer
> In vain they remind me of my garden at home

> *YFSJ* 22.329

While Chen Shubao does not mention the willow by name, his poem is replete with many of the conventional descriptions that would make direct mention redundant, especially the "long tendrils" (*chang tiao*) and drooping silken threads (*chui si*) of the first two lines.[9] This "drooping" (what we call "weeping") is found throughout the literati intratext, being most evident in the opening lines of the poem by Xiao Yi quoted above, where the word appears in a repeated duplicated adjective.

The "silken threads" mentioned by Chen Shubao is also one of the most conventional references to the willow's delicate branches. This silken image not only heightens the feminine associations, both sartorial and sericultural, of the tree, but it also enhances the theme of parting by playing on the common pun (which we saw in the Six Dynasties' "Jiangnan nong" poems) on "thoughts, longing" (**si*). For example, the silken thread image appears in the unusual compound of "boughs of washed silk" of the second line of this poem by Liu Miao (fl. 525):

In my high chamber alone for ten years now
Weeping willows with boughs of washed silk
Picking leaves I was surprised by your quick departure
Twisting tendrils I resent the long separation
Year after year with no word or news
Month upon month I grow less attractive
Who doesn't have hopes when spring comes
I think of you as you must know

YFSJ 22.329

The pun on "silk" and "longing" is heightened in Liu's poem by the final line that contains the term *xiang si*, (think of you). Moreover, these silken boughs end in the tendrils (*tiao*) of the fourth line that are picked as the parting gift and with which Chen Shubao began his poem. More than simple terms for branches, the tendrils imply the delicate and supple quality of the willow, again bringing to mind conventional descriptions of the woman in the poetry of that period.

The supple quality of the willow branches is also reinforced by, or encourages the use of, the verb *pan* (hold on to and pull oneself up), especially in the compound *panzhe* ("to reach up and break off"—translated here and elsewhere as "twist" and "twist off" respectively). In traditional usage this verb's direct object is exclusively vegetation, and consistently willow boughs. *Pan (zhe)* occurs in twenty-one of these twenty-five poems and is especially concentrated in the latter half of the series (in fifteen of the last seventeen poems). We have already seen this usage in the poems by Xiao Gang, Liu Miao, and Chen Shubao; another example of it is seen in the sixth line of Jiang Zong's (fl. 575) poem:

Across these ten thousand miles all news is lost
By the thousands, the weeping willow tendrils entwine
You would not expect flowers in the courtesan's garden
To be like the faraway snows on the Heavenly Peaks
Spring thoughts are deep and overwhelming
For now, boughs twisted off spring trees

We share these close and clinging feelings
But separated year after year, what can we do?

YFSJ 22.330

The etymology of *pan*, originating in "to pull oneself up," not only yields the derivation "to rely on," but necessarily implies the tensile strength of its object. These boughs are not just "plucked" (*cai*), as were the mulberry leaves and lotuses in Chapter 4, but rather must, like the separation they represent, be twisted off and pulled apart; the willow branches, as their name (**liëu*) suggests, want to remain, to linger, to be kept.

Jiang Zong's poem contains another word that implies this "staying quality," the modal *liao* (**lieu*), which can be read as a near-phonetic and graphic pun on both "willow" and "to remain." Moreover, its usage and meaning here, "for a while," fit well into the general sentiments of the poem (i.e., "would you remain for a while"). A similar use of *liao* is seen, again combined with *pan*, both in Chen Shubao's seventh line (above) and here in Lu Zhaolin's (fl. 650) poem (also line 7):

Shutters of a courtesan's chamber open to the sun
Garden willows are now close and clinging
Bird songs let her know that it's the new year
The new grown tendrils tell her spring has returned
Dew droplets on leaves could be tears on a face
Flowers in the wind mingle in her clothes as she dances
She twists a bough to entrust to him for a while
When one is in the army letters are rarely written

YFSJ 22.330

Lu's poem is an excellent example of the blending of the tree's feminine associations and the parting themes. These associations are constructed out of imagistic and modal elements similar to those seen in the poetry of Xiao Gang—the specific dew and tears analogy is found elsewhere in the series (Liu Xian, below). *Liao* (for a while) is used here in an adverbial manner, but its basic verbal meaning, "to rely/depend upon," is perhaps also relevant (i.e., she relies on this to detain him for a while), especially as it joins with *pan*, whose basic meaning is similar.[10] This sense is reinforced by the descriptive *yiyi* (close and clinging) of the second line, whose "willow" pedigree is among the best.[11]

At one point we find the *yiyi* descriptive used parallel to another descriptive, *ruoruo*, one with somewhat similar associations. This is seen in the opening lines of a rather elaborate poem by Xu Ling (507–583):

> The trees along the river dike waft and wave
> They surround the Wei barracks close and clinging
> In the South, Jiangling has its old song
> North near Luoyang they play a new tune
> Here I face the garden of Tall Poplar
> While you climb the wall of High Willow
> When spring returns we should see it together
> But my wanderer does not care anymore

YFSJ 22.329

Several points are worth noting about Xu Ling's poem. First, his opening couplet apparently mirrors that of Xie Lingyun's *xianghe* poem discussed in the opening pages of this chapter, thus constituting a rare intratextual reference to the *xianghe* poems. We should also note that Xu Ling's poem only mentions the willow as part of the archaic place names, *chang yang yuan* and *gao liu cheng* (an imperial palace, and a northern commandery in the Han, respectively), and thus is somewhat consistent with Xie's poem's avoidance of explicit reference to the willow.

Xu Ling's various references to music and song are not only found throughout this series, but, as we saw with Xiao Gang's poetry, are a common characteristic of late Six Dynasties *yuefu* poetry in general. It is not coincidental that these references occur here in Xu's rather archaizing and self-conscious poem. We should remember that music can lead back to the anonymous "songs to a Hun flute" introduced above. Similar associations with those early songs are found in the final lines of Yu Yanshou's (Tang) "Yangliu" poem:

> The great road connects the gates of the capital
> On both sides of it they plant weeping willows
> They are clustered together, but you are not here
> Gracefully they droop—it's been so long
> Evening birds are roosting in the boughs
> The male leaves, the female sings alone
> The remaining flowers resent the end of spring
> A faint moon rises in the autumn sky
> I sit gazing at butterflies in the window
> Then rise to twist off a bough full of leaves
> A pleasant wind blows through the long tendrils
> Full of grace how they are like me
> I see the willow garden is fresh again
> Four or five springs spent in these high chambers
> Please don't play the Hun border song
> Such melancholy destroys the person at Longtou

YFSJ 22.332

The "melancholy that destroys" of Yu's last line is a specific reference to the anonymous Northern poems (the first poem of each subset), and Longtou is a mountain in the far northwest. His invoking of the image of music and the abandoned woman, here joined in the allegorizing female bird singing by herself, is a more general reference to those poems. A similar merging of the woman and her song is also found, for example, in this poem by Tang poet Liu Xian:

> The sand-filled border near the Tri-river road
> Gilded bedrooms in the second month of spring
> Emerald mists, weeping willow colored
> Rouge powdered, the lady in gossamer silk
> Dew drops on leaves are lovely tears on a face
> Wind blown flowers remind one of dancing scarves

I twist and hold them, but you cannot see
So here listen to what is new in this song

YFSJ 22.331

Compared to the smitten young woman of the early anonymous poems, who sits cross-legged, listening to the simple flute song and watching her boyfriend chase his horse around the open pasture land, the woman portrayed in these literati poems is more urbane and mature, one who is generally identified as a "palace lady." Liu Xian's depiction of willow-colored mist, rouge, and gossamer silk (*qiluo*) speaks of this reorientation, and the comparison of the dew and her tears is common in the literati literature, with another example in Lu Zhaolin's poem above.

This woman is found throughout the "Yangliu" series (and in fact throughout the genre), as seen in the following poem by Zhang Hu (fl. 825), which may derive from Liu Xian's, especially in the corresponding "dancing scarves," "dancing sashes," both of which are variations on the "swaying skirts" of the women and the willow:

Days of rouge and painted chambers
In the mid-month of spring there are drooping willows
These boughs are twisted again because I miss you
It's not that I am jealous of their slender waists
Dancing sashes twirl, their silken threads break
Delicate eyebrows face the leaves furling
The horizontal flute can play a number of songs
But this one alone makes me the most melancholy

YFSJ 22.332

Zhang follows Liu Xian's lead in concluding the poem with a self-referential remark, and this time one that also refers to the poem's own (as well as the original "Hun" song's) musical associations. Moreover, Zhang has transformed the often-seen tree and woman images into a conflation of floral and feminine "slender waists" and "dancing sashes," with threads/twigs/thoughts that are broken. Here a woman reacts to the feminine charm of the willow, disclaiming her jealousy and pledging her affinity with those trees that are invoked to keep her husband at her side. The identification of the woman's eyebrows with the slender willow leaves is clearly made in the somewhat earlier "Yangliu" poem by Wei Chengqing (fl. 700):

> Out there on the border an endless wall
> Here the third month is weeping willow season
> The leaves resemble eyebrows in a mirror
> The blossoms are like snow beyond the passes
> Troops on the march have faraway thoughts of home
> A courtesan is alone in her high chamber
> She can't bear to lose the flower of her youth
> Filled with love, she sends it with a twisted bough

YFSJ 22.331

Wei's poem entwines the woman and the willow, until she becomes a flower herself, but all this is set against the muted, silent background of the northern border, which haunts that southern landscape.

The North and the South

Here I would like to consider one aspect of this intratext in a little more detail, namely, adaptations of certain "Hun" images originally found in the anonymous poems. While the literati poets are certainly not chasing their unsaddled horses through the grasslands, they are nonetheless always aware of the Northern musical and, more important, thematic associations of the title, even as they mix them with the more indigenous associations of the willow. We saw specific reference to those anonymous poems in the closing lines of Yu Yanshou's poem quoted above. The earliest reference of this sort comes in Chen Shubao's other "Yangliu" poem.

The weeping willows stir feelings of spring
In the courtesan's garden she is often startled
A blush of rouge enters her chamber
And the breeze brings the music of wood winds
At Wuchang she sees the new planting
At Guandu there are only tatters of trees
To sing then the song "Leaving the Pass"
Still accompanied by the Hun reed flute

YFSJ 22.329

The Northern orientation of this poem can, as with the others in this set, be attributed to the origins of its title/theme, but Chen Shubao's biography might give that orientation more personal relevance. Often disparaged as a incompetent ruler and decadent poet, Chen spent his last years as captive in the North under the emerging Sui dynasty, which would in the end unify all of China but itself had Northern origins. Thus for him, "out of the passes" could represent more than a mere tune title; it could have meant escape.[12] His singing of the song "still" (*reng*) accompanied by a Hun reed flute would be a very personal lament. We should note that Chen's concept of the "North" is defined by political reality, not by geography. Guandu, while substantially north of Wuchang, is still in the Yellow River plain; the implied disparity in seasons resides more in Chen's anguish than in actual miles. This is of course true for a number of the Six Dynasties poems, where the area of Luoyang represented the North to the literati poets of the Song, Liang, and Chen Dynasties of the South. The real focus of Chen Shubao's poem is, however, the woman who is very much a product of his Southern imagination. Not only is she accompanied by the appropriate willows that surround very feminine and Chinese (Southern) architecture, but she is also entertained by music from appropriately Chinese "woodwinds." How Chen would have preferred to have been there in Wuchang, singing his "Out of the Passes" in the past tense, accompanied by these real Chinese musical instruments rather than the "Hun flute." Chen's use of different types of wind instruments to mark the contrast between the North and the South reflects the importance of the musical element in the original anonymous poems, especially in the ironic lines, "I am a child in the enemy's family / I don't understand the Chinese song."

The disparity of North and South is seen throughout the series in a number of different dichotomies, though few as appropriate to the genre as those of music. The poem by Chen Shubao's contemporary, Cen Zhijing (fl. 575) is a somewhat muted example:

> When I first came to know the general
> Around the barracks the delicate willows drooped
> Dangling silken threads brush the wall and turn
> Flying catkins blow through the inner palace
> Those leaves crossed through border gates
> The boughs darkened across the mouth of valleys
> The song was sung where boughs were twisted
> Now I can only say how I resent this separation

YFSJ 22.329

Cen Zhijing's poem is concerned with the same Northern landscape that we see in Chen Shubao's, but in this case, that landscape is depicted almost entirely from a Southern perspective; the North is portrayed in vague and conventional terms—"border gates," "mouth of the valley." The thinness of that description becomes apparent when we compare it to Chen Shubao's first poem, quoted at beginning of this chapter. In that poem the woman is placed within the Northern setting, including the appropriately martial music, and she recalls the South where she is not. In Cen's poem the willow imagery is, however, stronger, especially as it provides the link between the two worlds: the woman imagines her gift of willow boughs traveling through those passes. In Chen's poem the view is from the North, recalling the South; in Cen Zhijing's poem, the view is from the South, imagining the North, thus making it closer to the mainline of the "Yangliu" intratext.

We saw a similar disparity of the North and South in the "Yin ma" poems discussed in Chapter 3, especially as the series' originally Northern orientation developed a more Southern, and in that case, feminine perspective, when the "abandoned wife" was drawn into the reflection of those border poems. The situation in the "Yangliu" poems is more complicated since the willow image necessarily has Southern associations, but the tune title was traditionally assumed to be of Northern provenance. Into this formula enter the tree's associations of both women and parting, yielding a particular complex assemblage of thematic material—the destination of that parting is almost universally understood as the northern border. Unlike the "Yin ma" poems, the Southern images of the willow generally overpower those Northern associations, testifying to the textual power of the titular theme. Consider, for example the following "Yangliu" poem by Wang Cuo (fl. 575) also of the Chen dynasty:

> There's no hint of spring beyond the Northern borders
> But the Shanglin willows are already in summer yellow
> The shadows of their branches sneak into the palace dark
> The shine of their leaves confused with starlight
> Along the lane they hide the playful birds
> In the upper chamber they conceal the fresh makeup
> Boughs twisted these are meant to be given as gifts
> The heart knows the road separating them will be long

> *YFSJ* 22.330

There is only a token effort to give this poem a Northern frame: the conventional reference to the "springless border" in the first line, and the even more vague reference of "long road" in the last line. The center of the poem is entirely concerned with China proper, specifically referred to in the euphemistic term "Shanglin," and with the willow, the woman, and her palace prison. A similar orientation is seen in the following poem by Cui Shi (fl. 710), though its Northern imagery is slightly expanded:

> By the second month spring is half over
> From the three borders our soldiers do not return
> In the flower of my youth I pity myself

> Just for you I twist this weeping willow
> Falling catkins stick to the sleeves of my blouse
> Drooping tendrils brush my coiled hair
> No word no letters, how can I stand it
> With flowing tears I look toward Yang Pass

YFSJ 22.331

Again the poem opens with a bow toward China's borders and closes with a specific reference to the far Northwest. Since the poem is a product of the Tang, we now have true border references, especially to Yang Pass, which was the last point of Chinese sovereignty along the southern silk route and a standard reference to that border area. Chang'an, which was the "North" to the Southern Six Dynasties' poets, such as Chen Shubao, becomes again (as it was in the Han) the center of China. The floral, decidedly nonborder, aspects of Cui's poem dominate—not only where the woman and the willow blend together (catkins and sleeves, tendrils and hair), but even in the reference to her flower of youth. The South still is south, but its conventions have been imported north to Chang'an.

In the next, particularly floral, poem by Tang poet Ouyang Jin, Cui Shi's "flower of youth" is placed in direct contrast with the border:

> Drooping willows brush the dressing table
> Clustered together the leaves half open
> The flower of youth appears on boughs
> Thoughts of the hinterland come with this song
> Soft colors appropriate to the new rains
> Light blossoms accompany falling plum petals
> Morning after morning drowsily boughs are twisted
> The marching troops, in what season will they return?

YFSJ 22.331

Most of this language describing the vernal willow has already been seen: the drooping, clustering, and delicate coloration. The addition of the plum flowers to the formula is a rare occasion of mixing of conventional language for the early and middle spring. The border imagery is there, along with its musical associations, but it is a border purely of reflection and not of actuality. Such also is the "hinterland dust" in the closing of the following poem by Zhang Jiuling (678–740):

> Slight and slender I break off the weeping willow
> To send off to my lover
> How could one bough be so valuable?
> It's lovely this spring in the garden back home
> How can this lingering scene last
> Flowing fragrance cannot stay fresh
> Even more melancholy for the marching troops
> Their hair turning old in the hinterland dust

> *YFSJ* 22.332

Then, in a similar vein, we have the second of Meng Jiao's "Yangliu" poems. Meng relies more on place names to set out the North-South dichotomy (and these are areas of the far North and South), and he is somewhat more specific in his mention of the border and concern with parting.

> Through the upper chambers the spring wind passes
> Before the wind floats the "Weeping Willow Song"
> Boughs sparse from the bitterness of parting
> The song laments how many years it's been
> Flowers startle us like snowflakes of Yan territory
> But their leaves reflect in the waves of the Chu pool
> Who can bear to part, leaving this behind
> The marching troops are now at Jiaohe

> *YFSJ* 22.333

This self-referential "Weeping Willow Song" ("Yangliu ge") exploits a number of floral/border images in innovative ways. The "sparse boughs" that open the second line bring easily to mind the lack of vegetation commonly associated with the barren border areas, but the conclusion of that line brings us back to the south. But then we discover that the unnatural lack of vegetation *is* the fault of those northern borders, since the boughs have been stripped as parting gifts for the men who have left for those regions. Similarly, the falling flowers of line 5 startle the women in the deep South (Chu) because they suddenly look like a snow storm in the far Northeast (Yan). This flower/snow imagery is a clever reversal of the conventional topos where the snows of the North are always reminding the lonely men there of the showers of spring flowers in the South. The most extreme border reference in this poem occurs in its last line, but in fact we have there only a place name, and this name, Jiaohe, is heavy with a sense of "non-China." Jiaohe was the Han name for the city in the Turfan basin, which even in the best of times was only tenuously under Chinese control. Like the mixed imagery of the rest of the poem, this has the effect of referring back to China more than to the border. This is, of course, exactly what the penultimate line clearly suggests.

Even when references to the border figure prominently in a "Yangliu" poem, the movement, whether actual or imaginary, is more from the South toward the North, as in the following poem by Weng Shou of the Tang. This is the last poem in the series, and the only other poem besides Chen Shubao's second poem that does not mention the willow by name:

> Along Purple Lane and Metal Dike shines the gossamer silk
> Everywhere travelers are moved to sing parting songs
> As time passes, old forts are lost in the grasslands
> Flowers carry fragments of sunlight falling on distant waves
> On the terraces the young men in white blown snow
> In the chambers worried women knit dark eyebrows
> With care twisted off and presented to the traveler
> Leaving here snow falls deeply in mountain passes

YFSJ 22.333

Weng has formed a truly eclectic poem out of the entire range of willow images and associations, built up in parallel couplets that focus on the contrast of North and South. The elaborate language of the seven-syllable lines (one of the few in the "Yangliu" set) masks some of the contrast, but it is evident in almost every phrase. While the willow is not mentioned, the penultimate line with its standard verbs, "twist off" *(panzhe)* and "present" *(zeng)*, are clear references to the boughs of the tree, just as the eyebrows in the line before are a more muted allusion to the leaves. In contrast to the references to the capital city area of the first line (Purple Lane and Metal Dike), the last line contains the most actualized references to the border, but we still have the sense that the border lies ahead and that we are still "here" with the willow tree, readying ourselves for the very real snow of the border. Weng does not make the explicit comparison between flying catkins and border snow, yet by this time in the development of the intratext the conventionality of the analogy would ensure its implication. Weng's use of the image is not without its own innovations, however. It is unclear, for example, whether the young men are already on the border standing in the wind-blown snow, which reminds them of the spring flowers, or if they are still standing in a "snow storm" of catkins in the south, which foretells their cold fate.

The Web's Edge

The "Yangliu" intratext touches a number of other groups of poems in the *yuefu* corpus. The thematic connection between the "Yangliu" and "Yin ma" poems suggests one such place. In that regard, we might say that the willow of the "Yangliu" intratext tends to keep the point of view, as the bough was intended to keep the traveler, with the one who stays behind (i.e., the woman in the South), just as the horse in "Yin ma" carried the man, and the point of view, off to the border. Those connections can then be extended into the wide range of border poems that fill the *yuefu* corpus, especially the large set entitled "Cong jun xing" ("In the Army").[13] But there are other more titular, and "Southern" connections to be pursued in the corpus.

The central set of twenty-five literati "Yangliu" poems comes to an end with the Late Tang poem by Weng Shou. But the "Yangliu" intratext does not die out there. In the Middle Tang there begins a new "Yangliu zhi" ("Boughs of the Weeping Willow") title sequence that extends through the Five Dynasties period to encompass seventy-nine additional poems by fifteen poets, starting with Bo Juyi (722–846) and including poems by Li Shangyin (813–850) and Wen Tingyun (812–870).[14] These poems, which betray "Wu sheng"/"Xi qu" origins with their five-syllable, four-line poems in sequences, form intratextual relationships with many of the "Yangliu" poems already examined here. The most prolific poet in this new title/theme, Xue Neng (fl. 850), with nineteen poems in two sequences, offers these comments on his own work:

> Poems with the title "Yangliu zhi" are [the same] as the poems with the old title "Zhe yangliu." In the fifth year of the Qianfu period (879), I was made magistrate of Xuzhou. Once giddy on wine, I had the department's young singing girls perform the fast dance to "Weeping Willow Boughs." For this new music I again composed these lyrics entitled "Yangliu zhi." (*YFSJ* 81.1142–43)

Indeed Xue's poems, as do many of the other "Yangliu zhi" sequences, engage primarily the feminine associations of the willow, leaving its "parting" theme almost unexplored. The complexity and extension that these new poems bring to the "Yangliu" intratext can be clearly seen in Xue's first sequence of ten poems.

1

Tall trees of Huaqing park rise above the villa walls
In the southern lanes soft tendrils carry the warm wind
Who can see their light shadows there this fine night
By the sound of the waterfall under the silver moon?

2

In the sunlight the shadows of Luo Bridge cover the river
   boats
The autumnal sounds of a Tibetan flute are soaked in border
   mists
Quietly I imagine the end of the official banquet at Xi pool
Water reeds, wind-blown catkins, evening descends over the
   bright sky

3

Soft green lightly hanging like knotted tassels
From the road he gazes on palace chambers beyond the wall
Who is able to approach those at her vermilion steps
That can spread on august winds through the Nine Provinces

4

The warm wind and the clear sun settle the floating dust
By the abandoned road, new tendrils grow on Angler's
   Terrace
There and everywhere light shadows make one solemn and
   sad
Where former people planted trees, people now twist them

5

By the pool at the river's edge weakly they droop
The sun is high, the wind still, catkins follow each other
But no one is seen near the lone tree by her painted chamber
It is now just the time when the girl is waking

6

A million tendrils hang high above the Bian River
The wind is fresh, both banks sway in unison
Sui power is exhausted, they were planted there in vain
Limitless spring winds now belong to our sagely rule

7

The peaceful flowers and misty trees in the nine-walled city
A hundred thousand encampments line the road in the
      spring shade
But in the direction of the border one cannot stand to gaze
A lone tree dry and withered, few people traveling this way

8

Outside her window on evenly drooping fronds the first
      sunlight
Beside her chamber they are light and lovely in the warm
      breeze
Don't let the wanderer say that such planting is not
      beneficial
So much better than the sparse shade of pear and plum trees

9

It's still cold, but the clump of trees has already turned
      green
Beside the imperial canal bridge there's Twisting River
      Pavilion
Tao's place of old days would have been like this
A courtyard of spring's green tendrils surrounds its halls

10

Supine within bed curtains surrounded by drooping wispy
  tangles
This brings to mind the garden of the Shi household
In wind-blown tendrils the moon reflections are doubled
Why would the noble mansions prefer to plant a day-lily?[15]

YFSJ 81.1147

Part of the beauty of this poetic series lies in the complex relationships that connect the various poems to each other and to the "Yangliu" intratext. This is especially so in its exploitation of the feminine associations of the willow. In Xue's rendering there is no mention of the act of parting, only the woman in isolation, the victim of that parting. Xue brings to this series not only a plethora of literary and historical allusions, but also many of the "Willow" conventions we have seen above. From the willow-shaded "southern lanes" of the first poem, which remind us of Luofu, to her willow-shrouded "empty bed" in the last poem, we see the tree/woman in her many manifestations. And almost every possible metonymy for the willow is here, including some innovative ones—tendrils, catkins, wispy tangles, misty trees, drooping fronds, swaying river banks, Tao Qian. We should note, however, that the word *willow* never appears; every line is about the willow, but none mentions it. The willow's absence fills the poem, just as the unmentioned parting fills the woman's world. The ephemeral day-lily, as beautiful as it might be, pales beside those tendrils that can retain, those unmentioned trees that remain.

6

R/endings: The Disruptive Poetics of Li Bo

Of the nearly six hundred authors in Guo Maoqian's collection, Li Bo (701–762) is the acknowledged master of *yuefu* poetry, not merely in the size of his corpus, but also in its range and power. Li's work represents the genre at its maturity, and his literary verve revivified the intratextual poetics that identify *yuefu* poetry as a functioning genre. No poet before Li identified so consciously and closely with the genre, and all those after him who sought to write in the genre necessarily worked in his shadow. Moreover, several of the earlier poets conventionally associated with the genre, especially Bao Zhao, were drawn retroactively into that association by Li's imitation of them. Li Bo is to *yuefu* poetry what Du Fu is to regulated verse, and together their work has been traditionally considered the zenith of the Chinese literary tradition. The Song dynasty literary critic Yan Yu (fl. 1200) was perhaps first to align these two poets together in this appreciation of their work:

> Poetry has an ultimate goal, that is to penetrate the spirit. When poetry penetrates the spirit, that's perfection, that's completion, one should not add to it! This is what Li and Du attained. Generally very few others attained it. . . . The two gentlemen Li and Du did not have the same strengths and weaknesses. [Li] Taibo had several

marvelous qualities that [Du] Zimei was not able to follow; Zimei had several marvelous qualities that Taibo could not recreate. Zimei did not have the creative energy of Taibo; Taibo did not have the profound complexity of Du.[1]

Like the clichéd *yin* and *yang*, Li Bo and Du Fu have formed the composite literary strength of China; they are her bipolar Shakespeare. Here we shall discuss only Li's half of that composite strength; as we shall see, his is of a more *yang* coloration, despite claims made otherwise.[2] While Du Fu's art has the resonance of depth and substance, which finds its full tones especially in his highly personalized verse, Li has more theatrical flash, a moment of daring brilliance that catches our eye and then quickly fades. In the establishment of Li's poetic style, *yuefu* poetry necessarily plays a central role.

In the spectrum of poetry and poetic types during the High Tang, Li Bo and Du Fu were more alike than this common bipolar comparison suggests. Stephen Owen remarks, "With some justification, Du Fu would have seen himself as a poet in the same tradition as Li Bo, and the more significant contrast lies between a kind of poetry represented by the work of Li and Du, and the capital poetic tradition represented by Wang Wei." [3] In contrast to Wang Wei's highly crafted and contemplative verse, what most united Li and Du, besides what Owen calls "their shared admiration of Li himself," was the importance poetry had for each of them as an act manifesting and, more importantly, signifying their personal character. For both Li and Du, the writing of poetry was the veritable creation of the individual personality in art, rather than art as a social, philosophic, or aesthetic exercise. Thus, it is within that rather narrow aspect of Chinese poetic endeavor, art as individuation, that the bipolarity of Li and Du must be viewed, not in the context of Tang poetry in general.

Du Fu's interest in this art of personal signification is, however, somewhat masked by his own poetic virtuosity and the complexity of his biography, and this in part accounts for his poetry's more subdued quality. I do not believe Du Fu was less interested in writing about himself, but rather that the "self" of which he wrote was of a more socially attached, integrated sort. Du's personality, both biographical and poetic, most often found its significance as part of a group, whether that group was his family, the city of Chengdu, or the imperial court. Du Fu and his poetry were always striving for human interaction, but personal circumstances meant he was often lamenting the suspension (but never the denial) of that interaction. Even in his highest poetic style and language, as seen in the "Autumn Meditations," he complains primarily of his inability to interact with those groups that give his life meaning. Du was not outside those groups (for he always felt part of them), but rather he was *separated* from them. This understanding of poetry as the means of *human* interaction and not of interaction between man and something other than man—nature, the gods, a muse—is a central concept of the Chinese poetic tradition.

While Li Bo is similarly concerned with his poetic personality, the formation of that personality, both its actual shape and the means by which it was formed, is quite different from that of Du Fu. As Owen has clearly elaborated, Li was the consummate outsider. He was politically, economically, and ethnically outside the mainstream in which Du and most other poets of the High Tang dwelled. And Li wore this outsider status, which he consciously enhanced in a multitude of ways, like a badge on his sleeve. Even when he was within the groups that Du Fu and others so often felt separated from but never outside of, Li was not part of them. And when he was separated from these groups, he would ponder his lack of interaction with them not as the suspension of a natural order, but rather as a manifestation of a natural disorder, which was himself. He was, as he was so willing to tell us, the young knight errant from Chengdu, the wild spender, the carefree drunk, and always "the banished immortal." According to the few biographical details that we have—and most seem to have been promoted if not invented by Li himself—his life began in myth that gave him his name, cavorted through a fairyland of Taoist magic, and ended in the legend of the tipsy embracer of watery moons.[4]

Li identifies with the borderland of China and the eccentrics of its tradition, does not seem particularly well-read, never sits for an exam, takes a "degree" in esoteric Taoism, marries perhaps for money, and stuns the inner circles with his studied disregard for them. In Li we have a poetic personality that never seeks to be merely part of the group—not the warmth of the family, nor the camaraderie of drinking friends, nor the shared reclusion of the untainted, nor even the flow of human history. Li was forever seeking to be the marvelous poetic artifact, an object for consideration, and an object of an audience, especially of the imperial audience. His claim of being a "banished immortal" and the thought that his verse was "strange on top of strangeness" *(qi zhi you qi)* naturally needed the highest legitimization and proof. Neither the well-crafted verse of the court poet nor the quotidian charm of occasional verse would do; he had to write above the crowd and his acceptance had to come from the highest sources. His most appropriate admirer was the one human close enough to heaven to know if that were where Li really belonged.

While Li was not, nor did he want to be, part of those common human groups, he certainly needed to find his sustenance, both physical and spiritual, from them. Owen has suggested that "even the archindividual, Li Bo, attained his separateness by laughing at convention, by a stance of defiance that required something to defy."[5] Li Bo's *yuefu* poetry operates exactly in this way, defying convention and radicalizing the contexts of its intratextuality; it is undoubtedly the most important element in the formation of that "outsider on the inside" stance.

Li Bo's *Yuefu* Corpus

One simple measure of the strength of Li Bo's position in the *yuefu* genre is in the size of his *yuefu* corpus, especially compared to that of Du Fu. While Li has approximately 120 *yuefu* titles, Du has only twelve, even though Du has at least five hundred more poems than Li in his total works.[6] And in this Du certainly better represents the central line of High Tang poetic trends. The other major poets of the High Tang have similarly sized *yuefu* corpora: Meng Haoran has only one *yuefu* title; Cen Shen three; Li Qi five; Gao Shi eight; and Wang Changling eleven. Even with the emergence of the "new *yuefu* poetry" of the mid-Tang poets the situation does not change dramatically, for while we begin to approach the actual numbers of Li's corpus, the percentages fall sharply (Bo Juyi's sixty-six titles are set in a total poetic corpus of over two thousand poems). Among fellow High Tang poets, only Wang Wei's work begins to approach Li's (twenty-seven *yuefu* titles of approximately four hundred poems, but still only about half the per-centage of Li's). Interestingly, the one major Tang poet who does out-perform Li's *yuefu* percentages is his successor in the poetry of the extreme, Li He (791–817) with forty-four *yuefu* titles in a total corpus of approximately two hundred and fifty.

Another objective measure of Li Bo's *yuefu* work is the spread of his poems across Guo Maoqian's twelve *yuefu* categories. Li's poems are found in all but one category, with just over half of them in the central *xianghe* and *zaqu* groups. Li even has one poem among the stilted ritual poems of *jiaomiao ge ci* (but we shall see that his is anything but stilted), and seven now designated as "new *yuefu*" (which may represent more Guo Maoqian's inclusive sweep than Li's con-scious praxis). It is true Li Bo leaves no *yuefu* stone unturned, but he does tend to center his efforts in those areas of the genre that were most popular with earlier poets. This includes, by the way, a very healthy nod to the poets associated with the "Southern style" in the *qingshang* category, such as Xiao Gang. While Li made some theoretical denun-ciations of this Southern poetry, in actuality he often wrote, and often well, in this mode. Thus we can say that while Li was out to make a name for himself in the genre, he did not plan to do this by experiment-ing with innovative categories, as would the mid-Tang "new *yuefu*" poets. The sheer exuberance of Li's *yuefu* efforts tended to spread his work throughout the genre, but his efforts remained mainstream, at least in the categories in which he wrote.

These numbers actually do not tell the full story of the importance of Li Bo's *yuefu* poetry in the formation of his poetic identity. Not only did Li write frequently in the genre, he apparently also wrote best therein.[7] Except for his fifty-nine "Gu feng" poems, almost every famous poem by Li is a *yuefu* one. These include the common anthology pieces: his startling "howl" poem "The Road to Shu is Hard" ("Shu dao nan"), his rowdy drinking poem "Bring in the Wine" ("Jiang jin jiu"), and his vivid antiwar poem "Fighting South of the City" ("Zhan cheng nan"). Even his quintessential palace poem, the "Jade Stair Lament" ("Yu jie yuan"), is actually a *yuefu* poem—it "imitates" poems of the same title by Xie Tiao (464–499) and Yu Yan (fl. 500).[8] Of the best known poems that celebrate the personality that we identify as Li Bo, only his "Drinking Alone under the Moon" ("Yuexia du zhuo") is not associated with the genre.

Li Bo's overriding investment and ability in the *yuefu* genre should perhaps strike us as odd, inasmuch as this genre, by virtue of its intratextuality, led easily to conventional writing. While *yuefu* poetry was relatively free in prosodic form, it was thematically restricted, either specifically to the titular themes or more generally to its intratextual markings. Owen has suggested that it was these very conventions that attracted Li, for they allowed him to write in adopted voices outside of the quotidian world of *shi* poetry. They allowed him "all the various roles he assumed in his poetry—the immortal, the bravo, the drinker, and the eccentric—[which] were all models of behavior that lay outside the twin roles of scholar-official and serene recluse."[9] But we shall see that they also allowed Li to write outside of their prescribed contexts, for once Li adopted such a role, he did not so much write within the conventions as he wrote against them. Li seemed to join in the praxis of intratextual poetics only so he would have something to disrupt; he was not so interested in weaving a text as he was in unraveling it.

The Willow and the Lotus

Li Bo was not always so disruptive when he wrote in the *yuefu* genre; within his large corpus there are a number of poems that participate in a more benign type of intratextuality. For instance, Li's "Zhe yangliu" contribution to the large corpus of similarly titled "Willow" poems discussed in the last chapter is an example of his relatively straightforward intratextual poetics. The Ming critic Hu Zhenheng has described this poem in its *yuefu* context: "The original *hengchui* text is lost, but after the Liang and Chen the imitations all describe the women in their apartments thinking about their soldiers far away. [Li] Taibo's poem also has this theme."[10]

> Weeping willows droop to brush the green water
> Wafting their beauty in this easterly spring wind
> Their blossoms are bright as the snow in Jade Pass
> Leaves are soft and warm in the gilded window mist

The beautiful woman is consumed by unending sorrow
Facing them her heart is filled with pain
Twisting a tendril, breaking off spring color
She sends it far off to Longting on the border

YFSJ 22.332

Here we have a well-formed amalgam of many images that form the "Yangliu" intratext: the drooping willow and the wafting skirts, the spring wind and the lonely woman, the delicate leaves and the pained heart. The flying catkins fuse with their conventional contrapuntal comparison, the snowflakes of the Jade Pass, to yield the often-seen South/North dichotomy. Befitting the title, the poem "remains" in the South with the woman; only the willow branch vainly reaches out to the border region where the woman's lover/husband is stationed. There is little here that would distinguish this as a Li Bo poem; he conforms to the conventions of the intratext to produce a pleasant, but not startling, "Yangliu" poem. Only in the penultimate line do we see any hint of Li's disruptive poetics, and while it is a minor example, it is typical of his *yuefu* style. In that line Li adopts three conventional images from the intratext—the nearly obligatory *panzhe* verb, the common "tendrils" *(tiao)*, and the straightforward reference to the spring scene/color *(chun se)*—but he joins these in a unique configuration. First we should note that while many "Yangliu" poems mention the "tendrils," these are not usually what are "twisted off," but rather these are what "waft" and "brush"; they are an arboreal metaphor for the woman's delicate skirts—usually the branches *(zhi)* are the object of the verb *panzhe*. Moreover, and more importantly, in Li's poem the verb *panzhe* itself is disrupted. Like the branch from the tree, it is broken off from itself to form two independent verbs *pan* and *zhe*, the first taking the almost conventional object "tendril," and the second taking the highly unusual object, the "spring scene/color." The woman twists off not a branch, but a delicate tendril, and that tendril is the vernal color itself, which easily alludes to her romantic desire (especially with the sexual connotations of the word *se)*. All of *this* is then sent to the border. Thus, Li reworks the most conventional topoi into an imaginative restatement of the principal theme of the intratext. Like his "Willow" poem, Li's "Cai lian xing" participates in a similar but slightly more marked reconfiguration of its "Lotus" intratext, which we discussed in Chapter 4. Composed largely of the elements from the conventional water-borne, semi-erotic scene of lotus picking, only at the end does Li's poem veer off in new directions:

> Along the Ruoye stream the girls plucking lotuses
> Laugh from behind their flowers, talking with others
> The sun shines on fresh makeup, bright in the depths
> The wind blows fragrant sleeves wafting in the air
> Who are those playboys who wander along the shore
> By threes, by fives in shadows of the drooping poplar
> The neighing of roan stallions enters falling flowers
> Seeing them hesitate there, in vain a heart is broken

YFSJ 50.733

The first half of this poem mirrors very closely the "Cai lian" intratext that Xiao Gang and his school created: we have the requisite women giddy with the dalliance on the river, hidden among the erect lotus plants, and caressed by the spring wind. The women are "appropriately" overdressed and the river has the common erotic associations that remove the women from any semblance of practical work. Moreover, the Ruoye stream (also called Huanshaxi) is specifically associated with the model of femininity, Xi Shi, who is said to have washed her yarn there when she was young.[11] But Li gets carried away with the conventions of intratext: suddenly the men, who are never mentioned but who are always implied in other "Cai lian" poems, come loping into view. Li has destroyed the convention of discretion; these "playboys" are wandering around in veritable gangs ("by threes, by fives"—an expression Li himself creates for use here), seeing what they can see. Then, as if that is not enough, in place of the conventional playing fish and startled egrets, Li introduces that prototypical animal of terra firma and male proxy, the horse. And instead of the boat and oars sliding through the falling petals, the neighing of these horses penetrates *(ru)* deep into that feminine world of the lotus. The last line finalizes the break with the "Cai lian" intratext by introducing the image of the hesitating horse from other *yuefu* intratexts, such as the "Yin ma" or similar border poems. The horse's hesitation actually represents the man's own, and is usually seen at parting or when he first faces the hostile world of the border.

Li Bo and the Border

The roan stallions *(ziliu)* in Li's "Cai lian" poem have actually wandered in from another large set of poems with the title "The Roan Stallions" ("Ziliu ma"). This group of twenty literati poems, which was initiated by Xiao Gang (but with related anonymous texts), yields a rather conventional intratext of horse and border—similar to the "Yin ma" intratext but without its distinctive titular narrative line. Li's "Roan Stallion" poem is nestled comfortably among those, but is elaborated with a certain amount of distinct imagery:

> The roan stallions neigh as they travel on
> In pairs they fly along on jasper hooves
> But at the current's edge they won't cross
> As if they regret muddying the brocade guard
> White Snow troops are far beyond Pass Mountain
> The Yellow Clouds are lost among the border forts
> Cracking their whips they go for a myriad miles
> How can they recall those spring apartments?[12]

YFSJ 24.355

Wang Qi remarks that, compared with the other imitations by Xiao Gang, Xiao Yi, Chen Houzhu, Xu Ling, and others, which "described only the horse itself," Li's poem did not "lose the theme of the old text," which is to say that he "described both the horse and the troops that had been dispatched far away, and not the joy of the love-nest."[13] While horses are a common topic of *yuefu* poetry, and of Tang culture in general, they seem to hold a particular fascination for Li Bo, especially with their inherent association with the western border regions that he explores here.

Li Bo's apparent fascination with the horse is most easily explained by his personal identification with the West and his self-professed abilities as a knight errant. Li regularly seized any opportunity to raise the foreigner, the border, and military prowess above their poetic commonplaces. A particularly lusty rendition of such hyperbole occurs in his "Song of the Youzhou Traveler on a Hun Horse" ("Youzhou hu ma ke ge") where these three topics are united:

> The Youzhou traveler on a Hun horse
> Has green eyes and a tiger cap
> Laughing he can shoot a pair of arrows
> And a myriad men cannot block them
> When his bow curves like a rounded moon
> Snow geese fall from the high clouds
> In pairs the Huns come swinging their whips
> Hunting they wander off towards Loulan
> Once out of the gate they don't look back
> How could dying for the state be difficult
> The five Khans are as proud as Heaven
> Rapacious like wolves they love destruction
> Horses and cattle scatter over the northern expanse
> The freshly killed are the tigers' meal
> Although they live on Yanzhi Mountain
> They don't notice the cold of the Ordos snow
> On horseback their wives and daughters laugh
> With complexions like carnelian plates
> Flying and turning they shoot bird and beast
> These beauties are drunk in the saddle
> But when the Hun star is in ascendance
> They join the battle like a swarm of bees
> Silver blades glisten red with blood,
> And Flowing Sands are turned crimson
> In antiquity who were the famous generals?

The exhausted soldiers can certainly sigh
And when will warlike Sirius be extinguished
So fathers and sons can rest in peace?[14]

YFSJ 25.372–73

The most distinguishing aspect of this poem is its pervasive and sympathetic "Hun" perspective. While Li writes almost entirely in the conventions of border poetry, he infuses the enemy with the romantic bravura of the knight errant, and transforms their common negativity into a positive quality. This is true compared with his "Roan Stallion" poem quoted above, but even more so when compared with more conventional border poems.[15] This transformation is entirely the product of the positive power with which Li imbues these foreigners. The cold of Ordos snows, a prototypical object of the border poem's complaint, is, for example, denied by the Huns' power to overlook it, thereby increasing their stature. Likewise, even the clichéd cruelty of the carnivorous wolf and tiger is transformed into an almost positive trait of military prowess. Compared with almost all other border poems, this "Youzhou Traveler" by Li Bo is much more a celebration of the border and its nomadic people with whom he is said to have identified; this is especially so in the passage that describes the women. While Hun women do turn up in *yuefu* poems with some regularity, they are nearly always represented merely as an object of sexual curiosity, often associated with the wineshop.[16] In contrast, the women in Li's poem take on full and exciting personalities. In fact they take on Li Bo's own favorite persona—the tipsy warrior, wild in appearance, with *joie de vivre* and great physical reserves. Here again Li is not so much creating something out of whole cloth as he is twisting the poetic commonplaces; to these women he attributes the heightened masculinity often associated with the Hun warriors and with which he opens his poem. These women are also the product of his romanticization of the "noble warrior."

Thus, it would appear that Li's apparent attraction to the horse was simply part of his identification with the bravura of the border; yet more generally we might note that the horse, especially the celebrated

Arabian horse, was the quintessential outsider on the inside of China.
While loved, nearly worshipped, the Arabian horse was always recog-
nized as essentially different from its Chinese cousin: the Arabian
sweated blood, could run one thousand *li*, and was considered the
off-spring of the Heavenly horses.[17] Certainly here was an animal equal
to Li Bo, the "banished immortal." Here was an animal that was to be
judged by different standards and allowed access to the highest audi-
ences. Li's interest in this type of horse is clearly seen in his "Heavenly
Horse" ("Tian ma") poem, the first of only a few literati imitations of
two ritual poems written during the rule of Emperor Wu of the Han.
The original "Heavenly Horse" compositions were composed as part of
the celebration of successful Chinese military campaigns in far
western Chinese Turkestan that secured these animals from the To-
charian *Dayuan* tribe of Ferghana. The horses, first discovered by the
Chinese in 120 B.C., had become the object of a near religious quest for
Emperor Wu. These two poems (one written at the inception of Wu's
desire, the other at its satisfaction) mark the beginning of what became
a pervasive Chinese obsession with the animals.

1

Composed in 120 B.C. When the Horses Emerged from the
Wowei River

A gift of the Ultimate One
The Heavenly Horses descended
Soaked in red sweat
Mouth foaming sepia
With expansive will
And marvelous power of spirit
Prancing over floating clouds
Galloping through the darkness
In a style carefree and at ease
They run more than a myriad miles
What now could be their mates
They have dragons for friends

2

Composed in 101 B.C. After Smiting the King of Ferghana and Seizing His Horses

The Heavenly Horses have come
From the Western Reaches
They have forded the Flowing Sands
The nine foreign tribes have submitted
The Heavenly Horses have come
Out from the source of rivers
With tiger manes doubled
They change like ghosts
The Heavenly Horses have come
They have crossed the barrens
Along trails of one thousand miles
They have taken the eastward roads
The Heavenly Horses have come
With Jupiter in the northwest
When they were about to rise
Who was there to meet them
The Heavenly Horses have come
With distant gates opened
We stand at attention
They leave the Kunlun Mountains
The Heavenly Horses have come
The matchmakers of dragons
They wander at Heaven's Gate
And gaze on Jade Terrace[18]

YFSJ 1.6

Nothing so represented the marvelous but forbidding West as did these exotic "foreigners" in China, and we can well imagine Li Bo's personal affinity with them. They are striking in spiritual and physical power; they are held in awe because of their extraordinary nature, and are even allowed to peer into the emperor's own Jade Terrace. The only equal they have in the pantheon of Chinese creatures is the dragon, itself an extraterrestrial, often celestial, guest. These are all things Li had in mind when he wrote his own flamboyant "Song of the Heavenly Horse" ("Tian ma ge"):

> The Heavenly Horses came from a Scythian cave
> Backs with tiger stripes, bones of dragon wings
> They neigh at blue clouds, shaking their green manes
> Running on orchid sinews and marvelous power they
>   disappear
> Over Kunlun Mountain and beyond the Western Reaches
> Their four hooves never once stumble
> At cockcrow groomed in Yan, at dusk foddered in Yue
> Like spirit's flight and lightning's flash they run in a blur
>
> The Heavenly Horse calls out, the flying dragon moves near
> Eyes bright and constant as Venus, double-duck breasted
> A tail like a comet, a head of a thirsty-crow sprinkler
> His mouth spews red light, rivulets of sweat run crimson
> With the Dragon of the Season he hurtles Heaven's streets
> The gold halter bridles its bright moon eyes in the august
>   city
> His superior air, proud and pleased, covers the nine regions
> Who would dare buy so mountainous a medallion of white
>   jade
> But in a moment they laugh at Roan Swallow
> Believing that his breed is so foolish
>
> The Heavenly Horses run, longing for the lord's carriage
> Rein-whipped startled, vaulting high floating clouds
>   spinning
> After a myriad miles they hesitate their steps
> And gaze from afar toward Heaven's Gate
> If they do not meet Horsemaster Hanfeng
> Who will know to select these scions of a shadow?

White clouds in a blue sky
Hills and mountains are far and steep
The salt wagons climb the precipitous grade
Against traffic, counter current, fearing the day's end
Bo Le's loving care for the horse has been lost
The youthful strength gone, I am abandoned in old age
I wish I would meet Tian Zifang
With kindness he would understand my grief
Although I might have Jade Mountain grain
It could not cure this bitter hunger
A severe frost in June withers the cinnamon branches
Kept in the stall, bridle and bit press on my brow
I plead with you to redeem me as a gift for Emperor Mu
To play again with those shadows in a dance at Jasper Pool[19]

YFSJ 1.9–10

While we have come to expect a certain amount of radicalism in Li Bo's intratextual poetics, the liberties that he has taken here with the Heavenly Horse theme are astounding. He certainly had the two Han "Tian ma" poems in mind when he wrote; this is seen in the close paraphrase of the opening two stanzas, but even there he exploits the commonplaces of these horses in innovative ways. Most apparent is the development of the draconic parallels and extraterrestrial qualities of horses that fill the entire poem. This begins with the derivative tiger and dragon images of line 2, and expands through the second stanza in a series of celestial images, many of which are derived from extra-*yuefu* sources. All of these images conclude with a plea for reunion on Kunlun Mountain with the most celebrated of all royal travelers, King Mu of the Zhou, whose fabled journey to the western regions is described in the *Mu tianzi zhuan*. (Mu, not incidentally, was a spiritual antecedent for Emperor Wu of the Han.) But between those two references to the fabled mountain in the West (lines 5 and 38), Li Bo interjects a more personal story—the story of the neglected, unappreciated foreigner in China, the story of the aging Heavenly Horse, told by the horse himself, who is obviously a voice for Li. Elling Eide has argued cogently and meticulously for Li Bo's Turkish background, and specifically he has shown how many of the details of this poem dovetail with the projection of that identity:

> These various identities and affinities do not, of course, make a good poem or even an autobiographical poem in and of themselves. It is important, therefore, to note how well elements of the poem correspond with what we know about Li Bo's career: exotic origins (lines 1–8); early evidence of great talent (also 1–8); pride, self-confidence, and ambition (especially lines 6–12, 15–16, 19–20); overnight fame and success at the capital plus association with the emperor and high officials (lines 9–16); rather inexplicable rejection (lines 17–18); desperate efforts to return to service (lines 19–28); disgrace, jail, and exile (lines 31–38); and old age spent far removed from the splendors he had once known (lines 25–38). In many of his poems Li Bo uses "blue clouds" and "cinnamon twigs" as symbols of honors and aspiration to high office. In this poem the progression of this career from youthful ambition to an old age of rejection and neglect seems emphasized by the "neighing to the blue clouds" in line 3 and the "withered buds of the cinnamon tree" in line 35.[20]

Eide continues and expands this line of argument with this poem and others. I would only note here, adopting Owen's more recent argument, that the poem actually corresponds more with Li's poetic persona than with his supposed biography, as well it should, since both poem and persona are products of Li's selective creative powers. While we do not know whether that identity is actually biographically grounded or not, Eide is right in that the poem is a testimony to Li's personal affinities with the West and with the Heavenly Horse. While it is possible that biography, psychology, and poetics unite to yield this poem, that would be highly unusual in both the genre at large and in Li's corpus, both of which tend to celebrate intratextual personae rather than actual personalities. I would also note that the assumption that a poem's progress consciously represents an actual life progress implies that the poem was written late in the poet's life, which is far from certain, though possible. Be that as it may, we should turn our attention to how the poem works in its intratextual context.

Viewed against its two Han model poems, Li's interjection of his own biographical and/or psychological story into the poem undermines the fantastic advent and celebration of the horse in the opening of his poem, as well as in the original Han poems. The first two stanzas are certainly infused with the highly charged style so commonly associated with Li Bo, both as he manipulates the Han poems' imagery (e.g., lines 2, 4, 5, 9, 12, 22), and as he introduces new material, especially from Yan Yanzhi's (384–456) "Rhapsody on a Light Sorrel Horse" ("Zhe bai ma fu") and the Liang Dynasty *Xiang ma jing (Classic of Horse Physiognomy)*.[21] The simple fact that Li was writing with seven hundred years between him and the original Han poems (and these were seven centuries in which the horse rose to prominence as a cultural artifact in China) ensured that his poem would be richer than its models.[22]

The poem as a whole, however, veers off from the Han model at the end of the second stanza, where the fine horse Roan Swallow (figurative language whose origins are found in the late Six Dynasties) is suddenly the object of laughter and his breed *(er bei)* is considered foolish. Thus, the exotic foreigner is ridiculed even though he strains to display his supernatural powers in the next stanza. Then in midstanza the horse suddenly pauses to gaze longingly back toward the Heavenly Gate (either celestial or imperial) where his Han counterparts had wandered leisurely and peered into the imperial gardens. This hesitation is transformed into a properly allusion-laden question, "If they do not meet Horsemaster Hanfeng / Who will know to select these scions of shadows," which is basically the same question asked by Qu Yuan (third century B.C.) and every other neglected literary talent thereafter: Who will be able to recognize my inner quality?[23] Yet even with that hesitation and question we are startled by the final stanza where we find the Heavenly Horse, who a few lines earlier had been vaulting through the skies, reduced to a mere draft animal laboring behind salt wagons on dangerous mountain roads, a metaphor with its own history.[24] Here Li is experimenting with that particular style of intratextual poetics that will come to mark his most memorable *yuefu*, which startled traditional readers as it "violated their sense of poetic order and decorum."[25] The poem then ends with the image of the Queen Mother of the West and

her Jasper Pool where the abused horses might find extreme refuge, a
fitting tribute to both the Heavenly Horses and to the Han, and of course
a compliment to Li himself.

The Radical Conservative

We have seen that the disruptiveness of Li Bo's *yuefu* poetics finds
several forms, such as the revision of a titular theme, the interjection
of a strong personal presence into an otherwise intratextual composi-
tion, or the conflation of conventional elements from disparate in-
tratexts. Another, and one of Li's most distinctive, methods of rewriting
the intratext is what might be called a radical conservative revision. Li
uses this type of revision when he encounters an intratext that has
evolved far from its original thematic sources; in other words, the
intratext has diverged from its original configurations and that diver-
gence itself has become conventionalized. When this happens Li can
then use the oldest, most conservative part of the intratext to effect a
radical rewriting of it. Such radical conservatism not only provides Li
with another distinct intratextual signature, but it also abets the estab-
lishment of his "outsider on the inside" persona. By breaking away from
the developing lines of a given intratext he places himself outside
convention, but by retrieving buried intratextual elements to rewrite
that convention he returns himself to its innermost circle.

   As an example of this method of rewriting, we can turn to some of
the oldest intratextual lines in the *yuefu* corpus. Among them is this
small, perhaps fragmentary piece, included in the *xianghe* poems:

> In the village there is a boy weeping
> He seems to be your father's son
> Turning my carriage around I ask of him
> His anguish is overwhelming[26]

YFSJ 38.563

The comments by Cui Bao and others, which presumably would have
been available to the poets who wrote intratextually, provide a general

context for these lines. Cui Bao first says: "Shangliutian is a place name. There was one whose father died and who neglected his orphaned younger brother. The neighbors created a sad song for the younger brother in order to criticize the older one, and it was called 'Shangliutian.'"[27] Wu Jing then comments that the poem, which he quotes as Cui did not, is probably a Han text.[28] Whatever its origins, this poem strikes one as appropriately "folk" in style and of a certain narrativity that would lend itself to imitation.

The first imitation of the "Shangliutian" poem in a group of six is one by Cao Pi that explores the commonality of man's suffering, whether rich or poor, with the term *shangliutian* acting as a [musical?] refrain. While there may be some very generalized thematic connection between Cao's poem and the "model," it would be difficult to prove any conscious one. Since much of Cao's poem deals with different types of grain, one suspects that he has been influenced by the title, which might be literally translated "Going to the Liu Fields." The next poem in the set is by Lu Ji, and it fits well the general configurations of the poetic voice that we saw in our considerations of his *yuefu* poetry in Chapter 4. It is a highly derived poem that portrays the theme of suffering and travel with somewhat clumsy and difficult language. While not as abstract as some of his other poems, his "Shangliutian" has a more philosophic, rather than mundane, coloration. There seems to be no thematic or linguistic connection with either the Han poem or with Cao Pi's; nor is there even a nod to the title.

Xie Lingyun, the early master of landscape poetry, is the next poet to adopt the "Shangliutian" title, and his rendition is an interesting interweaving of certain parts of the developing intratext, combined with an individualized signature. Like Cao Pi he uses the title as refrain throughout the poem, but like Lu Ji he takes up the theme of travel. In several places Xie includes subtle linguistic nods to the two poets and to the title. Xie's poem is, however, much longer than the previous two, more narrative, and written in a language whose perspicuity more closely approaches that of the original. Its most distinctive feature is the repetitiveness of its prosody, which not only interjects the refrain after every line, but also repeats every third line verbatim. The thematic connections between Xie's poem and the original are, however, extremely tenuous, if they exist at all. The last pre–Li Bo imitation is Xiao Gang's seven-syllable quatrain, which pushes the language and themes of the original even further into the background, though it seems superficially closer in its prosody. While Xiao Gang's poem refers to the farming village, his poem is a ritual celebration of the advent of spring, not a poem of rural life.

> At the first of the year the earth begins to ooze fertility
> The Heavenly Horse's bright gaze ignites the star of farming
> The families of the field ladle wine and work together in
>   groups
> Making a song of praise to the Golden Phoenix Dais in
>   Chang'an[29]

YFSJ 38.564

While Xiao obliquely acknowledges the title in the term "families of the fields" *(tian jia)*, nothing could be farther from the death and abandonment that surrounds the orphaned boy of the original than this very imperial perspective on the advent of spring in the countryside. And nothing could be further from Xiao Gang's poem than Li Bo's "Shangliutian" poem.

Li Bo's rendering of the "Shangliutian" has the length of Xie Lingyun's and opens in language reminiscent of it and of the original, but in the end Li Bo's work turns to a pedantry that makes Lu Ji look tame by comparison. That pedantry is closely connected to the thematic thrust and narrative line of the original poem, which had been almost entirely lost in the other imitations:

> In my travels I came to Shangliutian
> And saw a lone tomb tall and imposing
> Gathered there was the anguish of a myriad ages
> Where the spring grasses never grew again
> A grieving wind blew round its four sides
> The white poplars cried with broken hearts
> I asked to whose family did this land belong

Buried here in its spirit house of the dead
An old man explained it to me
That this was Shangliutian
The horse-mane mound on the tumbleweed plot now leveled
In the past a little boy died, his brother didn't bury him
Then some others set up a funeral banner for him
When a bird dies, a hundred birds cry out
When an animal runs, a hundred animals are startled
The sparrows of Huan mountain were bitter with parting
About to leave, flying in circles, not able to go on
The Tians were hastily going to split up the family
So the hot sun in the clear sky seared the purple thorn
It was the same as the tree of reciprocal yielding
When the east branch withers the west flourishes
Even things without human emotion are like this
How could Orion and Lucifer be celestial warriors
In Guzhu and Yanling they yielded power and rose to fame
The high wind blows long, the cascading waves surge and
    sparkle
Plug your ears so you can't hear the foot-of-cloth song[30]

YFSJ 38.564–65

Here is Li Bo at his most conservative, and that conservatism is double-edged and disruptive. It is double-edged in that (1) Li returns to the original (if slightly reconfigured) "neglected little brother" theme of the Han poem; and (2) he illustrates that theme with an array of examples from the orthodox "Confucian" iconography of sibling piety. The duality of the poem is reflected in the type of language out of which it is formed; it opens with a simple narrative style very similar to the original, but once the "story" is told, the poem is propelled into paratactic allusions. Li's conservatism is radical: he bludgeons the intratext with an archaizing and hyperbolic tract of itself.

    The other example of Li's radical conservative rewriting I want to offer here has a similar textual history, but yields a more graceful poem. The original poem, which has two titles, but which I will refer to as

"Konghou yin," is similar in style and size to the "Shangliutian" poem, and it is again found with an accompanying entry in Cui Bao's *Gu jin zhu*:

The "Konghou yin" poem is a composition by Liyu, wife of Zigao of the Jinzu hou village in Korea. One morning Zigao got up and was out punting his boat. There he saw a crazy old guy with his white hair hanging loose and a pot of wine in hand. The old man jumped into the current and tried to cross. His wife chased after him to stop him, but she was too late. He sank into the river and drowned. Thereupon his wife took up her lute *(konghou)* and sang this song:

> Old man, don't cross that river
> But old man, you crossed that river
> And sank into the river and drowned
> Oh, old man, what will we do now

Her voice was filled with anguish, and when she had finished her tune she also threw herself into the river and drowned. When Zigao returned home he told Liyu about it. Liyu saddened by the story, took up her lute to describe the woman's voice. Whenever anybody heard this tune they would sink into tears and sob. Liyu then taught the tune to a neighbor woman, Lirong, and this was called "Konghou yin."[31]

The whole energy and pathos of this anecdote would have appealed to Li Bo. Not only the crazy old man with his bottle of wine, but also the response of the two women, harbors a certain romantic appeal that befits Li's persona.

There are two poems between this anecdotal version of "Konghou" poem and Li Bo's imitation, both of which are from the late Six Dynasties, and in them we see a definite movement away from the language and theme of the original. The first, by Liu Xiaowei of the Liang, is a translation of the theme into language and setting more befitting the palace-style poetry of that period. The voice is not that of the wife of a crazy old man, but rather of a palace lady singing to her lord; the simple language and straightforward context of the original are elaborated into ornate phrasing and the problems of the leisured class. The poem opens with an echo of the original, "Please sir [old man] don't cross that river / The river is wide and the wind full of danger," and closes with a fanciful description of the double death, "You my lord will be a minister to Stream Lord / I shall become the little sister of the River Maiden" (*YFSJ* 26:378).[32] The center section is, however, filled with atmospheric description that has no relation to the original. The second of these Six Dynasty imitations is by Zhang Zhengjian and is even further removed from the original, but does take certain linguistic cognizance of Liu Xiaowei's poem:

> The Metal Dike divides the embroidered hawsers
> The white horse crosses with the lotus boats[33]
> The wind is strong, the sound of the song lost
> Beside the rolling waves someone is melancholy
> The oar is dropped in the peach-blossom water
> The sail is set, the bamboo arrows stream
> What would one say if sunk in the emerald palace
> A thousand years to accompany the Lord Yang

> *YFSJ* 26.378

Like Liu Xiaowei's poem, this poem can be read as a very elaborate transformation of the "Konghou" poem, and the transitional nature of Liu's version makes that reading all the more possible. By this we can understand the highly ambiguous lines, such as the final proclamation, in a relatively new light. The refinement of these lines of intratextuality could not, however, be carried much further without disappearing altogether.

While Li Bo's version is also a transformation, it does not continue the type of revision initiated by Liu and continued by Zhang, but in fact turns violently against them. In Li's "Konghou" poem the story of the "crazy old man" returns with a vengeance.

From the west the Yellow River pierces the Kunlun range
Roaring for a myriad miles it rams into the Dragon Gate
When its waves inundated heaven
Yao sighed aloud
While Yu regulated the hundred streams
He did not look in on his crying child
After he had stilled the currents and dammed the flood
Silk and hemp flourished throughout the Nine Provinces
Its harm gone, the wind blown sands expanded[34]
The old man with hair hanging loose, crazy and dumb
Why would he want to ford its currents in the early morn
No one there pitied his wife when she tried to stop him
"Old man, don't cross the river, it will be terrible to cross
Tigers can be wrestled, but to wade a river is hard"
In the end he drowned, swept by its currents to the sea
Where a leviathan with white teeth like snowy peaks
Dragged his skeleton, Oh that old old man, in those teeth
But even the grieving lute could not bring him back

YFSJ 26.379

Li draws on various elements of the flood myth of China and the legends of the Yellow River to decorate the simple narrative of the crazy old man. In this expansion there is some affinity with the elaboration of the river motif that was carried out by Liu and Zhang; yet, unlike those other "Konghou" poems, it is that old narrative with all its elements that forms the core of Li's version—his central lines (10–14) read like a prose gloss of the original folk poem. The wildness of Li's imagery, coursing from the Kunlun mountains down to the teeth of the leviathan in the East China Sea, is a poetic analogue to the craziness of the old man. Again the radicalism of the poem is directly tied to a spectacular reaffirmation of its oldest associations. Here we are very aware of Li's distance from the general lines of the developing intratext, but his stance is one that again places him simultaneously inside and outside the tradition.

Li Bo and Bao Zhao

Among the critical commonplaces concerning Li Bo's *yuefu* poetry is the claim of his affinity for and indebtedness to the *yuefu* poetry of Bao Zhao. I have already noted the extensiveness of Li's imitation of Bao's poems—nearly one-half of them have been imitated by Li. Here I would like to look more closely at some of those imitations, in order both to explore further the relationship between the two poets and to shed more light on Li's *yuefu* poetics. While Li imitates throughout Bao's corpus, there is a marked concentration of imitations among the *zaqu* (miscellaneous) poems, many of which are found in sets that were initiated by Bao himself. Here I want to concentrate specifically on those imitations by Li of titles Bao initiated. In this way, we can keep the web of intratextuality relatively simple, and focus more on the interrelationship of these poets alone.

First we should note that the poetic persona commonly associated with Bao Zhao's *yuefu* poetry—the drifter/military man/outsider—would complement nicely the poetic persona that I have described for Li Bo. Both men rose out of relative obscurity to become well-known literati of their times, though Bao never reached the levels of fame enjoyed by Li. The extrametrical quality of their personal and poetic lives vis-à-vis the centers of political and literary power tend to draw them together, and their poetic style shows some affinities as well. This style, a relatively lucid and narrative one, is often used to link them with Cao Zhi, thereby creating a lineage of disaffected poets in the *yuefu* genre; yet certainly the relationship between Bao and Li is much more conscious and attestable than is their relationship with Cao.

The intratextual relationship between these two poets is clearly seen in Li's important imitation of Bao Zhao's central *yuefu* series, his nineteen "Hardships of Travel" ("Xing lu nan") poems; these poems most often draw the critics' attention, especially the sixth poem by Bao and the first in Li's three-poem series. Bao's poem reads:

Facing the table I am unable to eat
Drawing my sword I strike the pillar, sighing deeply
Just how long can a man's life in this world last

How can I bear to hobble about with folded wings
I should simply quit my post and leave
Return to my home to take my ease
At dawn I left saying goodbye to my kin
This evening I return to their sides
To play with my child by his bed
To watch my wife weaving at her loom
Since antiquity the good and wise have lived in poverty
How much more so for men of my age, upright and alone[35]

YFSJ 70.998

After a large number of intervening imitations by other poets, Li follows with his derivative but extravagant version:

A golden goblet of clear wine, a gallon for ten-thousand
    coins
A jade plate of the choicest food, it is worth a myriad cash
I put down my cup, toss aside my chopsticks, unable to eat
Drawing my sword, I look all around, my mind in a daze
I want to ford the Yellow River, but ice blocks the streams
I would climb the Taihang range, but snow fills the
    mountains
Then peace of mind comes, dangling my line in emerald
    rivers
Suddenly I'm taking a boat dreamily past the sun again
Hard traveling
Hard traveling
Byways are many
Where am I now
There will come a time when winds will smash the waves
Then I'll just hoist my cloud sail and cross the dark sea[36]

YFSJ 71.1008

Li's poem may have other intratextual connections, both with Bao's large set and with the imitations that come between the two poets—such as the doubling of the title into two verses, which is also seen in Monk Baoyue's poem.[37] Yet the clear model for Li's poem is Bao's number 6. On this relationship Wang Yunxi has remarked: "With just a glance we can see that there is an integral relationship between the imagery here and the imagery depicted in Bao Zhao's poem. When Li created these images they were naturally closely related to his own life and feelings; yet it would not be wrong to say that the imagery of Bao's poem gave him important references and starting points."[38] Wang is forced by the orthodox interpretation of "realism" to support the biographical nature of Li's poem, but he must also acknowledge the blatant intratextuality (if he will pardon my term) of Li's poem, even though he does so in a deflecting double negation. These two poems have also drawn Stephen Owen's comparison:

> While Li Bo might begin a poem in the Bao Zhao mode, he quickly turned off in a direction entirely his own . . . [in this case] Li completely undermined the starkness of Bao Zhao's lines. . . . From Bao Zhao, Li Bo has borrowed only the gestures of dissatisfaction. A deeper understanding of Bao Zhao's poem would have drawn a poet to Bao's psychological starkness, its nervous energy and uneasy resolution. Li follows the stages of Bao's poem until the closing, but his hyperbolic frenzy is an act of poetic bravura that has nothing to do with Bao's credibly human dissatisfaction.[39]

Some of Owen's criticism might be extended to describe more generally Li's textual relationship with Bao, especially the distinction between the "humanness" of Bao's poetry and the pyrotechnics of Li's rewriting.

Of course, Li's intratextual variations on Bao's *yuefu* poems also occur in patterns other than the specific relationship described here by Owen. These are relationships that range from those closer to the benign mode that Wang Yunxi describes down to some that seem entirely disengaged. Below, I want to look at three specific examples from that spectrum of intratextuality, moving from the least to the most engaged, from the negation of intratextuality to its strong affirmation.

The Moon

There are three *yuefu* titles that were initiated by Bao Zhao and that
were imitated first by Li (i.e., without any interceding imitations): one
on the north wind, one on the spring sun, and one on the bright moon.
All three of these titles display only the most tenuous of intratextual
relationships between the "model" and "imitation," but in comparison
each exposes the distinctive voice of the two poets, especially Li's.
Since Li Bo is commonly regarded as China's "moon-struck" poet,
perhaps we should turn to the last of these as an illustration of such
"non-imitation."[40] First Bao's "Song of the Bright Moon" ("Lang yue
xing"):

> The bright moon rises over east mountain
> To shine before my gauze-curtained window
> By the window there pass many fine ladies
> Dressed in robes rare and exquisite
> I sit inside the curtains preparing my makeup
> Facing the door, I play the crystalline strings
> For her lovely coiffure the lady in Wei was selected
> Because of her slim waist Feiyan was promoted[41]
> For you sir I now sing a tune
> This "Bright Moon Composition"
> The wine arrives and then your smile relaxes
> Voices harmonize, and my thoughts are known
> How could a thousand cash be more valuable
> Than the sudden emotion captured in this song?

YFSJ 65.942

Nothing in this poem suggests the "traveling military" persona com-
monly associated with Bao Zhao's poetry; we have a rather straight-
forward treatment (though not without flourishes) of the woman as
entertainer. Instead of the voice of Bao Zhao's military official, we
again have his companion singing her song about singing her song—all
within very appropriate *yuefu* conventions. There is in this poem the
human warmth of which Owen spoke in conjunction with Bao's "Hard-

ships of Travel" poem, but not the dissatisfaction. These are all joined under the titular bright moon, giving Li Bo much material upon which to build a variation. Yet Li completely ignores Bao's poem and takes this lunar theme in an entirely different, but not atypical, Li Bo direction:

> When small I did not know what the moon was
> I called it the platter of white-jade
> Or maybe a mirror of the Jade Terrace
> Flying on the tops of gray clouds
> The immortal there dangled his two feet
> And its cassia tree kept growing round
> The white rabbit ground up the elixir
> But to whom, I asked, would it be fed
> The toad chewed away at its circle
> And that great light was eroded in the night
> When Yi brought down the nine crows
> The skies were clear and men were at peace
> But this essence of *yin* was sunk in worry
> Going, going, not enough to even gaze upon
> When sorrow comes what is it like
> Depression sits heavily on my heart

YFSJ 65.942

Wang Qi's introductory note to this poem says "Bao Zhao has a poem entitled 'The Bright Moon,' this is probably whence this poem originates";[42] yet the material from which Li Bo forms this poem seems completely divorced, both in language and in tone, from that of the "model" poem by Bao Zhao. It is a negation of intratextuality, a frustration of the reader's expectations, which casts Li's poem in a strong contrastive light. Li's poem does not borrow from its "model," but rather from the lunar myths of China, which Li turns into elements of a personal childhood fantasy. The immortal, the cassia tree, and the rabbit are the sum total of the various explanations of the patterns seen on the face of the moon, and the voracious toad an explanation of the lunar waning; moreover the white jade platter and the mirror of the Jade Terrace (i.e., of the immortals) are common figurative descriptions of the full moon. By appropriating these as his personal fantasy, Li implies that his childhood and the mythology of China are nearly equivalent. In addition, his poem suggests, especially in light of the opening line, that he himself has moved beyond such "superstition"; he now knows what the moon is, as a "banished immortal" very well should. This "insight" into the nature of the moon even allows Li to add to its mythology—the anxiety the moon (essence of *yin)* feels about Archer Yi's solar exploits is apparently a product entirely of Li's imagination.[43] And the implication of the final couplet is that Li's sorrow is as momentous as the moon's darkening and gradual eroding. Thus, the identity is brought full circle: the myth was the poet's, and then the poet is (through the moon) the myth.

The Battle

The next pair of poems by Bao Zhao and Li Bo to be considered, with a title Bao initiates and Xu Ling and Yu Xin follow, is centered in Bao Zhao's acknowledged home territory, the military expedition. True to the common appreciation of Bao's poetic voice, his poem is filled with the soldier's suffering and sacrifice. In it he exploits both conventional and more innovative border imagery but never wanders far from the typical treatment. Wu Jing's introductory note is clear about Bao's pedigree:

> The "Out from the North Gate of Ji" ("Chu zi Ji bei men") poems are just like the "In the Army" ("Cong jun xing") poems; they describe both the physical scene around Ji in the Yan [northeast] area, and the nature of the attack cavalry's bravery and hardship. Thus, Bao Zhao's poem describes in detail the bitterness of the expeditionary war.

> The winged commands arrive from the border towers
> Beacon fires enter the capital at Xianyang
> The cavalry reserve is encamped at Guangwu
> Troops are dispatched to rescue Ordos positions
> In the harsh autumn their archers are formidable

The enemy ranks are spirited and strong
The Son of Heaven grasps his sword in anger
The envoys gaze at each other from afar
Like a file of geese they follow rocky paths
Like a column of fish they cross flying bridges
The flute and drum carry the Han message
Banners and armor are coated with Hun frost
A sharp wind blows through the passes
Sand and pebbles fly easily through the air
The horse manes stick up like hedgehog quills
The horn-tipped bow cannot be bent for the cold
In times of danger a subject's discipline is seen
In periods of turmoil a man's loyalty is known
Sacrificing themselves for their brilliant leader
Their bodies become the country's fallen soldiers

YFSJ 61.891

The imitations by Xu Ling and Yu Xin that follow this one are some-
what briefer treatments of the same theme, distinguished by a slight
softening of the scene described, a reduction in technical military
vocabulary, and a somewhat more upbeat conclusion. Both imitations
incorporate the "Ji" signature in the opening lines, but neither appears
to have any overt echoes of Bao's poem itself. Yu's poem does,
however, seem to include subtle variations on Xu's, especially in the
opening couplet. Xu begins,

North of Ji for a moment we gaze afar
In the dusk we are alone and melancholy

And Yu rewrites,

Returning to the gate of Ji we gaze northward
Every conscript is exhausted and stung with pain

YFSJ 61.892

Then we have Li Bo's poem, which opens without the Ji signature, but on a similar "Northern" note:

> The enemy ranks spread across the northern wastes
> The Huns' Star of Fortune sparkles bright
> The winged letters fly like lightning
> Beacon fires stream across the night sky
> Tiger tallies go to rescue the troubled borders
> Their war carts are already as thick as trees
> The brilliant leader does not just sit idle
> But grasps his sword, flying into a rage
> He offers command to the fierce general
> Whose banners stream onto the battle field
> Our troops break through their desert shield
> The smell of death rises into the vaulted blue
> Files of our soldiers are near Red Mountain
> They are setting up barracks beside Purple Pass
> At the height of winter the wind is filled with sand
> Flags and banners flap with the sting of cold
> The painted horn grieves under the lake's moon
> Battle dress is rolled up in the sky's frost
> Brandishing our swords we chop down Loulan
> The curved bow shoots down their prince
> Once the Khan's lands are suppressed and pacified
> Their clans and tribes scattered and lost
> Merit is ours reporting to Son of Heaven
> As the victory songs return to Xianyang

YFSJ 61.892

This is certainly a fine example of the border poem, one that within its conventions shows elements of Li Bo's celebration of the warrior that we saw above, and one that participates in the intratext, but in a nondisruptive manner. While the upbeat, celebratory tone of this poem is more akin to that by Xu Ling, whose final couplet sings, "In peace the people of Yan are in accord / And will obtain noble positions," the actual language and narrative style finds its model in Bao Zhao's poem. This is true not only in the level and type of vocabulary the poems share, but also in specific terms. Of course, any border poem has conventional vocabulary upon which it can draw, but the frequency of the repetition of phrases and terms between the two poems betrays Li's conscious reworking of Bao's poem. Some of these are mere borrowings—enemy ranks, beacon fires, brilliant leader—or minor substitutions—"winged letters" for "winged commands," "rescue the troubled borders" for "rescue the Ordos positions"—but others are more elaborate variations. For example, Bao Zhao's "The Son of Heaven grasps his sword in anger" is reformulated in Li's poem as "The brilliant leader does not just sit idle / But grasps his sword, flying into a rage" ["brilliant leader" *(ming zhu)* appears elsewhere in Bao's poem]. Under the influence of such evidence, we might even suggest that Bao's middle verses,

> The flute and drum carry the Han message
> Banners and armor are coated with Hun frost
> A sharp wind blows through the passes
> Sand and pebbles fly easily through the air

are reformed by Li's poem in these the lines:

> At the height of winter the wind is filled with sand
> Flags and banners flap with the sting of cold
> The painted horn grieves under the lake's moon
> The battle dress is rolled up in the sky's frost

Throughout the poem, Li engages in this relatively low-key rewriting of Bao's text—making his presence felt, while not drawing undue attention to himself.

This type of reading of Li Bo's "Ji Gate" poem against Bao Zhao's model is most productive, however, when we compare the poems at a level above that of language and verse. For at that higher level the similarity between the poems allows us to read them as variations, or even continuations of the same narrative. The clue to this reading is found in the last line of Li's poem, which in context can be considered as a variation of the second line of Bao's poem. Bao begins this narrative,

> The winged commands arrive from border towers
> Beacon fires enter the capital at Xianyang

and Li finishes his with,

> Merit is ours reporting to the Son of Heaven
> As the victory songs return to Xianyang

In between those two couplets, and between the centuries and personalities that separate the two poets, a complex narrative is unwound. The story that Bao begins to tell, the deployment of forces into the Ordos, does not reach a narrative conclusion in his poem, but rather, like the frozen bow that cannot be bent, stagnates in battle fatigue and death, even though in the end some nobility is attached to that death by literary allusion.[44] When Li picks up the story he quickly moves it towards a more heroic conclusion: this time the bows are bent, arrows fly, and the enemy is struck down. The troops that were the country's fallen in Bao's poem are in Li's poem resurrected and rewarded upon their return to Xianyang. Li's rewriting is not so much an undermining of Bao's poem as it is a "correction"; it brings the story to its "appropriate" heroic conclusion—appropriate to the poetic persona of Li Bo, and perhaps to his intended audience, the emperor.

The Song

The last poem by Li Bo to be considered here is a variation on Bao Zhao's "A Song in the Night" ("Ye zuo yin"), which we discussed in Chapter 4. Li's imitation of this poem displays the subtlest type of intratextual poetics; here, he is not as strident as in his more disruptive moments but instead sets up vibrations between the poems that resonate stronger and deeper than the imitations and variations examined thus far. Generally the relationship is in quality more akin to that of the "Ji gate" poems, but in actual force is closer to the power described by

Owen in his comment on the "Hardships of Travel" poems. As in the "Ji Gate," Li picks up the thread of Bao's poem and draws it out far beyond itself, but as in "Hardships," this is seen at several levels of the text, and is more associational than narrative. Once again I would like to trace these variations through the poems section by section.[45]

Bao

The deep winter night; deep in the night you sit singing
I already know your desires before you speak

Li

In the winter night; the night is cold, the night is long
Deeply singing I sit forever, sit in the north hall

While Li's couplet is thematically merely a restatement of Bao's first line, on a verbal level he is engaging in elaborate word play. Prosodically, the most noteworthy thing about Bao's couplet, and indeed about his whole poem, is the structure of the first line, with its reduplicated *shen shen* (deep, deep) that separates the two "nights" *(ye)*. Li atomizes that verbal entity and reconfigures it throughout his entire couplet: the two occurrences of "deep" are reduced to one and used in the opening of the second line to modify "sing" *(yin)* (under the influence of Bao's line, this might be understood as a contraction of "in the deep night"). Li then replaces Bao's *shen shen* with a reduplication of *ye*, which allows him then to expand Bao's repetition of "night" into a triplication, an outrageous example of "waste" of poetic space, by which Li outdoes Bao at his own game. But Li still is not finished. Having lost Bao's reduplicated *shen*, he recoups it in the second line with a reduplication of *zuo* (sit), which appears by itself in Bao's first line. Such elaborate verbal relationships should prepare the reader for an heightened intratextuality throughout the poem, and we are not to be disappointed.

Bao

The frost enters the curtain
The wind blows through the grove

Li

Ice freezes over the well, the moon enters my apartment

Here Li continues the seven-syllable prosody of the first couplet to match what is usually considered Bao's two three-syllable lines, but syntactically we have near-perfect parallelism between Bao's two lines and Li's one. This time Li works his alchemy thematically. First, in the opening phrases of the two passages we see the simple progression from frost to ice, and in the second phrases from wind to moon—the first being an aqueous transformation, and the second an atmospheric one (understanding moon as moonlight). Thus, Li intensifies and deepens the scene; the world becomes colder and more luminous as it moves closer to the interior scene in his poem.

If we turn our attention to the two main verbs of the two passages, we find other subtle intratextual clues. First, the parallel verbs have switched phrases; *ru* (to enter) moves from Bao's first phrase to Li's second, and Bao's second-verse *du* (to cross = "blows through") is matched semantically by Li's first-phrase *he* (join together = "freezes over"). This leads to a particularly complicated set of relationships between the images, which can be represented graphically by the accompanying diagram.

The relationships outlined in this diagram might be described as follows: First, the exterior and interior scenes are reversed: Bao's couplet moves from the interior to the exterior, while Li's line moves in the opposite direction, despite the retention of the aqueous and atmospheric phenomena in their original positions. This is accompanied by the cross-use of the *ru* verb, which places the frost and moon in an analogous relationship, a relationship that is strengthened by the parallel analogy of curtain and apartment. This allows us to appreciate Li's play on the visual similarity between moonlight and frost, an image Li

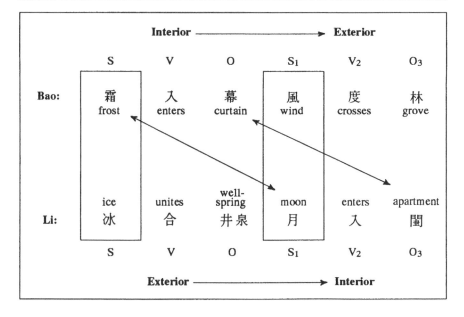

Relationships between Bao Zhao and Li Bo Couplets

himself made famous (but did not invent) in another, nominally *yuefu*, poem:

Seeing the moonlight at the foot of the bed
I thought it was frost on the ground
Raising my head I gaze at the mountain moon
Lowering my head I think of my old home

YFSJ 90.1274

This little poem can be understood as Li's synchronic reformation of the relationship he establishes retroactively between Bao's "Song in the Night" ánd his imitation of it. In Li's rewriting of Bao's couplet he informs the reader that Bao was mistaken: what Bao saw on the curtain was not frost, but moonlight. From this point on Li's imitation begins to diverge ever more widely and wildly from its model.

Bao

The rosy lamp is put out
And your rosy face is sought

Li

The gold lanthorn's chilling-green flame shines on sad tears
The gold lanthorn is put out
And her weeping becomes louder

While Li's first line of this section is prosodically linked to its preceding line, thematically it is part of an obvious echo of Bao Zhao's couplet, which Li *does* mirror prosodically in his next two lines. This echo is, however, one that introduces a particular set of vibrations, vibrations that approach Li's disruptive style of intratextual poetics. Li's first line is certainly most disruptive and, in light of his model, totally unexpected. Bao's interior world where human warmth, both literal and figurative, keeps the cold at bay is replaced by a nearly macabre scene of ancient lamps, sad tears, and *qingning*. He transforms the relatively straightforward language of the model into a strained vocabulary. Li's *gang* (lanthorn) is a rare term and *qingning* is his own morbid hapax legomenon, which has been rendered by another translator as "deadly green."[46] Whatever Li meant by *qingning*, the connotations are quite opposite those of the rosy lamp in Bao's couplet; Li turns that erotic and tipsy scene into one of morbid grief. This is also clearly seen in the rewriting of the couplet, where Li's first line echoes Bao's perfectly, but his second, after the light is out, replaces the woman's rosy face with a flood of tears.[47] Following this plunge into morbidity, Li unexpectedly returns to the upbeat themes of Bao's poem, and in fact goes beyond them.

Bao

Following your song
Pursuing its sound

Li

Wiping away my tears
I listen to your song
The song has its voice
I have my desires
Desires and voice harmonize
They are without conflict

On the surface Li has here merely expanded (and diluted) the imagery of Bao's model lines. In order to continue Bao's line of development, Li first must rid his poem of the morbidity of the preceding section; this he does with the wipe of a sleeve and the striking up of a song. Here Li's rewriting appears to be a rather repetitious, heavy-handed gloss of Bao's suggestively subtle lines. "Pursuit" is turned into blatant "togetherness." More interesting is Li's clarification of the identities of the singer and the audience. While Bao's poem is, as Kang-i Sun Chang suggests, somewhat ambiguous about the gender of the singer, Li is very clear, and we are surprised to find that he gives the song to the man, and its appreciation to the woman. In his fourth and fifth line of this section, Li retrieves the woman's "desire" *(qing)* from Bao's second line. The voice *(sheng)* that harmonizes with that desire can be traced textually either to Bao's following, final couplet, or perhaps even to a variant writing of that second line of Bao's poem, a variant that reads "I already know your voice *(sheng)* before you speak." We might even suggest that Li decided to reconcile these two readings by suggesting an identity (harmony) between the two variant writings; if that were true then we would have an example of the most complicated type of intratextuality. Certainly his final couplet lends weight to that suggestion.

Bao

Not valuing the voice
But rather its deep intent

Li

Let any word that does not engage such intent
Fly like dust off beams swept by your myriad tunes

Similar to his extension of Bao's "Ji Gate" narrative, Li moves these gentle lines by Bao far beyond their subdued scene. Their darkened moment of whispered romance becomes in Li's rendering a passionate aria that not only erases any remaining discord, but does the house-cleaning as well. Li's poem becomes more a riot of public celebration, replacing the very private joy of Bao's. The poems' intratextuality centers on the single, but poignant, word "intent" *(yi)*, which is "deep" *(shen)* in Bao's use and "not engaged" *(bu ru)* in Li's. Of course, *yi* is a very common term and the assumption of its role in Li's intratextual poetics is only possible when it is viewed in the context of the entire poem, especially as we have seen Li's intratextuality become more and more refined in the progress of the poem. Bao's *sheng* (voice) was moved to Li's preceding section, but it does leave echoes here in Li's final couplet. It is heard in the two principal manifestations of the human voice, speech *(yu, words)* and song *(qu, tune)*.

With this last line Li moves resolutely beyond Bao's poem, not only in its thematic intensity but also in its textual connections. First we have the flying dust image *(liang chen fei)*, which Wang Qi traces back through a poem by Lu Ji to a Han-dynasty anecdote that tells of how the purity and grief of a famous singer's voice *(sheng)* "stirred the dust on the beams" *(dong liang chen)*.[48] Secondly, the somewhat odd term "myriad tunes" *(wan qu)* leads in a different direction (i.e., to another *yuefu* poem by Bao Zhao, which is the term's apparent *locus classicus)*. Any objections that this is mere coincidence or unrelated to the construction of Li's poem should be dispelled upon close examination of Bao's other poem. This poem, "Song of the Hall" ("Tang shang ge xing"), is entirely one of public display and celebratory song:

Sit all around and quit your chatter
Listen to our "Song of the Hall"
When once serving in the capital of Luo
The noble house overlooked the river long
They came and went from those palaces
Making friendships as close as Cao and He
Carriages and horses raced after each other
Colleagues and guests enjoyed the flower faces
It was springtime of the first vernal month
Morning rays scattered through the flowing clouds
She walked lightly in search of the fragrant wind
Smiling she played with the crimson flower buds
Her rosy face glowed with the blush of wine
The Weaver Girl's loom was bursting with silk
Throughout the hall there were many fair ones
But eyes were on this Beauty of the Xiang
While she waited on her man's pleasure
Her clear makeup shown above silken gauze
The lute and flute were strummed and played
Her soprano voice was in lovely harmony
While a myriad tunes might not touch her heart
There is one that stirs her desires deeply
To know if she is full of desire or not
Then listen to her coursing voice again

YFSJ 65.943

The several connections between this poem and Li's "Song of the Night" certainly suggest his conscious use of it as a source, especially with the repetition of the cluster of terms "desire" *(qing)*, "voice" *(sheng)*, and "harmony" *(he)*. And of course there are also a number of links between the two Bao Zhao poems. Li's use of this poem moves his "Song of the Night" onto new thematic ground, and into associations with other texts, especially those in the *Songs of the South (Chu ci)*. While the concluding lines of these three poems share slightly different configurations of the same motif—the harmony of emotion and song—the extension of these associations by Li contributes to a major rewriting of Bao's poem. Li literally moves the private "Song of the Night" out into the display of daylight. The darkened bedroom becomes the teeming halls, courtyards, and byways of the capital of Luoyang. The beautiful women—and there are halls full of them and they are likened to goddesses—have the same rosy blush of wine *(zhu yan)*, but none of the sweet reserve that asks that the lamp be put out first. And, of course, the deep winter night has been recast into the warmth of a spring morning.

Conclusion

In Li Bo's imitation of the *yuefu* poems of Bao Zhao and others we see the persistent presence of a highly energized, often violent, form of intratextual poetics. This intratextuality ranges from studied disregard, through different types of disruptive techniques, to a deep and disturbing revision. Certainly Li has many *yuefu* poems that participate more benignly in the genre, but it is the more radical ones that distinguish his voice and that make him the master of *yuefu* poetry. By the fullness of his participation in its conventions, Li brought the genre to completion and exhaustion at the same time. Li stood at the center of the genre and consumed it with itself, thereby turning the center into the edge, once again transforming himself into the solitary figure that must be judged by different standards.

7

Remnants: *Yuefu* Poetry in Context

Despite the tremendous pyrotechnical force of Li Bo's *yuefu* poetry, the genre obviously did not collapse immediately after him. In the Middle Tang we see the flourishing of the "new *yuefu*" poetry *(xin yuefu)* that is associated with Bo Juyi (722–846) and Yuan Zhen (779–831). At the same time, and perhaps not coincidentally, we have the rise of *ci* poetry, which was itself often called *yuefu*. While both of these new poetic forms have something to add to our discussion of intratextuality, they escaped Li Bo's looming shadow by avoiding his intratextual company. There was, however, also a smoldering effort to write in the central, intratextual part of the genre, and this effort would yield moments of brilliance throughout the Middle and Late Tang, and even into later periods.[1] I shall not pursue those lines any further here, but rather shall discuss the broader literary contexts of the genre as it reached a definitive form in Guo Maoqian's anthology.

Theme and Variation

In the criticism of *yuefu* poetry there is a latent but pervasive tendency to discuss the themes of the genre. This tendency is specifically exploited in a study by Hans Frankel, which discusses fourteen early literati poems that center around twenty-five "*yuefu* themes."[2] In his discussion of these themes, Frankel indicates at several points the integral relationship that imitation has in the generation of those themes, commenting on one poem that "three literary *yuefu* imitating the title and atmosphere of this poem are extant," and of another, "The title seems to indicate that this *yuefu* (at least its music) is a variation on a combination of earlier *yuefu* patterns, and Cao Cao's poem in turn inspired later *yuefu* poets."[3] While for every theme or style associated with *yuefu* poetry we can offer counterexamples from non-*yuefu* literature, there is still a rationale behind this argument, but that rationale lies, as Frankel implies, in the complications of intratextuality, not in simple thematics. By its very nature, intratextuality encourages the exploration of titular themes and the propagation of stylistic lines. This is, after all, *thematic* intratextuality, and we can easily identify important themes and poetic styles associated with the genre by the power of that praxis—the border lament in the language of a military officer; the abandoned woman telling her tale in words of willow and lotus; the wandering immortal who couches his quest in sylvan esoterica. Some of these themes and styles intersect to form complex webs, such as the border poems and the "Willow" poems, but in the end they too are just a list of types held together by virtue of Guo Maoqian's collection. We are again back at the problematic supposition that the corpus defines the genre and not vice-versa.

We can, however, account for the general thematic characteristics of the genre that unite and divide it by arguing that it is the *process* of intratextual writing, the defining convention of the genre, that generates those themes and styles. In his definition of literati *yuefu* poetry Frankel actually alludes to the generative intratext that produces his "themes": he says the literati *yuefu* poem is "a member of a chain of *yuefu* poems with a common title and affinities in form, theme, and wording."[4] We can see that as titular themes gained strength and began to expand under the pressure of the accumulating intratext they would not only invite diverging imitations and innovations, but would also encourage the inclusion of new poems into the genre by *association* with the developing titular theme. In other words, poems that were not strictly intratextual (i.e., were not originally written or read within a particular intratext) could join the genre by thematic association if there already were an intratext to which they could be attached.

Intratextuality led to the development of thematic webs and stylis-
tic lines that subsequently give the impression that the genre is united
by these themes and styles, but in actuality the themes and styles are
more or less coincidental to the genre and are a secondary characteristic
of it. When we look more closely at the genre, we discover that it is the
method by which these themes are sustained that is the genre, not the
themes themselves. The genre is not a corpus, but a process.

Six Types of Intratextuality

Throughout this study I have noted previous efforts to formulate typo-
logies of the *yuefu* genre, which I have invariably faulted for being
tautological or merely descriptive. But typology seems endemic in the
study of *yuefu* poetry, and I too must surrender to the urge to codify my
understanding of the genre. Since I feel it is the *process* of intratextual
writing that defines the genre, I want to offer a typology not of texts
but of methods of intratextuality. I divide intratextuality into six types,
labeling them with Chinese terms of my own invention.[5] These terms
are derived from early Chinese poetics and literary criticism, but I have
appropriated them for this typology. I believe that these are concepts
yuefu poets themselves might have brought, albeit unconsciously, to the
genre; if they thought about the process by which they wrote, it could
have been in these terms. I have arranged these six types of intratextu-
ality to mark boundaries of increasingly free variation, all the while
acknowledging that these boundaries are only rather broad zones with
ample overlapping between any two contiguous types.

   As instantiation of this typology of intratextuality, I offer poems
drawn from another set of literati imitations, the Luofu poems.[6] The
Luofu set is headed by a famous *gu ci* poem, the Han "Moshang sang,"
that tells the story of Luofu, a faithful wife who resolutely rejects the
overtures of a traveling official. In my discussion of these types of
intratextuality I have also drawn on the comments of a late *yuefu* poet,
Yang Weizhen (1296–1307).[7] Yang, who wrote intratextually and am-
bitiously in the genre, has a corpus of more than four hundred *yuefu*
poems, many of which are prefaced by his own comments. Yang's
comments are especially useful since he speaks so self-consciously of

the intratextual nature of the genre, a self-consciousness resulting in part from the influence of Guo Maoqian's and Zuo Keming's anthologies.

The original Luofu poem, which comes from Shen Yue's set of sixteen Han poems and is included in almost every anthology of pre-Tang poetry, is perhaps the best-known *yuefu* poem in both China and the West. Its stature in the literary tradition has done much to reinforce the common understanding of the *yuefu* genre as one characterized by balladlike folk poems, which this one certainly is. The Han poem begins this story of Luofu's feisty fidelity in a straightforward and engaging narrative:

Mulberry along the Lane

The sun rises from the southeast quarter
To shine on the chambers of our Qin house
The Qin family has a fine daughter
She calls herself Luofu
Luofu skilled with silkworms and mulberry
Picks leaves south of the city wall
Blue silk are her basket ties
Cassia branches are her basket handles
On the side of her head a cascading chignon
In her ears bright moonlike pearls
Yellow silk is her skirt
Purple silk is her jacket
When passers-by see Luofu
They put down their loads and stroke their beards
When young men see Luofu
They doff their hats and adjust their hair-bands
Those cultivating forget their hoes
Those plowing forget their plows
When they return home they complain
All because they have seen this Luofu
A governor comes up from the south
His five-horse team stops and lingers
The governor sends a runner,

Asking to whose house this beauty belongs
The Qin family has a fine daughter
She calls herself Luofu
What is the age of Luofu?
Not yet a full twenty
But somewhat more than fifteen
The governor asks Luofu
If she would like to ride with him
Luofu answers straight to his face
"How can the governor be so stupid?
You already have your own wife
And Luofu has her own husband
In the east somewhere with a thousand cavalry or more
There my husband positioned at their lead
And how will I recognize my husband?
Their white horses follow his black steed
Blue silk binds his horse's tail
Yellow gold halters his horse's head
At his waist a sword with an ornate hilt
It is worth more than a million
At fifteen he was a grandee
At twenty he was minister at court
At thirty he was a Palace Gentleman
At forty he is Prefect Mayor
He is one with fair clear skin
And a fine light beard
Stately he walks the halls of his office
Slowly he moves about his residence
Seated among a thousand others
All say my husband is quite special"

YFSJ 28.410–11

This poem offers much for imitation: a strong narrative, easily identifiable characters, and poignant descriptive scenes. We can easily see how it fits into several other intratextual lines already discussed, but its

own legacy is one of the richest in the genre. The poems derived from
it offer various examples of the process of intratextual writing.

Ji (Continuation)

Continuation is the most common type of intratextuality found in the
genre and is close to, if not identical with, "imitation" *(ni* or *xiao)* in
the common sense of that term. The story/theme of the original model
is reformed to be offered anew to another group of readers. This type
of intratextuality ranges from nearly verbatim "translations" (limited to
language substitution) to much wider variations, involving structural
changes such as abbreviation, expansion, and modification.[8] In the
early tradition Fu Xuan often wrote in this manner, and his version of
the Luofu story is an excellent middle-range example of this type of
intratextuality:

> The sun rises from the southeast quarter
> To shine on the chambers of our Qin house
> The Qin family has a fine daughter
> She styles herself Luofu
> Her hair is fastened with gold and emerald ornaments
> Her ears decorated with bright moon-pearls
> Of pure-white silk is her skirt
> Of crimson embroidery is her jacket
> With one look she topples the market place
> With a second the state becomes a wasteland
> Ask where the lady makes her home
> Its halls stand south of the city wall
> The painted chambers overlook a great lane
> Its secluded gate held with double hinges
> A governor comes from the south
> His four-horse team stops and lingers
> He sends a runner to ask this noble lady
> Could she share his carriage with him?
> The lady kneels in respect to answer
> "Governor, how peculiar are your words
> The governor already has his own wife

And I, your servant, have a lowly husband
Heaven and earth give each his proper place
I trust you will, sir, change your plans"

YFSJ 28:417–18

Fu's major revisions are abbreviation of the narrative and deletion of some of its more folklike passages, especially the long description of Luofu's husband that concludes the *gu ci* version. He has also translated some of the images into more elaborate language—gold and emerald ornaments in her hair, crimson embroidery for her jacket, and literary allusions instead of village scenes. With this comes a weakening of the strength of Luofu's resolve; she politely suggests the Governor has made some mistake.[9] A more extreme version of this type of intratextual writing is Fu Zai's (531–585) version of the Luofu story:

Luofu once went out to pick mulberry leaves
Going out and entering south by the city wall
In silken blouse and shining pearl earrings
By silk cords she lifted the jade-inlay basket
Across her body she gathered the leaves
Stretching her arms she reached the long branches
In a vain attempt the governor asked for her
"I already have my own Palace Gentleman"

YFSJ 28.416

This is obviously the same story of Luofu and the governor, just drastically reduced. It introduces not only important language but also structural changes, while still retaining the integrity of the narrative. It is a refined, portable version of the original.

Fu (Amplification)

The term *fu* has an extremely long pedigree in Chinese literary criticism. Not only is it the name of a major poetic genre (the rhapsody), but it is also one of the six poetic principles in the *Shi jing*—usually

understood as display/narration/enumeration, which leads to the epide-
ictic rhapsody. Moreover, the term is used later in the context of salon
and court poetry to mean "to extemporize on an assigned topic," visible
in the titular formula "*fu de* . . . ." The term is also used commonly in
yuefu poetics, as seen in Yang Weizhen's remark, "I wrote on (*fu*) the
theme of the birds of Huan Mountain."[10] Here I want to use the term
more to describe that type of intratextual writing that inflates a theme
of the model with a different level of rhetoric and/or meaning. Of the
poets we have considered earlier, we see this type of intratextual writing
especially with poets such as Lu Ji and Chen Shubao, who enriched
their *yuefu* topics by the infusion of a new rhetorical style, one abstract
and the other refined. As an example, here is Chen Shubao's version of
the Luofu story:

> In her springtime chamber she combs her chignon
> Then hastens along the southern lane with the others
> They leave after the blossoms are scattered
> With wind sending their fragrance everywhere
> Her wide sleeves catch the morning sun
> Her long tresses tangle in the thick branches
> The new sprigs come off with an easy twist
> The leaves are taken soft before they wither
> Plucking a bunch her arm is weak on the handle
> She wilts, fine perspiration in her makeup
> But she should not go home early by herself
> She is worthy of the governor's company

YFSJ 28.416

While we still recognize this as the story of Luofu, Chen has enriched
it with an elegant rendering of the woman/spring motif. He retains
enough of the vocabulary of the original to maintain direct contact with
the intratext, but at the same time introduces heightened language from
the court poetry of his time. An even better example of this type of
amplification is Xu Boyang's (516–581) lovely rendering into seven-
syllable verse:

Over the vermilion wall the sun's orb rises near the
    vermilion door
Painted chambers hold the glow, always brilliant and bright
Far off, lighting up spring mulberry leaves in the lane
Slanting rays penetrate her silk-twill blouse in the Qin house
Luofu with her makeup is so elegant, so beautiful
In the mirror she recombs her hair into a cascading chignon
Her round basket is delicately tied with blue silk
With iron handles more slender than sweet-olive
The silkworms are hungry, the day wanes, her sadness
    grows urgent
Suddenly she meets a governor along the southern lane
His five-horse team quiets its bridle bells, he sends someone
    to inquire
Her two cheeks possess delicate beauty, a fine coyness
"My husband was a minor official in district headquarters
These days he comes and goes with the Prefect Mayor
I will recognize him returning from the east with a thousand
    horsemen
In billowing clouds, at sunset the red dust will rise"

YFSJ 28:421

Compared to Chen Shubao's poem, Xu's version maintains closer
contact with the original, which means that on one level it verges toward
the intratextuality of continuation, but the longer length also gives Xu's
poem more room for amplification. This sense of amplitude is particu-
larly sustained at the verse/couplet level by the use of the seven-syllable
line, which seems to expand the breadth of expression even beyond the
twenty percent that the two extra syllables represent (compared to the
original and almost all other members of the intratextual set). This is
clearly seen in the opening, where Xu takes the original's simple "rising
sun" and inflates into an elaborate element that integrates the external
and internal worlds where Luofu's story will be played out.

Hua (Ornamentation)

I derive this *hua* (flower/elegant/China) from the term *qing hua,* "light and flowery," that is used to describe the poetry of Xiao Gang, which his biography warns us "was not fit for gentlemen."[11] We have seen many examples of Xiao Gang's use of ornamentation of a *yuefu* title, which would sometimes build layers of refined language over the surface of the poem, and at other times choose one element of the poem to spin into an elaborate filigree. In the process of this ornamentation the thematic thrust of the intratext could very well be lost or deflected into an unexpected direction, which clearly distinguishes it from amplification. Ornamentation does not engage the thematics of the intratext deeply, but uses them only for lovely purposes, yielding a text in light relief, such as Xiao Gang's "Plucking Mulberries" ("Cai sang"):

> The colors of springtime glow in the air
> The garden plum is first to blossom
> Fine duckweed grows in thick layers
> The new flowers open in profusion
> A procession of jade pendants to the Qi River
> A line of carriage curtains off for Cong Terrace
> How lovely is the lady there
> At the windows she gazes at butterflies fluttering
> Anxiously she kneels working on her gown's collar
> With an iron she presses crisp its pleats
> Down from her couch she puts on her pearls
> At dusk she is worried for the hungry silkworms
> In conversation with the other mulberry girls
> The days are short this spring
> The limbs are too high for her to reach
> The leaves too sparse to fill her basket[12]

YFSJ 28.414

Here Xiao Gang has chosen to elaborate the physical charms of Luofu (assuming this is Luofu) into those of aristocratic femininity, filled with weakness, frailty, and incompletion. In ornamentation such as this, the realignment of the intratext is coincident to intratextuality, not integral to it. Of course it may be that such realignment becomes a distinctive part of the intratext in its evolution, as it has been with this transformed Luofu, but that is the result of later engagements of the ornamentation as theme, rather than of ornamentation itself. A smaller but similarly ornamented poem is Wu Jun's (469–520) "Moshang sang" that dwells not so much on Luofu at her toilette as on the trees of her work.

> The mulberries in the lane waft and wave
> They shade the lane and droop over the pool
> Long tendrils reflected by the sunlight
> Thin leaves concealing spring orioles
> My silkworms are hungry, again I worry for them
> I brush away my tears and pick up my basket
> How could my friend have left me like this
> The bitterness of separation inflames my heart

YFSJ 28.412

Despite its inherent inappropriateness, Wu has obviously drawn on the willow tree imagery to ornament this poem that is ostensibly about the mulberry. That conflation of willow and mulberry produces an interesting mixture of images that leads to consideration of her absent lover/husband, a relatively rare, unexplored theme in the Luofu intratext.

Yin (Extension)

Extension is the drawing out of a thread from an intratext and developing it into a new thematic line, one that often then ties into the web of another intratext. We saw this happening with the "Yin ma" and "Willow" poems, as they connected both with each other and with third-party intratexts—Wu Jun's Luofu poem quoted above suggests similar connections with the "Willow" poems.

    Yin (to draw a bow, to stretch, to lengthen, to extrapolate) appears throughout the *yuefu* literature, first as a musical term of uncertain meaning (perhaps a mode key or even melody type), but later as a type of writing in the genre. Yang Weizhen concludes a long preface (a review of musicality) to his "Zhou lang yu sheng yao" ("The Jade Flute of Mr. Zhou") with this comment: "I have written (fu) a song on the jade flute, which generally follows the rhapsodies of the various gentlemen, but I also extend (yin) them as follows."[13]

In the Luofu texts there are many such examples of yin especially where Luofu's feminine charms are extended to merge with those of the palace ladies that populate Six Dynasties poetry. There are also occasions when her confrontation with the governor is extended to connect with the "Qiu Hu" narrative, which shares a similar thematic line. This is seen in Wang Yun's (481–549) brief poem:

> They say the mulberry trees in the lane
> Before dawn are already aglow
> Layer upon layer, both shadows and light
> Faint and mild comes sweet fragrance
> When Qiu Hu first stopped his horses
> Luofu had not yet filled her basket
> "This morning the silkworms were already collapsing
> How can I have time to dally long?"

> > YFSJ 28:413

As I have suggested elsewhere, this linking of the Luofu narrative with the Qiu Hu one begins an elaborate interweaving of these two stories in later poetry and drama, and is the most productive "extension" in the Luofu intratext.[14] Once the extension begins, we can then read poems in the set in light of this new perspective, thereby allowing relatively minor references to take on special import. When read as part of the "Qiu Hu extension," the closing lines of Liu Xiyi's (772–842) Luofu poem figure much more prominently in the significance of the poem.

> The willows see the traveler on his way
> Green and lush, westward into Qin
> The mulberry picker of the Qin house
> In her chambers, she cannot bear the springtime
> Full and brimming the Ba River wends its way

She steps slowly through spring's fragrant greenery
By the sides of her rouged face bright pearls shine
Within her red lips is white jade
Turning to look east over the Wei River bridge
She admires the blending of spring colors in the distance
Blue silk ribbons are delicate in the sunset
Her yellow silk dress stirs in the spring wind
Lifting her basket she deeply sighs
Roaming on she is in love with the spring
Even the flowers seem full of feeling
Leaning on a tree as if without any strength
In the dusk her thoughts are sad and distant
The Governor is in the southern lane
When they meet they do not recognize each other
Returning home to dreams of painted chambers

YFSJ 28:416–17

Here the "willow extension" reconfigures Luofu from the nominal "mulberry picker" of the third line into an abandoned woman, but when the Governor arrives she does not recognize him as she should. Here she seems to adopt the role of Qiu Hu's wife, implying the Governor is the one for whom she is longing (i.e., her long absent husband).

Bian (Transformation)

Transformation is Li Bo's intratextual method in its most radical moments, when the intratext is turned on itself to undo itself. The term *bian*, with glosses that include "to change," "to transform," "to disrupt," "strange," "solar eclipse," and "to die," also has an appropriate poetic pedigree related to its subversive quality. It was first used to label those sections of the *Shi jing* that were not considered *zheng* (appropriate, correct, orthodox) and commonly understood as reflecting the decline/transformation of the proper way of government. In other words, the poems were deflected out of their proper orbit. *Bian* also appears much later in the term *bian wen* (transformation texts) in the popular narratives on marvelous themes in the Dunhuang manuscripts.[15] The *fan* ("contra") poetic writing that I have mentioned in connection with the *Wen xuan* is similar to *bian* intratextuality, but announces itself too clearly to be truly subversive. The usage I suggest is more actively and subtly subversive than these, as we have seen in Li's writing, and one that is inner-directed and self-transforming. The last two lines of Chen Shubao's "amplifying" Luofu poem that we saw above, which say that she "is worthy of the governor's company" and should not go home alone, are definitely a form of transformation. An even more integral and startling example of subversion is seen in this small Luofu poem by Xiao Hui (fl. 500):

> Dark and dusky, concealing distant mists
> Billowy and black, rising cloud formations
> And right there a lady of the Qin house
> With delicate beauty toasted the governor

YFSJ 28:422

Xiao has given us not an extension or interpolation of the Luofu story, but rather the Luofu story turned on its head. The confrontation with the governor is now a liaison, Luofu's rebuke is now a welcoming toast. Outside of its intratextual context this poem loses all its impact; it is merely a small filigree on the conventions of palace poetry. But within its intratextual context it finds its proper innovative voice; only there does it exist as a *yuefu* poem.

Fou (Negation)

In classical Chinese grammar, a *fou*-type negation is not a simple negation like *wu*, *bu*, and *wei*, all of which negate another word to which they are actually or implicitly attached; *fou* contains what it negates, it stands alone and complete. *Fou* means "it is not so," and the "so" is supplied by context. So it is with intratextual negation, which is not simply the nonexistence of a given intratext (that would include almost all Chinese poetry), but rather a self-contained denial. Xiao Gang's "ornamentation" of the Lofu poem is very close to this type of negation, but in that case the negation is not significant. For a more self-conscious and significant negation we might offer Yin Mou's (fl. 575) version:

A lovely beauty comes out from the Qin house
Just when the morning sun is shining down
In the lane the horses could halt
Flowers everywhere are fragrant again

YFSJ 28.421

Yin gives us enough information to let us know that he is avoiding an engagement of the Luofu theme, whose essence is in her confrontation/meeting with the governor. How do we know that the intratext is denied and not just absent? By the signals to the intratext that are revealed in the process of retroactive reading. In this case, that signal is in the very glancing dual references to her (Qin) house and the governor's horses. But once the reader recognizes this intratextual sign, his conventional expectations are frustrated. He has only the nonstory of Luofu, one that is in Yin Mou's rewriting only a potential story, a potentiality that centers on the horse that "could" *(neng)* halt in the lane.

By contrast, retroactive negation (when a poem is read back into an intratext, but does not participate with the central intratextual lines) is most easily seen in the inclusion of the "proto-*yuefu*" poems in the intratextual set, such as those by the early poets of the Wei dynasty. Thus Cao Cao's "Moshang sang" describes a celestial journey and quest for immortality.[16] If we want to understand this as a negation of the Luofu intratext, then we must recognize that that negation results from a post facto development of the *yuefu* conventions of intratextuality. A more productive example of this type of retroactive negation is the inclusion of Bao Zhao's "Cai sang" (a title he initiates) poem within the extended Luofu poems. While it explores the erotic world of mulberry pickers, it, unlike many that follow in the titular line, specifically disregards the mainlines of intratext.[17] We have similar combinations of authorial and retroactive negation in the Luofu intratext with the "The Sun Rises [from the Southeast Corner]" ("Ri chu [dongnan yu] xing") poems, some of which engage the intratext, while others are merely poems about the sun in various manifestations.[18]

As we have seen in several examples above, these six types of intratextuality are not necessarily mutually exclusive. A strong intratextual poet often joined several types into one powerful rewriting of an intratext. The prime example of such a powerful intratextual reading should be by Li Bo, and we are not to be disappointed:

> The beautiful lady east of the Wei River bridge
> Is at work with her silkworms when spring returns
> His five horses are like flying dragons
> Blue silk ties their gold halters
> He does not know who this girl is
> He flirts with her, bringing a teasing reply
> "I am after all Luofu of Qin"
> With fair complexion, a famous beauty of the city
> In the green branches shining white hands
> Pick mulberry leaves near the corner of the city wall
> Not even the governor is considered
> To say nothing of Qiu Hu
> The small dark cicada loves the emerald grass
> The singing phoenix perches on the verdant tree
> Her heart has its object of attention
> But for the foolishness of that guy over there
> Vainly he labors until the sun sets
> While the noble passengers linger to no avail

YFSJ 28.413

Li Bo's version of "Moshang sang" is a multifaceted engagement of the Luofu intratext. There is a sense of continuation in his retelling of the confrontation with the governor and his use of standard Luofu imagery; there is amplification in the recasting of the horses as dragons; and the cicada-phoenix couplet is a small diversion into ornamentation. The major effort of Li's intratextuality is, however, in the use of extension and transformation. Li not only extends the story to include Qiu Hu, but also, it would seem, the local boy (that guy over here) who so gawked at Luofu that he forgot his work in the original poem—a character who was politely ignored in every other poem of the Luofu intratext. This later extension is another example of Li's "radical conservative" intratextual writing. But Li is not satisfied with mere extension; he couples his rewriting with a multileveled subversion. Luofu is unmarried, and not only available but an actual tease; however, her affections are not with the governor or his alter-ego Qiu Hu (who both are apparently there), but seemingly with the local boy. But is the farm-boy doffing his cap and forgetting his hoe? No, he is so busy in the field he does not even notice his Luofu.

The Literary Context of Intratextuality

Within its literary context a given genre is defined by its relationship to the other genres surrounding it: both how it is similar to and how it is different from them. That is to say, the genre not only coheres through the acceptance of shared conventions, but also distinguishes itself from the other parts of the literary system by those very conventions. Thus the identity of *yuefu* poetry is very much a function of how it fits into the literary context of early Chinese literature, especially *shi* poetry. Here I want to compare *yuefu* poetry to the other poetic forms that surrounded it when it was a functioning genre.

Regulated Verse

The most important category of *shi* poetry during the Tang was *lü shi* (regulated verse). The overt defining characteristic of regulated verse is, of course, a strict prosody that easily distinguishes it from most *yuefu* poems.[19] However, *yuefu* poems could be and were written in the prosody of regulated verse, especially in the High and Middle Tang periods, so even that easy distinction is not entirely adequate. A more subtle and important distinction between these two genres was the nonfictionality of regulated versus the fictionality of *yuefu* poetry.[20] The assumed nonfictionality of regulated verse asked that poems be read as personal, biographical statements by the poets in their relation to the actual world. As we have seen, *yuefu* poems did not require the same reading; in fact, fictionality was assumed. That assumed fictionality was the direct result of the practice of intratextuality. By writing intratextually the poet chose to write in the voice of the intratext, not in his own. The intratextuality of the *yuefu* genre allowed the poet to experiment in fictional modes, themes, and personae. Of course, the personal voice of the poet and that of the intratext could merge in these fictions, yielding intratextual poems with particular individual signatures. No one was more adept and passionate in the fusing of his personal intent with the conventions of the intratext than Li Bo, and that is one reason why his *yuefu* poetry is so effective.

Old Style Poetry

The other major category of poetry in the *shi* genre, and one that is often viewed in contradistinction to regulated verse, is *guti shi* ("old style poetry"). *Guti shi*, a style whose intended model was the poetry of the Han, Wei, and Jin periods, was recognized as a distinct form of poetry only after the formation of regulated verse. Wang Li, the definitive voice in the discussion of the prosody of these genres, says:

> Old style poetry is also called poetry of the old manner *(gu feng)*. After new style poetry *(jinti shi)* [i.e., regulated verse and its related types] developed in the Tang, poets did not stop writing poems in the prosody of ancient times; there were poems that were not written according to the tonal restrictions, parallel couplets, or the prescribed syntax of the new style poetry, but rather modeled themselves on the relatively less structured poetry of the ancients. At that time regulated verse and the five-syllable quatrain *(jueju)* stood opposed to old style poetry forming two types of poetry.[21]

As Wang suggests, in the simplest of definitions old style poetry is really any *shi* poetry that regulated verse is not; thus it shares a great deal of territory with *yuefu* poetry. Yet old style poetry also had associated generic conventions that distinguished it from both regulated verse and *yuefu* poetry. The thematic scope of *guti shi* was similar to that of regulated verse, but there was a tendency for the poet to use it for the more historical and conceptional aspects of that range, which is to say that it had a less biographical but nonetheless nonfictional voice.

The historical/conceptual coloration of this poetry was because the term *gu* (old) brought it into association with the reactionary sentiment of the Tang *fugu* ("return to antiquity") movement, which gained strength in the Middle Tang period. Stephen Owen's description of this poetry shows its *fugu* associations:

> The *gu feng* had its own themes, its own turns of phrase, and its particular modal associations. True metaphor and allegory appeared most commonly here and were linked with the implications of moral seriousness carried by all *fugu* forms . . . . [And it] became the appropriate vehicle for hidden topical commentary, a means to express socially or politically dangerous feelings and opinions. The majority of *gu feng*, however, were not topical: despite its mild archaism, the form also served for intense emotional effusions and philosophical meditations that were not tied to occasion.[22]

It is this seriousness of purpose, along with the much more sparse intratextual, topical markings, that distinguishes old style poetry from *yuefu* poetry, and which unites it with the prosodically dissimilar regulated verse. Yet the nonregulated nature of old style poetry and of *yuefu* meant that, separated from the intratextual context, they could look alike. There were *yuefu* poems that would never be mistaken for old style poetry (for example, the *Wu sheng* poems and *yuefu* poems written in a regulated style), but old style poetry could enter the *yuefu* fold at any intratextual moment, whereupon it would cease to be old style poetry and become part of the *yuefu* genre.

Court Poetry

There are subcategories of *shi* poetry where a *yuefu*-like fictionality is more allowed. This is especially true in the court poetry of the Six Dynasties and Tang periods, which asked the poet to write in conventional, fictional rubrics. Court poetry has its generative origins in the literary games associated with the salons of the Southern Six Dynasties, such as that of Xiao Gang. As we have seen, *yuefu* also flourished during that period and was closely related to such verse. By the beginning of the Tang, such games had been transformed into the poetry of the imperial court, which Owen describes:

The court poets of the late fifth through seventh century practiced a kind of "creative imitation" similar in many ways to that found in lyric poets of the European Renaissance. Once the basic themes and forms of court poetry were set in the late fifth century, poets accepted their inheritance as the absolute limits of poetry; within this inheritance poets sought novelty of expression rather than true originality. What they lost in freedom and depth, the court poets tried to compensate for in craft, style, and cleverness.[23]

Owen goes on to describe the subtleties of that "craft, style, and cleverness," which produce a poetry of refined sensibility and propriety, where a premium was placed on speed of composition and graceful performance, all governed by a set of restrictive rules: "First among these unwritten rules was a sense of topical and lexical decorum. One of the first things that defines a court poem proper is that it is written to a prearranged topic (sometimes indicated by phrases such as *fu de)*, often to imperial command *(yingzhi)*."[24] These descriptions of salon and court poetry remind us again of the *yuefu* genre, especially in the encouragement of fictionality that excludes poetry with a biographical and personal expression. What distinguishes this fictionality from that of *yuefu* poetry is how occasional it is in court poetry and how textual it is in *yuefu*. Participation in court poetry was by definition limited to those in proximity to the center of political/literary power. This was not true for the poet who wanted to write in the *yuefu* genre, whose conventions were text-bound and relatively free of occasion. *Yuefu* poets could choose their own fiction and learn its conventions anywhere they found the intratextual poems. In this way *yuefu* poetry functioned as a court poetry for those literati who were not at the political and literary center of their society.

Yongwu Poetry

There was, however, a type of court poetry, usually considered a subgenre of *shi*, that did approach *yuefu* poetry's use of a textually assigned topic and implied a certain type of fictionality. These so-called *yongwu* poems, which also derive from the literary games of Six Dynasties, choose as their subject physical objects *(wu)*, either man-made or natural, which they would then describe *(yong)*, usually in short refined poems, sometimes with an overlay of allegory and riddle—in the simplest form these poems are recognizable by their use of *yong* in the title. The easiest distinction between these two types of poetry is that *yongwu* poems have a more limited topical range and poetic style, a style that unites the poems across their multitudinous topics. Needless to say a "topic" like "Watering Horses at the Long Wall Spring" is beyond the usual range of *yongwu* poetry. Yet many of the "willow" poems discussed in Chapter 5 approach the intent and style of the *yongwu* poetry (trees, including willows, are common *yongwu* topics), and there is occasional crossassignment of poems in the two genres. But the complication of the titular theme, especially into hypotactic narrative, is not associated with *yongwu* poetry. A *yongwu* "willow" poem would be concerned primarily with a physical description of the tree itself, while the *yuefu* would be more interested in pursuing the story of separation that the tree always signified. Conversely *yuefu* poetry does not necessarily expect the same playful cleverness and ingenuity demanded by the *yongwu* genre. Finally, the most important characteristic of *yuefu* poetry is the fictional personae that it provided the poet; while *yongwu* provided a topic, it did not offer voices for singing about that topic.

Songs

The musicality of *yuefu* poetry often places it in association with the common "song" *(ge* or *gexing)* poetic group. The *gexing*, like many *yuefu* poems, are free of formal conventions, and often are relatively irregular in their prosody, which tends to align them with the early *yuefu* poems. In this way there is no formal way to distinguish a *gexing* from a *yuefu* poem, but there are many *yuefu* poems that could not be mistaken for *gexing* (e.g., those that are written in the prosody of regulated verse). But even the *Wen xuan* has a category of "songs" *(ge)* distinct from the *yuefu* poems, and the major Song anthology of Tang poetry, *Wenyuan yinghua,* clearly separates the two poetries by placing the "songs" in their own category outside of *shi* poetry *(yuefu* is considered a subtype of *shi).*[25] If we accept the evidence of these two anthologies' separation of the "songs" from the *yuefu* poems, it appears that the titular theme is the *only* distinguishing feature of the *yuefu* genre. There are some problems using these criteria with *Wenyuan yinghua* groups, but they are minor; almost without exception the *yuefu* poetry of the *Wenyuan yinghua* is presented in intratextual sets, and the *gexing* appear as individual poem/titles.[26] Moreover, Stephen Owen has noted, "These two categories are only loosely differentiated, the former *[yuefu]* tending to adopt the personae of various *yuefu* 'types,' the latter tending to be the poet speaking in his own voice."[27] By offering intratextuality, and not musicality, as the defining criteria of *yuefu* poetry, we of course easily account for the differences that Owen points out between the two genres. Intratextuality is the method by which the *yuefu* personae are sustained. Consequently, the biographical voice of the *gexing* poetry places the genre closer to mainstream *shi* poetry in this regard, despite their formal differences.

Ci Poetry

In the Middle Tang period we have the emergence of another genre marked by its musicality, the *ci* (lyrics), which we have already noted was commonly called *yuefu* in the post-Tang period. This shared designation is part of the habit of the recycling of literary terms, and does not indicate any apparent generic identity between the two poetries. Yet there are fascinating parallels (some coincidental, some not) between *yuefu* poetry and *ci*. The origins of *ci* poetry have been debated for years, but certainly Marsha Wagner's recent thesis is well reasoned: *ci* poetry arose in the environment of performative singing, where courtesans entertained literati poets with popular songs, which influenced and were influenced by the men's more literary contributions.[28] We are struck by the contextual similarities that this theory of *ci* origins has with the earliest layer of the *yuefu* genre: the fitting of lyrics to established tunes (which probably were of foreign origin), the public performative nature of the art, and its association with women and with nonliterati singing. What is even more interesting is, however, the way the *ci* poetry grew into a central literati art form. That growth has parallels with our understanding of the development of *yuefu* as a literati genre.

Early in the history of *ci*, its generative tunes were used as the music for new poems, with lyrics *(ci)* adapted from already-existing poetry or composed specifically for the occasion, with the tune title remaining as the title of the poem. This is the very process that we assume for the early stages of the *yuefu*, for which we have only negative evidence. In *ci* poetry the evidence for this process (for which the music is also lost) is textually visible because the prosody for the poems written to a given melody is always the same, although the thematic material is usually unrelated to the tune title or to other poems in the title. But the ephemerality of music again disrupted this process. This time it was not, however, the theme that was conventionalized when the music was lost, but rather the *prosody*, which became the enduring signature of the tune title. The prosody for every poem written to a given title is identical line-for-line, whether written by Su Shi (1036–1101) or by Chairman Mao. This unifying prosody certainly helped sustain the lyrical nature of the genre, even after the poetry was divorced from its musical origins. Thus there is also an intratextuality for *ci* poetry, but it is prosodic not thematic. And once again it is that *process* of prosodic intratextuality that defines the *ci* genre, not the prosody itself, which was different for every titular tune in the genre. Thus, at a very deep level of poetic structure, *ci* poetry is closest to *yuefu* poetry; but once again it is not musicality but intratextuality that they share.

From this overview of the poetic genres that surround *yuefu* poetry we can argue that not only does thematic intratextuality hold the corpus together better than any other convention available for inspection, but it is also what most distinguishes *yuefu* poetry within its literary context. Other important defining conventions of the genre, such as common themes and assumed fictionality, can be viewed as manifestations of the process of intratextuality, which is truly defining. This explains how *yuefu* poetry can intersect with many other poetic genres and subgenres by sharing their features in conjunction with its defining intratextuality.

The "New *Yuefu*" Poetry

Stylistic affinities have long been offered as the rationale for inclusion of the last category of Guo Maoqian's typology, the "new *yuefu* poetry," which is closely identified with mid-Tang poet Bo Juyi (772–846). Guo Maoqian's introductory notes to his large set of "new *yuefu*" poems (which he extends far beyond, even predating, Bo Juyi) offers a thematic, nonmusical distinction for the "new *yuefu*" poems. His remarks are couched in an extended discussion of the genre's musicality, providing us with a convenient review of the traditional conception of the genre:

> The term Music Bureau comes from the Han-Wei period. In the time of Emperor Xiao of the Han, Xiahou Guan was his Director of the Music Bureau *(yuefu ling)*, and that is when the title for the office began. During his reign, Emperor Wu set up the Music Bureau, which collected poems for the nightly performances; there were tunes from the areas of Zhao, Dai, Qin and Chu. Having collected these popular songs, they put them to [new] music, which apparently also had come from afar. Of the *yuefu* song texts, some were composed to fit music, such as the poems to "three modes" of the Wei period—these were songs created to fit the music of the strings, pipes, bells and stone chimes. There are also some that were songs for which music was composed, such as the various tunes of *qingshang* key and Wu music—from here we first have songs that were sung *a capella*, which were then put to strings and pipes. There are also some for which the music and the lyrics were provided, such as the *jiaomiao, xianghe, nao ge,* and *hengchui* categories. There were also some for which there are lyrics and no music, such as those created in imitation by later writers, which were not put to the music of bells and musical stones. The "new *yuefu*" poems are all new songs *(xinge)* that were written during the Tang period. *Because their lyrics are fully* yuefu *but since they were not usually put to music, they therefore are called "new* yuefu." (*YFSJ* 90.1262 [my emphasis])

The last sentence is the one usually cited in discussions of the meaning of "new *yuefu*" poetry, but it is clear that these criteria are not entirely distinguishing for the category: certainly there are other Tang poems that fit this description, which basically says the "new *yuefu*" are like traditional *yuefu* without music. The confusion lies in what Guo means by "their lyrics are fully *yuefu*" *(ci shi yuefu)*. Guo does argue against the common criterion of "social criticism," which is derived from Bo Juyi's preface (quoted below). Guo claims (rightly so) that the Chinese literary tradition is full of such poems, and "If one were to put all those poems to music then there would certainly be many like 'new *yuefu*' poems!"[29] In his following discussion Guo obfuscates the matter further by becoming embroiled in the question of "old title" versus "new meaning." Here Guo says that, as we have seen, an old title with a new meaning and an old title with an old meaning but with new lyrics are both *yuefu*. From this argument it appears that Guo believes it is the *new title* that is distinguishing for the "new *yuefu*." In the end, Guo Maoqian's comments are again not very helpful because he seems to include too much, often contradictory, information for us to effectively use to define the category, or even to decipher his criteria for the category.

Perhaps we would be better served by turning to Bo Juyi's own preface, in which he introduces the term "new *yuefu*." Bo may not account for Guo Maoqian's enthusiastic anthologizing, but at least we will have a sense of how the issue began and perhaps how the genre ended. Bo introduces his set of "new *yuefu*" poems first with some statistics:

> There are here all together 9,252 word/syllables, divided into fifty poems. The poems are not of a set length, and the lines not of a set number of characters; the richness of the poems is in their meaning *(yi)*, not in their textuality *(wen)*. The first line announces the theme *(mu)*, the remaining lines develops the intent *(zhi)*. This is also the principle behind the three hundred poems of the *Shi jing*. The lyrics here are substantial and direct; if someone reads them, they will provide easy instruction; their words are simple and cutting; if someone hears them, they will provide severe warning; their content is true and verifiable; if someone has reason to use them, they will transmit their belief. Their form is free and unrestricted, they can be put to music and sung. Generally speaking, these poems are written for and about *(wei)* gentlemen, ministers, people, things and affairs; they were not written for and about texts *(wen)*.[30]

In Bo Juyi's eyes, what makes these poems *yuefu* poems seems to be that they are written in a prosodic style that is free and variable, and they are of a relatively unadorned poetic language. What seems to make these poems *new* to the genre had nothing to do with the issue of their nonmusicality (in fact Bo says that they are at least potentially musical), but rather that they are instructional—the preface ends with the listing of all fifty titles with their instructional intent—and they were focused on people and things of the actual world and not on texts *(bu wei wen er zuo).*[31] In other words, they are new because they are *serious, nonfictional, and not intratextual.* That would mean Bo was saying that it is the lack of intratextuality and its accompanying fictionality that makes these new; they are written based on life, not on intratexts. Those may not have been adequate criteria for Guo Maoqian, since he had included so many poems that are serious, nonfictional, and not intratextual in his anthology, but they do match our redefinition of the generic criteria of *yuefu* poetry. As we have seen, in its literary context a nonintratextual, nonfictional *yuefu* poem was certainly new, if it was *yuefu* at all.

Practice as Praxis

In many ways *yuefu* poetry, with its imitative core and intratextual elaboration, is a genre that practices all the other genres. One could, after all, write a *yuefu* regulated verse, a *yuefu* old style poem, a *yuefu* poem that is in another light a *yongwu* poem. Certainly a *yuefu* is also a "song" *(gexing)* with the intratextuality added, and perhaps even a proto-*ci* with its intratextuality reformed. Of the major poetic genres, only the *fu* (rhapsody) seems untouched by the range of *yuefu* poetic forms. Yet despite all the striking differences between *yuefu* poetry and the rhapsody (with the rhapsody's prolix style and difficult vocabulary, and the epic amplitude of its epideictic effusion), these two poetries do share an interest in intratextuality. Like the *yuefu* poetic sets, *fu*, especially in its classical (Han) form, had similar "intratexts" that were built around poetic themes upon which poets could and should draw when they wrote their own *fu*. These "intratexts" verged toward the more topical kind like those of *yongwu* poetry, but are more elaborated by epideictic display. This type of intratextual writing is clearest in the *Wen xuan* rhapsodies, especially those on the metropolises.[32]

The epideictic *fu*, especially in Tang times, was a genre that was often seen and used as a training ground for the potential degree holders, a form that allowed them to utilize and expand their accumulating exposure to the literary heritage in relatively easy and obvious ways. The intratextuality of the adolescent rhapsody was not the mature kind that would be seen in the literary rhapsodies *(wen fu)* or essays. It was exuberant and expansive, lacking the moderation of the older poet who would be more selective and more subtle.

We could argue that the position *yuefu* poetry held on the lyric side of the Chinese poetic spectrum was similar to that held by the rhapsody on the prosaic side. The intratextuality of *yuefu* poetry was also a relatively easy form of imitative poetics. It did not even require access to an encyclopedia; as long as another poem in the intratext were available then one could write intratextually. This form of writing would have been quite suitable to novitiates of literary culture of early China. They could learn to write well in a limited area of intertextuality (in the *yuefu* intratext), before venturing out into the textual sea of Chinese poetry. The introduction to *yuefu* poetry could lead them on to the more subtle and difficult writing of *shi* poetry, especially regulated verse.

Yuefu intratextuality may have been a training ground for the Chinese poet; *yuefu* poetry may have been the adolescence of Chinese poetry. This "adolescence" was not necessarily temporal, either in the literary history of China or in an individual's poetic work. It could have existed side-by-side with more "mature" poetic work; yet it would always represent the somewhat more youthful, playful, and experimental side of the poetic corpus, both culturally and individually. For most poets, *yuefu* poetry was a less serious concern, less serious both socially and philosophically. It was not the poetry in which they would take their personal stances. It was a poetry that allowed them to adopt the voice of others, and they could adopt that voice for no higher purpose than to write in another persona—fiction for fiction's sake. It allowed "serious" poets an outlet for fantasy; it allowed them to play pretend—pretend warrior, pretend woman, pretend Hun, pretend prince.

This brings us back to our consideration of Li Bo and Du Fu, one whose poetic reputation rests predominantly on *yuefu* poems, and the other with hardly any *yuefu* poetry to his name. To some extent this may reflect the presence of early works in Li's poetic corpus, and the absence of them from Du's, absence that may have been accidental or intended. But I suspect the reason for this difference is more fundamental to the poetics of Li and Du. Du Fu was not an adolescent poet; he wrote seriously and biographically. Even in his thirties (from which the earliest poems date) he was "a poet without an apprenticeship, a fully mature poet with a sure hand and a strong individual voice."[33] He was not so involved in *yuefu* intratextuality as in intertextuality with the entire poetic tradition, a tradition that he did not seek to consume but rather to transmit, revitalized and irrevocably changed, to later poets. Du Fu was not interested in fictionality as much as he was interested in historical truth; he earned his epithet as the "poet historian."

Li Bo, on the other hand, was very much interested in fictionality; in fact we have seen how he strove to turn fiction into psychological if not historical truth, to turn himself into a fiction. *Yuefu* poetry gave Li the voices that he adopted for his own persona; it allowed him to experiment in those poses, for it was one place where the tradition encouraged fictionality. The genre also gave Li relatively easy access to the early Chinese literary world through the ready-made tradition of intratextuality. While Li was no literary incompetent, neither was he raised in the rich literary environment that Meng Haoran, Wang Wei, and Du Fu were. He was by his own reckoning a novice to the world of Chinese letters (whether that entry was from a foreign culture or from the land of the immortals was dependent on the pose that he struck). Li Bo was the preeminent *yuefu* poet because he was essentially an adolescent poet, a young poet all his life. His love of fictional poses, his avowed interest in the shock value of language, and his exuberant display of radical intratextuality were all manifestations of that adolescence. He took the conventions of the genre very seriously. He used the genre's fictionality and intratextuality so violently as to exhaust it for the poets who came after him.

The traditional critical appreciation of the poetry of Du Fu and Li Bo is that one should study/emulate/imitate *(xue)* Du's poetry but not Li's. As Owen says,

The rationale for directing young poets away from the model of Li Bo was that Li's art was perfectly natural, uncontrollable, almost divinely inspired. But the real reason that Li Bo was inimitable was that Li Bo's poetry primarily concerned Li Bo: its goal was to embody a unique personality, either through the person of the poem or through an implied creator behind the poem. Imitation necessarily failed because it contradicted the very reason for the style's existence.[34]

The inability to imitate Li's poetry is testimony to the success of the poetry he chose to write. Li wanted to separate himself not only from his predecessors and his contemporaries, but also from those that followed. He wanted to be inimitable, not to be a model for the young. How different this is from Du Fu, who would have been pleased with the great line of students, imitators, and kindred souls who followed in his wake.

Li chose the stance of the most extreme solitude, a stance that a mature poet would "outgrow," a stance that would soften in middle age into one of quiet camaraderie, and in old age into deep human compassion. His flamboyant poetics of fictionality isolated him not from, but within, the poetic tradition, and this certainly makes Li one of the most tragic voices in the Chinese literature. Li was constantly and profoundly alone, as his search for poetic autonomy forced him to cut and drift from those, such as the younger Du Fu, who offered him community.[35] Yet without Li Bo, the Chinese poetic tradition would have been infinitely less interesting, less problematical, and more comfortably middle-aged.

This is, of course, also the position that *yuefu* poetry held in *its* literary context. The convention of intratextuality allowed *yuefu* poetry to adopt a stance within the other genres without actually entering into them. Moreover, since it broke the conventions of the quotidian and biographical voice, which held most of the Chinese poetry in its grip, *yuefu* poetry could infuse into the tradition a sense of play, excitement, and freedom that would not otherwise have been allowed. Thus, in its literary context, intratextuality did not represent limitation, but rather innovation; it did not restrict the poet, but rather freed him. *Yuefu* poetry freed the poet to speak in the voice of others, in a voice larger than the biographical self.

Notes

Introduction

[1] Heather Dubrow, p. 31.

[2] Jonathan Culler, *Structuralist Poetics*, p. 116.

[3] The Chinese literary tradition does not have a critical text as seminal as Aristotle's *Poetics* in this regard. Zhi Yu's work, available in my translation, is of a similar type, but much later and not as generative. Lu Ji's "Wen fu" and Liu Xie's *Wenxin diaolong* are nearly as important as the *Poetics*, but are of a quite different nature.

[4] Tzvetan Todorov, *The Fantastic*.

[5] Hans Frankel has a number of studies that deal with different aspects of the balladic nature of *yuefu* poetry, a critical approach that was adopted in Birrell's recent book of translations and essays of Han folk poems. Gary Williams' study also deals with these materials, especially in the context of their supposed orality. Also see the Bibliographic Note.

[6] Thais E. Morgan, pp. 1–2.

[7] A. J. Krailsheimer, p. 15.

[8] Thomas M. Greene, p. 51.

[9] Ibid., p. 50.

[10] The critical methodology semiology/semiotics has a complex history of its own. Briefly stated it is the study of the "signs" in any cultural context or system, especially the significance any referent has within a given system. Thus, in Chapter 5 I explore the various "signs" (words, phrasing, images, etc.) of the willow

tree not only within the Chinese literary tradition, but also within the subsystem of poems of parting. The opening chapter of Robert Scholes' *Semiotics and Interpretation* is one of the best statements on the method; Jonathan Culler's *The Pursuit of Signs* is an extensive review of the field.

[11] Morgan, p. 8.

[12] Julia Kristéva, p. 59; cf. Stamos Metzidakis, p. 133, n. 1.

[13] Metzidakis, p. 22.

[14] Jonathan Culler, *Pursuit*, p. 38.

[15] Vincent B. Leitch, p. 59

[16] Morgan, p. 9.

[17] Michael Riffaterre, "The Interpretant in Literary Semiotics," p. 41.

[18] Morgan, pp. 20–21.

[19] Metzidakis, p. 23.

[20] Culler, *Pursuit*. In this way I align myself more with Riffaterre and Scholes' methodology in that I interpret the system as well as describe it, realizing that my interpretations are among many possible "completions" of the intertextual system.

Chapter 1

[1] While there was no need to "translate" the classical Chinese texts into another language, there were certainly ongoing "clarifications" (annotations, commentaries, glosses, etc.) to those texts. This type of work really began in the Han (subsequently often identified as "Han scholarship" [*Han xue*]), had a burst of activity in the Tang and again in the Qing, continuing up to this day in the philological schools of Chinese and Western sinology. The depth and length of those clarifications or "corrections" (*zheng yi*) for any given text is directly proportional to the importance of the text in the tradition. When do these clarifications constitute a translation? Is a modern *bai hua* "translation" (*yi*) a translation? These are interesting and worthwhile questions for which I have no ready answer. Nevertheless, when we compare the Chinese medieval tradition with that of Europe, it appears very "translation-free."

[2] John DeFrancis, pp. 125–26.

[3] Miyazaki Ichisada, p. 16. He is discussing the exam system in the late imperial time, but these conditions have been relatively stable since the Tang, when the exam system was institutionalized.

[4] The literary games and contests played by Chinese literati were an important part of this process of becoming literate in China. John Marney's *Liang Chien-wen Ti* discusses various forms of these games as they were played in the Liang literati society; Richard Mather, *The Poet Shen Yüeh*, chapter 5, discusses similar praxis in *Yongming* poetry, including topical *yuefu*. For the Tang, see Stephen Owen's *Early T'ang* volume.

[5] Early in the twentieth century Wen Yiduo based much of his reconstruction of Chinese myth on such deciphering of the script. This work has been carried on by scholars such as Edward Schafer and William Boltz in the West. See my "Wen I-to" for a brief review of Wen's work.

[6] I here refer to the discovery of the Shang-dynasty oracle bones at the beginning of this century, which extended our knowledge of Chinese script half a millennium. A review of those discoveries can be found in K. C. Chang's two volumes, and elsewhere. Chang's *Shang Civilization*, as is David Keightley's *Sources of Shang History*, is largely based on these materials.

[7] Wilhelm/Baynes, pp. 328–29 (translation slightly altered); *Zhou yi*, p. 166. The *Zhou yi* is multilayered and difficult to date, but certainly this passage represents a very early conception on the origin of the sign/script system, of which the *Zhou yi* is itself the earliest product.

[8] James J. Y. Liu, *Theories*, p. 22. Also see Stuart Sargent's discussion of the meaning of *wen*, which he calls "an original language," in somewhat later sources, pp. 166–68.

[9] Stephen Owen, *Traditional Chinese Poetry*, pp. 12–53, which contains a detailed and sophisticated discussion of the whole question of what *wen* is and means.

[10] James J. Y. Liu, *Theories*, p. 8.

[11] The first lexicographic entry we have for *xue* (*Shuowen jiezi* [ca. A.D. 100]) is *jue wu*, "to realize," or as a variant for "to teach." The gloss *xiao* is first found in the *Guang ya* [ca. A.D. 230], but based on a passage in the *Analects*. The term *wenxue* first appears in the *Analects*, as does the form *xue wen*, from which

I postulate the grammatical transformation that yields *wenxue*. We see a parallel linguistic structure in such terms as *wen fu*, *wen xuan*, and *tianwen xue*, which are susceptible to similar transformations. For explicit evidence of this structure see Wang Yi's prefatory note to the "Tian wen" in the *Chu ci* (3, 1a), where he suggests the *tian wen* is a transformation of *wen tian*. Richard Lynn's discussion of the concept of *xue*, which he calls "emulation/imitation," in Yan Yu's (1180–ca. 1235) *Canglang shihua* is illuminating in this regard; he says, for example, "Emulation of the right masters was the cornerstone of his whole program for poetry" (p. 158).

[12] Wilhelm/Baynes, p. 320; *Zhou yi*, p. 157.

[13] The "old text" versus "new text" controversy centered on the debate over the authenticity of two sets of Han texts—those in the reformed (new) script, which were largely reconstructed from memory after the loss of texts in the Qin, and those in the old (pre-Han) script, many of which were said to have been found in walls of a house belonging to the descendants of Confucius. This controversy also had major political ramifications, with the new-text school being more progressive and supporting the growing strength of the emperor and his expansionist policies; the old-text school was more conservative and sought limitations of those policies. The authenticity problem was finally settled in the Qing, in favor of the new-text materials, but lingering debate was carried on, especially by some Western sinologists, into the twentieth century. See Liang Ch'i-ch'ao, esp. pp. 83–88; Michael Loewe, preface; and in Chinese, Pi Xirui.

Nonetheless, this controversy could only have existed in an environment of shared assumptions about language, and one that allowed texts to remain active and complete in the memories of living men. That is to say the debate did not center on the script itself, but rather on the contents of the texts in the two forms; and new-script texts were those that were transcribed into the reformed script from memory, independent of other written records.

[14] John Marney, *Liang Chien-wen Ti*, pp. 146–47; cf. the original passage in *Nan shi*, 80.1999.

[15] A. Wylie, p. xvii.

[16] This bibliography, compiled in 621 (*Sui shu* 32–35.903–1104) of 2,851 main entries and 2,327 supplementary entries, also contains numerous footnotes to books that had been lost since the Liang—in the formula *Liang you . . . wang* (the Liang had . . . but now is lost) appended to the entries of then extant books. The twenty-nine main entries for the *Shi* [*jing*] editions (32.915–18), for

example, list twenty-eight related texts that had been lost since the Liang. Most of these losses are assumed to have resulted from Xiao Gang's rather desperate action. See Teng Ssu-yu and Knight Biggerstaff, p. 9.

[17] Thomas Greene discusses these questions at length; for his thoughts on Dante see especially pp. 4–6.

[18] Ibid., p. 8.

[19] This attitude yields a rich and very "modern" tradition of lexicography in China, one to which we are still very much indebted. The "modernity" of Chinese traditional lexicography to which I refer is its early interest in source citation and objective recording of usage rather than evaluative discriminations. Compared to the history of Western dictionaries, Chinese lexicography is more concerned with retrieval systems and monolinguality. The history of Chinese lexicography is a neglected but fascinating intellectual endeavor that began around the third century B.C. and continues to this day. In English see Xue Shiqi or my brief "Chinese Script and Lexicography"; in Chinese Liu Yeqiu's work is definitive and comprehensive.

[20] A detailed introduction to the *Wen xuan* is provided by David Knechtges in the first volume of his translation.

[21] These two poems are found in the *Wen xuan* 25.1193, 1199, respectively— subsequent citations are given in the text; my partial translations of these poems are based on those by J. D. Frodsham, *The Murmuring Stream*, vol. 1, pp. 185, 149.

[22] Knechtges, *Wen xuan*, p. 39.

[23] Owen, *Early T'ang*, p. 105, discusses this type of poetry.

[24] The *dai* designation also appears with personal names/titles, in which case I understand it to mean "written in the voice of. . . ." See the contemporaneous *Yutai xinyong* 10.283, for two examples. While on the surface the *dai*-title designation appears to be a *ni/xiao* type of imitation, as its usage develops it becomes associated almost exclusively with *yuefu* poetry, and thus is not the imitation of one particular model text, but rather a designation of the poem's participation in the intratextuality of a set of poems with this title.

[25] James J. Y. Liu, *Theories*, p. 127.

[26] Du Fu is by all accounts considered the *best* classical poet of China and, by inference of the preeminence of the poetic tradition, the most important Chinese writer. That reputation comes not only from his technical strength and breadth of accomplishment, but also from the strong and comfortable personal voice that permeates so much of his verse. There are a plethora of studies of his life and work; in English the most comprehensive is William Hung's *Tu Fu*; one of the most recent is Stephen Owen's chapter on the poet in *The Great Age* volume.

[27] This line, "*du shu po wan juan,*" is found in *Quan Tang shi* 216.2251

[28] Walter Jackson Bate, p. 5; cf. Greene, p. 293.

[29] Bate, p. 6.

[30] Harold Bloom, p. 32.

[31] Sargent, p. 166. My understanding of Du Fu's position in the tradition is drawn largely from this excellent article. Also see Owen, *The Great Age*, pp. 183–85.

[32] Adele Austin Rickett, p. 110.

[33] Bate, p. 12

[34] Sargent, p. 168.

[35] Jonathan Chaves, p. 211.

[36] Ibid., p. 201.

[37] Ibid., p. 206.

[38] Ibid., p. 208. Chaves provides this translation of the anecdote:

> One day early in the springtime, Manqing [Shi Yannian (994–1041)] noticed that the newly sprouted blades of grass beside the stone staircase were bent like hooks, and that their color had not yet become green. A line came to him then: "Grassblades bend their golden hooks, the green not yet returned." Later he wrote a full poem entitled "Early Spring," which took him ten days in all to complete. This included the couplet,
>
> > Roof-eaves hang their muscles of ice [i.e., icicles], which only melt in the sunlight;

Grassblades bend their golden hooks
the green not yet returned.

The inferiority [of the new line] to the line which first came to him is considerable. From this I realized for the first time that in a work by a poet, any line or couplet which comes [to the poet] first will turn out to be the most outstanding [in the poem].

[39] Owen, *Traditional Chinese Poetry*, p. 161.

[40] Richard Lynn, p. 159.

Chapter 2

[1] Chinese *yuefu* studies have especially focused on the issue of taxonomy, while those in the West have generally dealt with *yuefu* poetry in more general or incidental ways, the exceptions being Jean-Pierre Diény's *Origines de la poésie*, William Nienhauser's "Two *Yüeh-fu* Themes," and the several studies by Hans Frankel. Frankel's earlier studies are closest to the Chinese in approach, although there is a certain comparative perspective to his work. Anne Birrell's recent work includes a thorough review of these problems, as well as description of the literary sources and developments of the genre. Unfortunately my study was essentially complete before I knew of her work. Be that as it may, since Birrell, like the early Frankel, is only concerned with the early "folk" tradition associated with the genre, my arguments remained relatively unchanged in light of her study.

[2] These passages are found in *Han shu* 22.1043, 1045, and 30.1756. Full discussion of them can be found in numerous studies, but perhaps best in Wang Yunxi, *Yuefu shi luncong*, pp. 8–10; and Hellmut Wilhelm, "The Bureau of Music of the Western Han." Birrell's introduction is a fine review and summary of these.

[3] This collecting of music is mentioned in the *Han shu* passages on Emperor Wu's establishment of the Music Bureau (see note 2), and is usually associated with the legendary *cai shi guan* (Official in Charge of Collecting Poetry) of the pre-Han period.

[4] Diény discusses the western origins of this "new music."

[5] *Han shu* 11.335. Michael Loewe, chapter 6, introduces this emperor (Ai) and his activities.

[6] These ritual poems are collected and discussed in the *Han shu*, especially 22.1046–1070, but see below regarding their tenuous relationship with the genre.

[7] See the Bibliographic Note in the end matter for a discussion of the *Yuefu shiji* (Hereafter, *YFSJ*) and its studies.

[8] Luo Genze, *Yuefu wenxue shi*, pp. 11–25, gives a full review of the history of these terms.

[9] *YFSJ* 26.376–77.

[10] Frankel, "Yüeh-fu," pp. 69–70. In a more recent essay that discusses early literati *yuefu* poetry, Frankel has modified his definition somewhat, including foregrounding the *yuefu* intratextual sets; see his "High Literary Genre," p. 255. I discuss his new definition of the genre in Chapter 7.

[11] Frankel, "Yüeh-fu," p. 71.

[12] These pre-Music Bureau poems are collected under category 11, "lyrics for miscellaneous songs and ditties," especially chapter 83. The rest of this category seems to be made up of poems that Guo Maoqian felt were musical (usually because of their title), but that did not have any established relationship with the Music Bureau or the genre. Birrell shows how Guo Maoqian inherited this category from the Tang anthologist Wu Jing. These poems cannot be given any serious consideration in the definition of *yuefu* poetry, by any criteria.

[13] *YFSJ* 90.1262

[14] The *Wen xuan*, chapter 28, has a small collection of "songs," separate from the *yuefu* poems; the *Wenyuan yinghua* has a substantial collection in chapters 331–50. I discuss these poems in Chapter 7 as part of an overview of literary context for *yuefu* poetry.

[15] *YFSJ* 17.223–24.

[16] *Song shu* 19.549.

[17] James Robert Hightower, *Outlines*, pp. 51–52. There are innumerable problems with the designation of the *yuefu* poems as "ballads," as I discuss in my dissertation, Chapter 2. While those problems do not affect Hightower's brief comments here, when his ideas are extrapolated by others, the whole problem of "balladic" literature comes to the fore.

[18] Frankel, "Yüeh-fu," p. 72. He suggests that this typology is derived from use of new criteria: "first, the difference between the oral and literary tradition; second, the dichotomy of hymns and ballads; third, regional differences; and fourth, differences of period" (71–72). His actual application of these criteria is, however, not clearly developed in this description of the corpus—he never explains, for example, what in these criteria establishes the second type as a "special class" of ritual hymns, although one suspects it is the rare combination of the ritual and the so-called oral nature of these poems that mark them as "special."

[19] Masuda Kiyohide, pp. 5–15.

[20] *Han shu*, 30.1701–81. This bibliography is based on Liu Xiang's (77–6 B.C.) "Qi lue," which would put its compilation right at the height of Music Bureau activity.

[21] A thorough review of those early anthologies can be found in the introduction of David Knechtges' translation of the *Wen xuan*.

[22] These are available in Xu Wenyu, pp. 67–84, and I have translated them in my *"Discussions"*—the reference to *yuefu* occurs in Xu, p. 74, and in the translation, p. 26. Masuda Kiyohide cites this as the earliest usage of the term in its sense of a literary type.

[23] Bao Zhao, p. 24.

[24] There is a good deal of confusion about which poems in this anthology were originally designated *yuefu*; in this count I have only included those so designated in the introductory passages and titles, considering designation solely in the table of contents as suspect.

[25] *Song shu* 19.549. At another point (21.603 et passim), Shen includes these poems under now-recognized *yuefu* categories (*xianghe*, etc.), but does not call them *yuefu per se*—Diény's *Origines* is a full-length study of these poems. Yet note that in Shen's postface (100.2459), he refers to the *yuefu* genre by name but seemingly as a minor type of verse; Anne Birrell, p. 7, claims this as the first reference to the *yuefu* genre.

[26] Be aware that the common citation of Cai Yong's (133–192) reference to ritual music (*jiaomiao*) as *yuefu* poetry is not accurate. Cai is only describing four types of Han music, not *yuefu* poetry (*Song shu* 20.565).

[27] My evidence is based primarily on the listing of source citations for *YFSJ* in *Gafu shishō no kenkyū,* back matter, pp. 205–45. Birrell (pp. 14-15) provides a list of sources for *YFSJ* based on this study.

[28] The text is held in the *Siku quanshu zhen ben,* 12 *ji,* vol. 200. The *Siku quanshu zongmu tiyao,* pp. 4180–81, describes Zuo's work and suggests a date of composition around 1346, only a few years after Guo Maoqian's collection (which probably was not seen by Zuo) was printed.

[29] For a discussion of this set of poems, see Chapter 7 and my "From Saint to Singing Girl."

[30] There are many problems with this identity of *gu ci* and *wuming* poems with "folk" literature. This is especially so with the Southern *wuming* poems, which are better understood as "unsigned" rather than anonymous, for they usually are as "literary" as the authored poems of the same type. The *gu ci* poems have a better claim to the "folk," but not entirely so, especially for those in Guo's collection of unknown provenance.

[31] Some exception to this prejudice is seen in the studies of Huang Jie and Xiao Difei, but Huang contains only Han and Wei poets, and Xiao is limited to pre-Tang materials. Zhou Zhenfu's essay is unusual in its concern with not only literati, but also Tang, *yuefu* poetry. Moreover, while he does not explore the intratextual contexts of the poems that he discusses, he is aware of them and mentions them in passing. In the Japanese studies, Masuda is more inclusive of literati poems. As a historical review Luo Genze remains the most balanced.

[32] Wang Yunxi, *Yuefu,* p. 1.

[33] These are (Tang) Li Bo, Bo Juyi, Zhang Ji, Li Ho; (Liang) Shen Yue, Xiao Gang; (Northern Zhou) Yu Xin; (Jin) Fu Xuan. These counts are by separate title, not number of poems. Since some poets have more than one poem under a title, the counts may be somewhat low.

[34] Many readers' assumption of the centrality of the early and/or folk *yuefu* poems is based on a limited exposure to the literati side of the spectrum. Just as the prejudice toward the early part of the spectrum is evident in the studies, so it is in the readings of students of *yuefu* poetry. The average student will read a selection from this narrow band of the Guo Maoqian's corpus (usually as part of a general survey of pre-Tang poetry), perpetuating the belief in the importance of "Han *yuefu* ballads." When important literati *yuefu* poems *are* read,

they are invariably read divorced from their intratextual context and treated just like other *shi* poems.

[35] See Yang Yinliu, vol 1., p. 141–95, where he gives all the available information on music in the post-Han, pre-Tang period, which is most pertinent here, a period Yang characterizes as full of disruptions and new influences. Much of Yang's information is derived from the *YFSJ* notes.

[36] *Jin shu* 13.701.

[37] *Song shu* 19.536.

[38] *Jin shu* 22. 679.

[39] The "Bo wei" poem is found in Ding Fubao, p. 1402.

[40] It is unclear whether Luo's two types of imitation by "title" are intended to be based on musicality or thematics; the assumption in most of these studies is that "title" refers to the tune or melody, thus it would be musicality. Despite such assumptions it is clear that the titles also became vehicles of themes as well.

[41] These are included in the more than forty poems surrounding the *gu ci* "Moshang sang" title, *YFSJ* 28.410–23.

[42] Okamure Tadao discusses the seminal role Fu Xuan played in thematic imitation of *yuefu* poetry.

[43] In Chapter 7, I discuss how the *yuefu* can assume the prosodic garb of almost any other poetic form. Hans Frankel and Gary Williams both take up the issue of orality, or at least formulaic composition, in their studies.

[44] Nienhauser's "Themes" is the major exception to this. Masuda Kiyohide also includes discussions based on themes (e.g., knight errant), but does not limit himself to subsets. While he does not recognize them as such, the "twenty-five *yuefu* themes" that Frankel discusses in his "High Literary Genre" are also a product of intratextuality—see below, Chapter 7. While she does not pursue the idea, Anne Birrell notes that the *YFSJ*'s organization by titular sets "enables the reader to compare the original with its later imitations and to contrast existing versions of the early text" (p. 9).

[45] Anne Birrell, pp. 154–56, translates and discusses two versions of this poem, the *gu ci* and one of Zhuo Wenjun's alleged authorship.

[46] Wu Jing, preface.

[47] Michael Riffaterre, *Semiotics of Poetry*, p. 99.

[48] The relationship between the *gu ci* and *ben ci* versions is often unclear, but in the case of "Bai tou yin," the *ben ci* version is that from the *Yutai xinyong*, while the *gu ci* is the *Song shu* text.

[49] A description of this transformation of Luofu at the hands of the literati poets can be found in my "From Saint to Singing Girl."

[50] See Richard Mather's discussion, pp. 64–66, of Shen Yue's participation in the genre.

[51] See Konishi Jin'ichi for an explication of the *Shinkokinshū* sequences.

Chapter 3

[1] This set, along with related poems, is found in *YFSJ* 38.555–63; most citations to the *YFSJ* hereafter are interlinear.

[2] Poem 5, by Lu Ji, is translated and discussed in the beginning of Chapter 4.

[3] Here and elsewhere in the study, I do not punctuate the translation of Chinese poems unless it is necessary for clarity.

[4] I have read *yi* (feather) for *ji* (hope).

[5] The Yellow and Luo Rivers are principal rivers of the northern China plain; the Central Mountains are just south of the capital city, Chang'an.

[6] See Owen, *Early T'ang*, pp. 22–24, where he translates and discusses this poem in its intratextual context, with a slightly different reading of the last line.

[7] "Formation Eight" (*ba chen tu*) and "Military Portals" (*liang he*) are technical military terms for deployment strategies and camp formations, respectively.

[8] Owen translates and discusses this poem, *Early T'ang*, pp. 21–24. My translation is heavily indebted to his.

[9] There is debate on how to read the closing of the poem, especially whether the abandoned woman speaks the last line to herself or to the husband. A review of that debate can be found in *Liang Han wenxue shi cankao ziliao*, pp. 574–75, whose conclusion I follow here.

[10] This more generalized and elevated type of language is what Fu Xuan adopts in his poem (no. 4), and, as is suggested by its alternate title, he may very well have had the first "Old Poem" in mind as much as the *gu ci* when he wrote his "Yin ma" poem (*YTXY*, p. 42, takes Fu Xuan's title from the first line of the poem, which is nearly verbatim from the first "Old Poem"). Fu's poem, which begins with a close rewording of the opening of no. 1, never ventures far from the theme of separation but diverges from most of the other poems in the series by its extensive use of more literary images.

[11] The invocation of this "meal motif" is rarer than we might imagine in early Chinese poetry; there is a similar usage in Mao no. 66 of the *Shi jing*.

[12] The "formality" of the main verb of the final line of this poem, *bao* (repay/retribute/reply), suggests an even stronger contrast between military duty and nutritive care, especially when we recall that this same verb answers the question, "How will I return my lord's favor?" in the closing couplet of poem 7. But there the object of *bao* is appropriately military: "[I shall repay] With horsehide coffins on the battle ground." I should note that there is a possible metaphoric extension of the couplet in Yu's poem, where the ultimate reference would be the fulfillment of political/ military duty. Even if that is so, the "meal motif" is still intratextual. Here two poetic moments reverberate as we read through the series, and that reverberation heightens the contrastive quality *within* the closing of Yu Shinan's poem.

[13] Under the influence of these letters and their invocation of the "meal motif" one might be inclined to assume a letter frame for the final lines of the first "Old Poem" as well.

[14] The Meng Jiangnü legend (taking winter clothes to her husband laboring on the Wall, she discovers he has died and been entombed in the Wall; her wailing brings forth his bones, which she buries properly) is found in Arthur Waley's *Stories and Ballads*, and is discussed by Wang Ch'iu-kuei. Marsha Wagner, pp. 94–96, describes a set of *ci* poems that center on the legend, whose relationship she calls *intertextual*.

[15] *Chu ci* 9.4a–4b; translation by David Hawkes, p. 225.

[16] Wu Jing, 2.2a, quoted in *YFSJ* 38.555.

[17] As mentioned above, the *Wen xuan* (chapters 30–31) and the *Yutai xinyong* (chapter 3) have sets of "*Ni gu*" ("In Imitation of the Old") poems, the most important by Lu Ji, as discussed below in Chapter 4.

[18] Diény, p. 3.

[19] This poem is also found in *WX* 27.1277–78; and *YTXY* 1.18. A translation appears in Frodsham, *Anthology*, pp. 1–2.

[20] *YTXY* 1.9–12, where several of the "Nineteen Old Poems" are attributed to Mei Sheng (Cheng) (ob. 141 B.C.).

Chapter 4

[1] The series is found in *YFSJ* 70.997–1001; translations available in Frodsham, *Anthology*, pp. 142–53. There are two counts of the poems, one at eighteen and another nineteen, the former being the most common.

[2] The actual number of poems in Bao Zhao's *yuefu* corpus differs according to the source. While Guo Maoqian lists thirty-seven poems, Bao's collected works (*Bao Canjun shizhu*) has forty-four *yuefu* titles in a corpus of about 140 poems. Kang-i Sun Chang, *Six Dynasties*, p. 81, says that Bao's *yuefu* poems "claim about one half of the entire corpus of his work," which suggests that there is an even more liberal counting. As I argue below, Bao's growing stature as a *yuefu* poet may have led to a gradual expansion of his *yuefu* corpus by enthusiastic editors.

[3] Sun Chang, pp. 80–83

[4] *Shi jing*, Mao no. 168, stanza 6.

[5] *Zhuang zi* 5.14a; *Han Fei zi* 1.5a. These references, as well as others mentioned in connection with Lu Ji's poems, are most often found in the notes to He Liquan edition and in Kang Rongji's annotation.

[6] In the notes to He Liquan (p. 12), and Kang Rongji (p. 139), but I am unable to locate the passage in the *Wu Yue chunqiu*.

[7] Cao Pi's poem referred to here appears under a different title in *YFSJ* 37.547.

[8] I assume the "red banners" (*chi chuang*) in line 4 were associated with the life of the immortals, as were the "magic mushrooms." This appears to be the locus classicus for the *chi chuang*.

[9] The "bamboo and fabric" (*zhu bo*) refers to writing surfaces, and according to the *Mo zi* (13.2b) is "where one's legacy is transmitted to his descendents."

[10] *Huainan zi* 1.9b, on the relative transience, therefore value, of an "inch of shadow": "The sage does not cherish a foot-long jade *bi*, but rather values an inch of shadow, since it is difficult to get and easy to lose."

[11] Liu Xie, p. 22.

[12] Zhong Rong, p. 5, cites these imitations as some of Lu's best work in five-syllable verse. Frodsham includes this poem in his *Anthology*, but notes (p. 89) that "a great deal of [Lu's] verse tends to be imitative, devoid of content, and given to rhetoric." This last fault is the one that repeatedly brought Liu Xie's condemnation (pp. 254, 362).

[13] The two sets of poems are both found in the *WX*, with these two poems at 29.1350 and 30.1428, respectively.

[14] Kang Rongji notes the *Li ji* origins of this association and (as does He Liquan, p. 46) Cao Zhi's use of it in another *yuefu* poem.

[15] In this line I accept variants *yong* and *yi* (already).

[16] Frodsham, p. 90, has a much different interpretation of this last line, which he translates as, "And homesickness cannot be borne for long." While I do not believe *li si* (parting thoughts/feelings) could be construed as "homesickness," an alternate reading might be, "My feelings on parting cannot be endured for long." Yet I still prefer the use of *shou* as "to protect," "to keep," especially since it allows this complicated intratextual reading.

[17] Zhong Rong, p. 177; on Bao Zhao's works collected in the *WX*, David Knechtges, p. 38, says the anthologist "seems to prefer Bao's poems on martial themes."

[18] *Sunflower Splendor*, p. 544.

[19] James J. Y. Liu, *The Interlingual Critic*, p. 33.

[20] Sun Chang, p. 104.

[21] Adapted from Sun Chang, pp. 96–97.

[22] Ibid., p. 96. I also deal with this poem at the end of Chapter 6 when I discuss Li Bo's imitation of it.

[23] This translation is adapted from John Marney, *Mulberries*, p. 62.

[24] Marney, *Liang Chien-wen Ti*, p. 112.

[25] Wagner, p. 62; cf. Marney, *Liang Chien-wen Ti*, p. 95.

[26] *Liang shi* 4.109

[27] Marney, *Liang Chien-wen Ti*, pp. 100–103, discusses this poetry.

[28] Ibid., p 81; *Liang shi* 49.691.

[29] The collected notes in Qian Zhonglian's edition of Bao's works (p. 69) contains various attempts to give the poem a biographical setting. I think the relative generative strength of the intratext is clear even with Bao's *yuefu* poems.

[30] The "minnows" (*tiao*) in this case are metaphors for Bao's home area of Chu, since the most famous *tiao* are those in the Zhuang zi's (also from Chu) speculation of the joy of swimming fishes (*Zhuang zi* 6,15a). By implication the cold North has few such minnows and few such pleasures for Bao.

[31] Lu Ji's "Boatman's Song" is first in the series with this boating theme (again we assume the Wei poem is only musically related to any original song by this name), but we can see that it could not have been anything but a very general model for Xiao, or even Bao Zhao; Lu is up to some very different kind of boating:

> Slowly springtime is about to close
> The day's air is mild and bountiful
> Great felicity fills the First Triad
> On Cleansing Day we wander along the Yellow River
> The dragon boats float with sea-phoenix prows
> From their plume banners hang variegated blossoms
> Capturing the wind they fly over the scenery
> Back and forth, freely they play in the waves
> A well-known tune rises on clear voices
> The oarsmen break into a boatsman song
> They cast their lines deep into the surging river
> Arrow-lines fly high into the purple clouds

YFSJ 40.593

[32] Adapted from Marney, *Mulberries*, p. 34.

[33] I might suggest here that as the genre develops, more and more *yuefu* poems foreground their musical associations with internal references either to music in general or to specific songs, such as this one. I would argue that those references do not indicate inherent musicality, but rather, because the poems feel the need to establish their conceptual musicality, they focus on it textually, unable to participate in it actually. Internal references to music will belatedly draw other poems (and groups of poems) into the genre to be canonized in the large collections made by Guo Maoqian and others, even when there is little else to support their inclusion.

[34] Wagner, p. 55.

[35] Sun Chang, pp. 153–54.

[36] It so happens that the oldest version of the "Water Chestnut" title is a set of seven poems (each in four five-syllable lines) by Bao Zhao. This set of poems is much in the spirit of, and now included in, the "Jiangnan nong." The first poem in the set is ample evidence of this:

> The swift vessel sails briskly by Cassia Inlet
> Resting our oars we dally at Pepper Pond
> Flute performances north of the placid Xiang
> "Water Chestnut Song" south of the clear Han

> *YFSJ* 51.739

While other poems in Bao's set of seven poems have more of a "travel" motif, those are more in the spirit of the *Chu ci* itineraria than the border poem expedition. Indeed, the entire sequence, including this poem, is filled with complex language and imagery from the *Chu ci*. Here is Bao at his most self-conscious, not only in those borrowings, but also in the self-referential song title and the very specific use of *nong* in the third line, which locates the poems in their larger intratextual grouping, the "Jiangnan nong."

[37] There is also a group of "Jiangnan" titles included in the *xianghe* poems (*YFSJ* 26.384, 385, 390), including "Jiangnan ge cai lian" ("You Can Pick Lotus South of the Yangtze"), which was originally the title of a poem collected by Shen Yue in his sixteen Han poems, from which Wu could have adapted his subtitle. This poem is now simply called "Jiangnan":

> You can pick lotus south of the Yangtze
> The lotus leaves are thick and lush

The fish play among the lotus leaves
The fish play east of the lotus leaves
The fish play west of the lotus leaves
The fish play south of the lotus leaves
The fish play north of the lotus leaves

YFSJ 26.384

This well-known folk song has generated several literati imitations in the *xianghe* poems, and it is not difficult to see how those imitations could have contributed to the inspiration for the later "Jiangnan nong" poems. In Wu Jing's note to the *xianghe* poems he specifically says that the Han folksong served as model not only for literati (including Xiao Gang's) imitations in that *xianghe* group but also for this new title and its subtitles in the *qingshang* category.

[38] Marney, *Liang Chien-wen Ti*, pp. 110–12, has a general discussion of Xiao Gang's treatment of this woman/boating/eroticism theme.

[39] This transformation is discussed in my "From Saint to Singing Girl." I also introduce some of these poems in the final chapter of this study.

Chapter 5

[1] I have not sought scientific accuracy in the translations of the various botanical references here, but I have tried to maintain strict consistency in the many poems in this chapter, not only for the names of trees, but also for the various conventional terms and attributes. I do this to aid the recognition of shared elements in the intratext, often at the expense of comfortable phrasing. Thus, whenever the term *yangliu* appears I translate it as "weeping willow," *liu* as "willow," and *yang* as "poplar."I have used the term "bough" only when the term *zhi* actually appears; *tiao* is always rendered "tendrils," *chui* as "droop/ing," *lou* as "[upper] chamber," etc. The verb *zhe* is always rendered "break off," *pan* as "twist," and *panzhe* as "twist off."

[2] In Shen Yue's *Song shu* the title of this poem is given as "Mo mo," with "Zhe yangliu" as the tune name, designated as the *air* by Diény, p. 138.

[3] This translation is adapted from Frodsham, *Murmuring Stream*, p. 110.

[4] Since the literary "palace lady" was mostly the creation of male fantasies, the presence of children would not have been an appropriate association. Children

are very much present in the early woman-oriented folk poems of the genre, such as in "Dongmen xing" and "Fu bing xing."

[5] In the latter part of the genre, especially those parts of it influenced by the poetics of the southern Six Dynasties, we see an increasing number of true sequences (i.e., sets of poems under a given title written consciously as sequences by a single author). I conclude this chapter with such an example. It is interesting to note that a large number of the problematic *xin* (new) *yuefu* of the Middle and Late Tang exists in such sets, suggesting that intrasequence intratextuality might mark their membership to the redefined genre. I deal with the "new *yuefu*" poems in slightly different terms in the final chapter of this study.

[6] This poem, and the sequence to which it belongs, are deeply immersed in the eroticism of southern customs and language. Here that eroticism is seen in the conflation of the "pure body" of the rice and that of the woman. She uses that rice to make "sweet buns," which in the original *(jiuzi zhong)* are a type of wrapped cake associated with a Buddhist fertility goddess.

[7] The first four lines of the "Mulan" poem are the same as the third poem of the second set; a translation is available in Frodsham, *Anthology*, pp. 104–6.

[8] While the horse is conventionally associated with the man, here and occasionally elsewhere the horse seems to stand nearly as a symbol for the woman—the possible sexual overtones of that relationship remain totally unexplored, as far as I know.

[9] The first poem in this two-poem set (translated and discussed below) does mention the willow by name, so if one reads them as an integrated set, we do have a named willow presence. But I treat these two poems separately, and in reverse order.

[10] The term *liao* seems to have had both meanings ("for a while" and "to rely on") from a very early date, there being pre-Han evidence for both. The original meaning of the term was "sound in the ears," which was used as a phonetic loan for "for a while." The meaning "to rely on" seems to derive from another loan usage (the modern *lai)*. All this information is contained in the *Shuowen jiezi* entry.

[11] The descriptive *yiyi*'s first occurrence is in the *Shih jing*, Mao no. 167.6, which is also concerned with parting and separation, although there is no evidence that the willow had its "retaining" connotations at this early date:

When we left the willows were *lush and luxuriant*
When we returned the snow fell hard and heavy
The road we took went on far and forever
We were thirsty and we were hungry
Our hearts were so pained with grief
But no one understood our sorrow

From this first meaning of "thick," or its alternative reading of "soft," the *yiyi* binome then gathers around willow trees throughout the tradition. At the same time, drawing from another semantic tradition, it builds associations of the sorrow of separation, beginning with Wang Yi's (fl. A.D. 130) lines, "With a sigh I look back at the Zhanghua palace, / And my mind was sick longing *[yiyi]* for it" *(Chu ci* 17.12b; translation Hawkes, *Songs*, p. 316). Yet behind all these associations is always the original meaning of *yi*, "to rely on, to cling," and thus in these poems I usually translate it, at the risk of overtranslating, as "close and clinging."

[12] Since there is no way to date this poem, it also could have been written before Chen Shubao's captivity in the North; my arguments for a biographical overlay to the intratext are therefore somewhat tentative.

[13] This group of sixty-six poems is found in *YFSJ* 32.475–33.490.

[14] These poems belong to Guo Maoqian's *jindai qu ci* ("Lyrics for Recent Tunes") category, a questionable musical grouping that he defines as "miscellaneous tunes from the Sui and Tang period"—but he also has poems under the "miscellaneous categories" *(zaqu ge* and *zageyao)* from the Sui-Tang period; thus, his seemingly logical definition falls apart on closer inspection.

[15] This set of poems is riddled with allusions and references, including a number of whose significance is unclear in this context. Generally there are a number of references to places near or in Chang'an, especially those associated with imperial life. The "Tao house" of the pentultimate poem refers to the poet Tao Qian (132–94), who wrote a fictional autobiography called the "Biography of Mr. Five Willows" (the willows were said to stand in front of Tao's house). I assume Mr. Shi of the last poem is Shi Chong (249–300), a wealthy official of the Jin dynasty who was known for his elegant residence, as well as for his womanizing and other hedonistic habits.

Chapter 6

[1] Yan Yu, *Canglang shihua*, pp. 153–55. Guo Shaoyu's notes to the second passage quoted here are a rich source of traditional comparisons of Li and Du, most of which are along these lines.

[2] Arthur Cooper, *Li Po and Tu Fu*, pp. 15–20, makes this *yin-yang* comparison, but considers Li as *yin* and Du as *yang*, presumably because Li is more "Taoist," therefore *yin*, than Du. A similar, but better wrought, comparison is found in Seaton and Cryer's introduction, esp. pp. ix–xi.

[3] Owen, *Great Age*, p. 188.

[4] The basic information, including the favorite legends of Li's life, can be found in several sources, but Elling Eide's "On Li Po" is by far the most sophisticated analysis in English. Owen's *Great Age* chapter 8 on the poet is best in the explication of the problem of poetic persona. Much of my argument is derived from these two sources.

[5] Owen, *Great Age*, p. 184.

[6] The various *yuefu* poem counts given in this section are based primarily on Guo Maoqian's corpus (by number of titles, not poems). Comparative figures for the poets' entire corpora are drawn from either the *Quan Tang shi* or standard collected works. There necessarily is some degree of variation in these counts, but the general configurations described are certainly accurate. Shinada Kumiko, "Ri Haku no gakufu ni tsuite," p. 19, has a convenient chart of numbers (titles and poems) and percentages of Li's *yuefu* poems by category, three of which account for the majority of Li's *yuefu* poems: *zaqu* poems (38 titles, 45 poems) account for 28% of his corpus; *xianghe* poems (27 titles, 32 poems), 20%; *qingshang* (15 titles, 18 poems), 11%.

[7] Owen, *Great Age*, p. 119, says that "during the Tang, Li Bo was best known for his *yuefu* and songs: not only were they the most widely anthologized of his works, they also occurred in anecdotes and comments about his poetry far in excess of their proportions in his present collection."

[8] Pauline Yu, *The Reading of Imagery*, pp. 190–91, discusses Li's poem in its intratextual setting, showing how much it differs from its models.

[9] Owen, *Great Age*, p. 135.

[10] Quoted in Wang Qi, *Li Taibai quan ji*, p. 338. Throughout this chapter I have consulted Wang's standard edition and annotation of Li's works, especially in regard to literary allusions and textual problems. While I do not provide a complete annotation of each poem, I do gloss what I consider necessary and relevant information from these annotations in my notes and text.

[11] Li has another *yuefu* poem where reference to the Ruoye stream is specifically linked with Xi Shi; see *YFSJ* 45.653.

[12] I follow Wang Qi's (p. 340) emendation of line 6; Wang also gives information about the military forces "White Snow" and "Yellow Clouds" in his notes, having no information about the latter other than citations of usage. I assume the "sea" *(hai)* of the sixth line refers to the border area (either the sea of sand or the large inland lake, known as Qinghai). My rendering of line 2 is tentative at best.

[13] Wang Qi, p. 340.

[14] While Wang Qi, pp. 269–70, has a number of notes to this poem, especially regarding the various place names associated with the northwest border area (Loulan, Yanzhi, Flowing Sands), as well as a note on the "Hun star" (whose periodic appearance was linked with the tribe's uprising—also see "Chu zi Ji bei men xing" below), he does not mention Li's intertextual reference in line 8, "Once out of the gate they don't look back." This must derive from the old *yuefu* poem "Dongmen xing," which tells the story of a disaffected man's abandonment of his family for a military/criminal life. The poem opens "Once out of the east gate, He gave no thought of [did not look to] returning" *(YFSJ* 37.547–48).

[15] The "border poem" is closely associated with *yuefu* poetry and the largest set of such poems are the "Cong jun xing" in *YFSJ* chapters 32–33, as I mentioned in the previous chapter. Guo Maoqian (24.352) quotes a *gu ci* of the Roan Stallion poem, in which there is an intertextual reference to the "Cong jun xing." Below we will see another example of Li's border poetry ("Chu zi Ji bei men xing"), which is also linked with the "Cong jun" poems.

[16] This type of Hun girl can be seen in another horse poem by Li, his "White-nosed Sorrel" ("Bai bi gua"):

> A silver saddle for the white-nosed sorrel mare
> By the green pool its mud guard is elegant brocade

As flowers fall in the fine mist and spring wind
He cracks his whip to go join the Hun beauty for a drink

YFSJ 25.373

[17] A complete description of these horses and their position in Han culture is found in E. G. Pulleyblank, "Chinese and the Indo-Europeans."

[18] These poems are orginally recorded, accompanied by their appropriate contexts, in the *Han shu*, 22.1060–61, quoted along with other Han sources in Guo Maoqian's notes. The poems themselves contain various references to the west and northwest border regions of China.

[19] This translation is adapted from Eide, pp. 391–94. Obviously the poem is filled with literary allusions, some of which are intratextual with the Han poems and all of which are explained by Wang Qi. The significance of many is clear from the context, and I comment on others in the following discussion. Among the notable ones not mentioned in my discussion below are: in line 7, *Yan* and *Yue* are terms for the most northeastern and southern reaches of China, respectively; lines 10–13 draw on highly metaphorical language to describe the horses—the "thirsty crow sprinkler" was a type of street sprinkler of the Han, the Heavenly Horses were thought to sweat blood (see Pulleyblank); Han Fengzi, Bo Le, and Tian Zifang were all noted for their ability to perceive the qualities of a good horse.

[20] Eide, pp. 395–96.

[21] Yan Yanzhi's "Zhe bai ma fu" is found in *WX* 14.621–31; the *Xiang ma jing* is no longer extant, but two editions are noted in the bibliography of the *Sui shu*, 29.1039.

[22] Li's poem does perhaps suffer from an overzealous incorporation of material, especially in the later part of the poem, as if he, like Zhou Danlong (644–674), copied freely and without much design from an encyclopedia entry—a weakness shared by many of Li's juvenile *fu*.

[23] Qu Yuan is the arch-unappreciated poet in Chinese literature, and his masterpiece, the "Li sao" (in the *Chu ci)* has always been read as an allegorical and elaborate plea for understanding from his ruler.

[24] Li borrows the salt wagon metaphor from the *Zhan guo ce*, where it represents the misuse or disregard of a person's true nature or talent. In that story it is Bo

Le who comes to the horse's rescue, thus the reference to him two lines later. There does not appear to have been any previous usage of the metaphor with the Heavenly Horses, however.

[25] Owen, *Great Age*, p. 111.

[26] This poem is contained only in the notes to Cao Pi's poem, suggesting that Guo Maoqian did not feel that it was complete and/or not actually the generative *gu ci* of the intratextual series.

[27] Cui Bao, *Gu jin zhu*, 2.4b; quoted in *YFSJ* 38.563.

[28] *YFSJ* 38.563. Wu's comment is slightly ambiguous; it may mean only that the subject of the poem is one of Han times, but generally such a comment in the traditional criticism would assume the composition was also Han.

[29] The "star of farming" *(nong xiang)* appeared in the first month of the lunar calender and marked the offical beginning of agricultural activities in southern China. The Golden Phoenix Dais was built in the Northern Wei period to replace the Bronze Sparrow Pavilion mentioned in Chapter 2 in association with Cao Cao, and thus had appropriate imperial connotations.

[30] There are a myriad literary allusions of varying importance in this poem (all duly cited by Wang Qi), a number of which refer to proper brotherly behavior. The "sparrows of Huan mountain" refers to young birds being separated from their mother, who was terribly grieved by their loss and called in a distinctly plaintive way. The most important allusion is in lines 18–21, which tell the story of the Tian brothers (incidentally, the same *tian* of the title) who were to divide up the family assets, including the purple thorn tree that stood in the courtyard of their home. When the tree heard about this plan, it dried up and died. Seeing this omen the brothers changed their minds, whereupon the tree came back to life. The "tree of reciprocal yielding" (which is from Wang Qi's variant of the line) that is mentioned in conjunction with this story is from another popular source that says that there was a certain tree whose east and west sides took turns flourishing every other year, thereby (it is understood) yielding to and assisting the other side. Orion and Lucifer were said to be brothers-turned-stars who were separated so they would not fight—the image is also used to describe separated lovers. Guzhu and Yanling are places associated with famous men who modestly yielded power to their brothers. The "foot of cloth song" in the last line was a children's ditty that referred to unfilial behavior between brothers.

[31] Cui Bao, 2.2b; quoted in *YFSJ* 26:377.

[32] My translation follows the variant line given in Guo Maoqian's notes.

[33] The syntax of the first two lines is elliptical at best, leaving me perplexed about the exact nature of the scene described. The (indestructible) Metal Dike *(jin ti)* is associated with metropolises, especially the capital of Chang'an, but how it divides (or perhaps is divided by) the hawsers is unclear. The "white horse" of the second line is also seen in Liu Xiaowei's poem, where it is a sacrificial animal (?), but how and why it crosses (with) the lotus boats here is also unclear. Ther verb "cross" *(du)* means to cross water, and is the same as appears in all poems about the old man "crossing."

[34] The dragon gate is where the Yellow River passes through the mountains in Shanxi, turns, and enters the central plain of China. It is said that a fish that makes it up through this section of river becomes a dragon. Yu is the mythological hero/emperor who brings the flood under control by carving the rivers of China, thereby draining the land. He served Emperor Yao in this capacity and was so devoted to his task that he passed by his own house three times without entering to see his crying child.

[35] This translation is adapted from Frodsham, *Anthology*, pp. 145-46; and from Owen, *Great Age*, pp. 141–42.

[36] This translation differs only slightly from Owen's, *Great Age*, p. 142, which has supplementary notes, p. 373.

[37] *YFSJ* 70.1001.

[38] Wang Yunxi, *Li Taibai yanjiu*, p. 212.

[39] Owen, *Great Age*, p. 141–42.

[40] Eide discusses the importance of moon imagery to Li's identity, and Wong Siu-kit, "The Genius of Li Po," has a section dedicated to the "Woman and Moon in Li Po's Poetry" (pp. 7–22), which includes discussion of this poem, but not within the context of *yuefu* poetry.

[41] The principal consort of the King of Wei was promoted because of her beautiful hair; in the state of Zhao the queen was said to be favored because she was skilled at the "flying swallow dance."

[42] Wang Qi, p. 259. In Wang's collection Li's title is rendered slightly differently, "Gu lang yue xing" ("The Bright Moon of Antiquity").

[43] Archer Yi's mythological accomplishments center on his shooting down nine of the ten suns when they inadvertently all appeared at once (there were ten days in the Chinese "week," thus ten suns). The term for the moon, "essence of yin" *(yinjing)*, appears to be Li's invention, as does the conceit implied here.

[44] Xianyang, which both Bao and Li use as the name of the capital, is an archaic but common term (it was the capital area during the Qin period). *Guo shang* (country's fallen soldiers) is a term derived originally from the "Guo shang" poem of the *Chu ci*, a tribute to soldiers who died for their country, which David Hawkes calls "one of the most beautiful laments for fallen soldiers in any language" *(Songs*, p. 117).

[45] These poems are found in *YFSJ* 76.1072–73.

[46] Wong Siu-kit, p. 51. *Qingning* is the variant as it appears in Wang Qi, p. 201.

[47] Unfortunately there is no way to understand this weeping *(bei ti)* as the result of sexual passion, only of grief; if one could, then there would be a simpler but more provocative progression of the action depicted here.

[48] Wang Qi, p. 201.

Chapter 7

[1] The most successful of the post–Li Bo *yuefu* poets was perhaps Li He (790–816), whose poetic corpus includes a large number of the *yuefu* poems. There is some problem counting the number of *yuefu* poems in Li He's corpus; I count forty-four titles (several with multiple entries) in a corpus of approximately 250 poems. Li He's early death accounts for the relatively small poetic corpus and may (as I argue in the conclusion to this chapter) account for the relatively high percentage of *yuefu* poems. Frodsham's *Li Ho* is a translation of the entire corpus, prefaced by a substantial introduction and accompanied by extensive notes. Li He has a voice nearly the match of Li Bo's, to whom he is often compared, but that voice is of a different timbre, and thus can be heard over the strong echoes of Li Bo's accomplishment in the genre. In the subsequent centuries there are occasional reengagements of the intratextual nature of the genre, including Yang Weizhen (1296–1307), whom I mention below (n. 6), and Liu Ji's (1311–75) corpus of 265 *yuefu* poems, on which William Nienhauser comments: "The *yuefu*, though on traditional themes . . . are unique

in that they include philosophic twists to the conventional subjects" (*Indiana Companion*, p. 575). There is even a small selection of poems by the contemporary poet Yang Mu that engages the poetry in high-modernist ways; Yang calls these "new *yuefu* poems" (*You ren*, pp. 111–53).

2 Frankel, "High Literary Genre." This essay differs from Frankel's earlier studies in that it concentrates on the literati poets, but it is limited to the earliest literati associated with the genre (some of which I consider "proto-*yuefu*" poets). Unfortunately I did not have an opportunity to read the essay until this study was nearly complete.

3 Ibid., pp. 259, 270.

4 Ibid., p. 255.

5 The inspiration for this typology, including the number of types and their inventive names, is Harold Bloom's *The Anxiety of Influence*, not Guo Maoqian. Here I also draw from Stuart Sargent's study of Song poetry, which derives from Bloom as well.

6 *YFSJ* 28.410–23; the set, considered in its widest range, is composed of over forty poems under several different titles.

7 See Owen's entry, "Yang Weichen," in *The Indiana Companion*, pp. 917–18. He characterizes Yang's *yuefu* collection this way: "This work consists of 416 *yuefu* on gods, figures from legends and history, and set *yuefu* situations [intratexts]. These are sensual, often wildly imaginative songs that belong more in the tradition of Li He and Wen Tingyun than in that of the original *yuefu*."

8 While I do not discuss them in this study, there are a number of cases where the poems of different provenance or authors seem to be nearly exact reproductions of each other. This may involve misattributions or variants of the same poem. In addition to these obvious "translations," there are more subtle ones where the literati poet "translates" the relatively simple language of the original into his more elevated vocabulary. Fu Xuan, whose poem I discuss below, was prone to this form of intratextuality.

9 The transformation of Luofu's resolve in these poems is a central concern of my "From Saint to Singing Girl" essay; I shall not repeat that argument here.

10 Yang Weizhen, 1.4a. For an explanation of the reference to the "birds of Huan Mountain," a motif introduced into the intratext by Li Bo, see Chapter 6, n. 30.

[11] *Nan shi* 4.109.

[12] There is a longer version of this poem in the *Wenyuan yinghua*, 208.1287, which includes an ending in which Luofu and the governor engage in an elaborate repartee (translated by Marney, *Mulberries*, pp. 14-15). I have taken my lines 11–12 from that version, but have not included its final lines, which are not part of the "ornamentation" of the poem, but do tie the poem closer to the intratext. I suspect that line 9 is corrupt, and perhaps Marney's emendation is correct: "To avoid stumbling she fixes the hem on her gown."

[13] Yang Weizhen, 2.15a.

[14] This connection is also discussed at length in my essay on the poems. In the Qiu Hu story his wife has a confrontation similar to Luofu's, except that her illicit suitor is her own husband, Qiu Hu, who does not recognize her (nor she him) after a long absence. She resolutely rejects his overtures, and then commits suicide after discovering his identity (in shame for him).

[15] This term and these texts are discussed by Victor Mair in his *Tunhuang Popular Narratives*.

[16] *YFSJ* 28.412. Cao Cao's nonengagement of the intratext is, of course, common since he is one of the "proto-*yuefu*" poets. Commenting on Cao's "Qiu Hu" poems, Frankel remarks, "The title 'Qiu Hu xing' derives from a story about a man named Qiu Hu which has nothing to do with Cao Cao's two poems" ("High Literary Genre," p. 273).

[17] *YFSJ* 28.414. Other poems that follow Bao's in this titular subset include ample contact with the Luofu intratext (such as Fu Zai's, which I offer above as an example of *ji* intratextuality), but Bao's does not do so. Thus, the negation may have been entirely the product of Guo Maoqian's inclusion of the poem in the Luofu set. But we can see how once Guo had included Fu Zai's truly intratextual poem, he would have been forced to include all the others in the subset, including Bao's "generative" poem.

[18] The Luofu set includes "Moshang sang" poems by Cao Cao and Cao Pi, a wandering immortal poem and a military traveler poem, respectively (28.412). These are preceded (28.411) by an unusual poem of the same title with the notation, "Copied from the *Chu ci*" ("*Chu ci* chao"). Indeed, this is a version of the "Shan gui" ("Mountain Spirit") poem of that pre-Han text. The "copy" reproduces the first fourteen lines nearly verbatim from the *Chu ci* poem, but always with the *xi* particle deleted; then it skips eleven lines, and closes with a

relatively free variation on the last couplet of the original. This is certainly one of the most striking examples of the musical associations of an early title, which would later be developed thematically. In all three of these early poems I assume that the musicality to which their shared title refers unites them.

Guo concludes this set with the "sun" poems, whose longer title is derived from the opening line of the Han "Moshang sang." The poems cited by Xu Boyang and Yin Mou have this longer title, while Xiao Hui's poem has the shorter title. Li Bo also has one by the shorter title, but it is entirely devoted to a celebration of the sun (similar to his "Moon" poem cited in Chapter 6), and thus is a retroactive, if not authorial, negation.

[19] The prosodic rules for the Chinese regulated verse are extremely complicated, involving a set number of lines (eight), either five or seven syllables per line (used exclusively of each other), end rhyme on the even lines, parallelism in the inner two couplets, and a strict tonal (similar to stress) pattern for each line that is determined by its position in the poem. A succinct description of these rules, especially the last, can be found in the introduction to A. C. Graham's *Poems of the Late T'ang*. A more elaborate appreciation can be found in Kao Yu-kung's "Aesthetics" essay.

[20] Owen argues for the nonfictionality of *shi* poetry, especially in *Traditional Chinese Poetry*, p. 15 et passim, and for the fictionality of *yuefu* poetry, especially in *Great Age*, pp. 9–10.

[21] Wang Li, p. 304.

[22] Owen, *Great Age*, pp. 8–9.

[23] Owen, *Early Tang*, p. 7.

[24] Ibid., p. 8.

[25] The *ge* in the *WX* are found in chapter 28, following the *yuefu* poems, both of which are a subtype of *shi* poetry. The *gexing* songs are found as a separate section in chapters 331–50 of *Wenyuan yinghua*; the *yuefu* poems, are part of the *shi* category, in chapters 192–211. The set of *shi* poems and the set of *gexing* poems are both organized according to (although not exactly the same) topics, with *yuefu* being one of the *shi* topics. The *yuefu* poems are themselves organized according to title, in the same way as they are in the *YFSJ*.

[26] As in the *YFSJ*, there are occasional isolated *yuefu* poems in the *Wenyuan yinghua*, and within the *gexing* poems there are a few titular sets, the largest

being a group of eight poems with the title, "Huaisuo shangren caoshu ge" (338: 1742–44). There is also one cross-reference (335.1730) from the *gexing* poems to the *yuefu* (the title is given in the *gexing* poems, but the reader is referred to the *yuefu* chapter where the poem actually appears). Some poems that are included in Guo Maoqian's *YFSJ* are designated as *gexing* by the *Wenyuan yinghua*, such as Du Fu's "Bing che xing." Interestingly, Du Fu's poem is designated a "new *yuefu* poem" (*xin yuefu*) by Guo Maoqian; as is common with that category, it stands alone with that title, thus the generic distinction of intratextuality is not applicable, which allows it to be easily considered a "song." Pursuit along these lines might be fruitful in reaching a better understanding of the *gexing* and *xin yuefu* genres.

[27] *The Indiana Companion*, p. 549.

[28] Wagner discusses the generative "intertextuality" of this contact, but one wonders if it might be more accurate to consider this as another type of "intratextuality."

[29] *YFSJ* 90.1262–63.

[30] Bo Juyi, 3.52.

[31] The expression *bu wei wen er zuo* could also read as "not written for literariness," (as *wen* is used above), but here we should understand *wen* in opposition to the actual (i.e., nonfictional) world.

[32] These rhapsodies have been translated by David Knechtges in the first volume of his *Wen xuan*.

[33] Owen, *Great Age*, p. 186.

[34] Ibid., pp. 109–10.

[35] It is a commonplace that Du Fu showed great respect for the somewhat older Li Bo, including writing several laudatory poems for Li. (Owen has an interesting, but very subversive, reading of one of those poems in his *Traditional Chinese Poetry* [pp. 211–18]). Li did not seem to return those feelings, however, tending to shower praise on the more marginal members of his community, such as Taoist adepts.

Bibliographic Note

This Note is offered as a supplement to the textual information contained in the main body of the study, especially in Chapters 2 and 7, although I have repeated myself on occasion when it seemed best for clarity. Needless to say, this Note is not exhaustive on textual questions or secondary literature, but it should provide the student with a convenient point of departure. The list of Works Cited should also be consulted for other relevant texts and studies. The entries for *yuefu* poetry and the *Yuefu shiji* in the *Indiana Companion* (pp. 961–65) both provide excellent bibliographic information. Anne Birrell's discussion and description of the *Yuefu shiji* and its textual sources (including several illustrative appendices) are well done and should be consulted first. Her bibliography is also extensive, although it obviously mirrors her narrow perspective on the genre.

All study of *yuefu* poetry is necessarily centered on Guo Maoqian's (fl. 1080) *Yuefu shiji*, a definitive compilation with few textual problems, especially since it exists in a relatively complete Song edition. Almost nothing is known about Guo Maoqian, other than a sketchy family tree and approximate dates (see the entry for his text in the *Siku quan shu zongmu tiyao*, 4146–47; but compare the entry in the *Zhi zhai shulu jieti*, 15:15a)—Birrell (p. 8) includes a summary of the biographical information contained in Masuda. We know that the *Yuefu shiji* represents the culmination of *yuefu* anthologies and studies that began in the late Six Dynasties and continued through the Tang, of which few are extant. A short list of *yuefu*-related titles can be found in the *Sui shu* bibliography (35.1085), including an eight-*juan* volume called *Gu yuefu* (*Old Yuefu*)—note how these titles are intermingled with "song" (*ge*) titles. Also note the list of lost (no doubt from Xiao Gang's infamous burning of the Imperial Library) titles that were extant in the Liang, which is attached to the *Wu sheng ge ciqu* entry. The *Tang shu* bibliography (47.2080) contains several volumes from the *Sui shu* list, but also adds a few new ones, most notably an anthology edited by Xie Lingyun. There are also several related volumes listed under the

"Music" section of the bibliography (46.1975). The Song *Zhi zhai shulu jieti* has only one listing besides that for Guo Maoqian's anthology. The student of *yuefu* poetry today should base his work on two important editions of the *Yuefu shiji*. The first is the above-mentioned Song edition that was photo-reprinted in the 1955, Wenxue guji kanxing she (Peking) edition (with some lacunae filled in from a Yuan text). More importantly one should see this text in the *Gafu shishō no kenkyū* of 1970, where it is accompanied by several useful bibliographic aids (the text unfortunately is reduced in size by fifty percent). For specific textual questions and day-to-day work, the second important edition, a 1979 typeset (standard characters), fully punctuated, and collated edition by Zhonghua shuju (Peking) supersedes all others. This is especially so in its collation of texts from a wide variety of sources, not only from other editions—the Ming edition by Mao Jin being the other important one (reproduced in the *Sibu congkan*)—but from other anthologies and individual collections as well. Variants are footnoted, and emendations marked. The punctuation is full and accurate, including all types of end-stops and quotation marks; this punctuation extends to Guo Maoqian's introductory notes, an extremely valuable source of information that is made more so by this work. The only place I have noticed any potential problem with the punctuation is in the delineation of text citations in Guo's notes; it is often difficult to tell where the citation ends and Guo begins, which leads to difficult judgment calls. In any case, this edition makes working with the collection infinitely easier.

Both of the Tokyo and Peking (1979) editions have author and title indices, which are essential for efficient use of the anthology. The Tokyo edition indexes by Japanese pronunciation; the Peking one is by total stroke count. While the student may find the Chinese system easier to use, the Japanese indices seem to be more accurate (but problems are actually fairly rare in the Chinese ones). The Peking edition has a very nice introductory note describing the text and related questions (this is better than Yoshikawa Kōjirō's preface in the Tokyo edition), and the table of contents provides an excellent overview of the text, especially as an insight into the way Guo Maoqian and the tradition viewed the intratextuality of the genre. The Tokyo edition provides, however, other research aids that are truly beyond expectations. First, it includes photocopies of prefaces to all other important editions, including the one to the Chinese 1955 photocopy (a very thin affair), and even Wang Yunxi's bibliographic note (but, of course, not to the more recent Peking edition). More importantly the text includes a great deal of information on pre-Song works related to *yuefu* poetry. It does this by listing all books (163) cited by Guo Maoqian in his notes (these are listed by Japanese pronunciation). Following each entry that is not to a well known, extant text one finds detailed bibliographic information and a note on other sources for given entries (usually in various bibliographies or encyclopedias); to all of this there are occasionally supplementary remarks. The value of the information is enhanced by a chart in which each cited text is listed with *every* poem associated with it, which is especially useful in charting the changing parameters of the genre throughout the centuries.

As I have indicated before, Guo Maoqian's notes themselves are a valuable source of information, especially as they cite other texts; but they are not definitive since they are encyclopedic and often suspend judgment between conflicting citations. There are entries for *yuefu* (usually under music, not literature) in several of the encyclopedias; these also have a great deal of undigested information—the *Tong zhi* entry (*juan* 25) seems particularly full. There are also the "Monographs on Music" in various dynastic histories, particularly the *Song shu* and the *Tang shu*, that are sources for information on *yuefu*. Most of this work, as well as other areas of traditional *yuefu* scholarship, is concerned with typology, nomenclature, and musicality, a direction of research that I believe will always be relatively unproductive, considering the problems of music and diachronic change that I discuss in Chapter 2.

As supplementary texts the student should consider Zuo Keming's parallel anthology and Wu Jing's collection of essays, which are so often cited by Guo Maoqian. There is also Yang Weizhen's personal collection of the early Ming that is an interesting anomaly in the post-Song literature. Parenthetically, one should be reminded that after the Song the term *yuefu* is most often used to refer to *ci* poetry, not to the intratextual *yuefu* discussed here.

The modern secondary literature on *yuefu* poetry is substantial in volume, if not always in critical weight. The standard literary history is still Lo Genze's, and all others derive from it; Xiao Difei is useful as another interpretation (but does not include the Tang). In critical essays, Wang Yunxi stands alone as the most reasoned and well-informed, especially compared to most of the nonsense that fills the *Yuefu shi yanjiu lunwen ji* volume. There is some interesting work coming out in Taiwan, such as Zhang Xiurong's work on mid-Tang *yuefu* poetry. Most is, however, rather repetitious of the work of the thirties; Qi Tingting's work distinguishes itself for its rigor in a limited scope. In Japanese, Masuda is voluminous and occasionally innovative; his opening essay on the definition of *yuefu* was especially useful to me. Frankel is the standard treatment in English, especially in the promotion of the "oral" background of the poetry— he has a number of studies of individual poems, etc. that complement his general essay. Birrell's work is much in this vein. Frankel's most recent essay, "High Literary Genre," develops a slightly different line of thought and is well worth considering. The *Indiana Companion* entries (pp. 961–65) by Chou Ying-hsiung provide a convenient, conventional description of the genre and the anthology, but are now superseded by Birrell's lengthy introduction. Stephen Owen's passing remarks on the genre in his two monographs on Tang poetry are always useful, especially since he tends to bring a fresh perspective to genre. Jean-Pierre Diény, *Origines*, offers an interesting reformation of the importance of the poetry and is probably the best extended work on the subject in a Western language. I do not have information on the bibliography in German or the Slavic languages, but do not sense it is substantial (there is Gimm's huge translation of Duan Anjie's [fl. 895] *Yuefu zalu*, which is a text on music, not poetry).

Modern anthologies of *yuefu* poetry are all flawed, perhaps necessarily, by the suppression of the poetry's intratextual context and the propensity to over-represent the "folk" side of the genre. The standard and rigorously annotated anthology of the early poems is Huang Jie's *Han Wei yuefu fengjian*; a broader treatment is found in Yu Guanying's anthology (which has particularly clear and helpful notes for the student), and there are other similar volumes available from Taiwan. Wang Zhong's collection represents the most balanced selection but is very thin on annotation, often including only the *Yuefu shiji* text (and not punctuated as fully as the 1979 Peking edition). Considering the availability and quality of the recent Peking four-volume edition, the student would best acquire it—it is also available in a two-volume pirated edition from Taiwan, hardbound but with paper of somewhat lesser quality than the original.

Since the completion of this study, two new *yuefu* anthologies have appeared that should also be consulted. While neither presents the poems in their intratextual context, both do offer a more balanced view of the genre. The first, *Yuefu shi jianshang cidian* (Peking: Zhonghua, 1990), contains a relatively full selection of the literati poems, including those from the post-Song period. This volume also provides the student with extensive annotations and paraphrases of the poems. The second work, *Yuefu shixuan* (Taipei: Zhengzhong, 1991), covers a similar range of primary materials but does not annotate as extensively as the Peking volume. While both anthologies still privilege the "folk" poetry associated with the genre, they do begin to give the literati poems more their due.

Works Cited

Abbreviations

SBBY: *Sibu beiyao* 四部備要.
SBCK: *Sibu congkan* 四部叢刊.
WX: *Wen xuan* 文選.
YFSJ: *Yuefu shiji* 樂府詩集. (see Guo Maoqian)
YTXY: *Yutai xinyong* 玉臺新詠.

Works

Allen, Joseph Roe, III. "Chih Yü's *Discussions of Different Types of Literature*: A Translation and Brief Comment." *Parerga* 3 (1976), 3–36.

——. "Chinese Script and Lexicography: Pedagogical Notes." *Journal for the Chinese Language Teachers Association*, 19.3 (1984), 35–66.

——. "Early Chinese Narrative Poetry: The Definition of a Tradition." Diss. University of Washington, Seattle, 1982.

——. "From Saint to Singing Girl: The Rewriting of the Lo-fu Narrative in Literati Poetry." *Harvard Journal of Asiatic Studies*, 48.2 (1988), 321–61.

——. "The Myth Studies of Wen Yi-to: A Question of Methodology." *Tamkang Review*, 8.2 (1982), 137–60.

——. "Records of the Historian." *Masterworks of Asian Literature in a Comparative Perspective*. Columbia University Press, forthcoming.

Analects. Arthur Waley, trans. London: George Allen & Unwin, Ltd., 1938.

Bao Zhao 鮑照. *Bao Canjun shizhu* 鮑參軍詩注. Taipei: Shijie shuju, 1962.

Bate, W. (Walter) J. (Jackson). *The Burden of the Past and the English Poet*. Cambridge: Harvard University Press, 1970.

Birch, Cyril, ed. *Anthology of Chinese Literature: From Early Times to the Fourteenth Century*. New York: Grove Press, Inc., 1967.

Birrell, Anne. *Popular Songs and Ballads of Han China*. London: Unwin Hyman, 1988.

Bo Juyi 白居易. *Bo Juyi ji* 白居易集. Peking: Zhonghua shuju, 1979.

Bloom, Harold. *The Anxiety of Influence: A Theory of Poetry*. Oxford: Oxford University Press, 1973.

Canlang shihua, see Yan Yu.

Chang Kwang-chih. *Shang Civilization*. New Haven: Yale University Press, 1980.

Chang, Kang-i Sun. *Six Dynasties Poetry*. Princeton: Princeton University Press, 1986.

Chaves, Jonathan. "Not the Way of Poetry: The Poetics of Experience in the Sung Dynasty." *Chinese Literature: Essays, Articles, Reviews*, 4.2 (1982), 199–212.

Chu ci 楚辭. *SBBY*.

Cooper, Arthur. *Li Po and Tu Fu*. London: Penguin Books, 1973.

Cui Bao 崔豹. *Gu jin zhu* 古今注. *SBCK*.

Culler, Jonathan. *The Pursuit of Signs: Semiotics, Literature, Deconstruction*. Ithaca: Cornell University Press, 1981.

———. *Structuralist Poetics*. Ithaca: Cornell University Press, 1975.

DeFrancis, John. *The Chinese Language: Fact and Fantasy*. Honolulu: University of Hawaii Press, 1984.

Diény, Jean-Pierre. *Aux origines de la poésie classique en Chine: Étude sur la poésie lyrique a l'époque des Han*. Leiden: E. J. Brill, 1968.

Ding Fubao 丁福保. *Quan Han Sanguo Jin Nanbeichao shi* 全漢三國晉南北朝詩. 3 vols. 1962: rpt. Taipei: Shijie shuju, 1969.

Dubrow, Heather. *Genre*. London: Methuen, 1982.

Eide, Elling. "On Li Po." *Perspectives on the Tang*. Ed. Arthur Wright and Denis Twitchett. New Haven: Yale University Press, 1973, pp. 367–403.

Frankel, Hans. "The Development of Han and Wei Yüeh-fu as a High Literary Genre." *The Vitality of the Lyric Voice*, pp. 255–86.

———. "Yüeh-fu Poetry." *Studies in Chinese Literary Genres*. Ed. Cyril Birch. Berkeley: University of California Press, 1977, pp. 69–107.

Frodsham, J. D. *An Anthology of Chinese Verse: Han, Wei, Chin and the Northern and Southern Dynasties*. London: Oxford University Press, 1967.

————. *The Murmuring Stream: The Life and Works of the Chinese Nature Poet Hsieh Ling-yün (385–433), Duke of K'ang-lo.* 2 vols. Kuala Lumpur: University of Malaya Press, 1967.

————. *The Poems of Li Ho (791–817).* Oxford: Clarendon Press, 1970.

Gafu shishō no kenkyū 樂府詩集の研究. Ed. Nakutsushama Wataru 中津濱涉. Tokyo: Kyuko, 1970.

Gimm, Matin, trans. *Das Yüeh-fu Tsa-lu des Tuan An-chieh: Studien zur Geschichte von Music, Schauspiel und Tanz in der T'ang-Dynastie.* Wiesbaden: Otto Harrassowitz, 1966.

Graham, A. C. *Poems of the Late T'ang.* Baltimore: Penguin Books, 1965.

Greene, Thomas. *The Light in Troy: Imitation and Discovery in Renaissance Poetry.* New Haven: Yale University Press, 1982.

Gu jin zhu, see Cui Bao.

Guangyun 廣韻. Taipei: Yiwen shuju, 1976.

Guo Maoqian 郭茂倩. *Yuefu shiji* 樂府詩集. Peking: Zhonghua shuju, 1979.

Hanfei zi 韓非子. *SBBY.*

Han shu 漢書. Peking: Zhonghua shuju, 1962.

Hawkes, David, trans. *The Songs of the South: An Anthology of Ancient Chinese Poems by Qu Yuan and Other Poets.* Middlesex: Penguin Books, Ltd., 1985.

He Liquan 郝立權, ed. *Lu Shiheng shi zhu* 陸士衡詩注. Taipei: Shijie shuju, 1962.

Hou Han shu 後漢書. Peking: Zhonghua shuju, 1976.

Huainan zi 淮南子. *SBBY.*

Huang Jie 黃節. *Han Wei yuefu fengjian* 漢魏樂府風箋. 1923; rpt. Taipei: Hu Shi jinian guan, 1969.

Hightower, James Robert. *Topics in Chinese Literature: Outlines and Bibliographies.* Cambridge: Harvard University Press, 1953.

Hung, William. *Tu Fu: China's Greatest Poet.* Cambridge: Harvard University Press, 1952.

The Indiana Companion to Classical Chinese Literature. Ed. William Nienhauser. Bloomington: Indiana University Press, 1986.

Jin shu 晉書. Peking: Zhonghua shuju, 1974.

Jiu Tang shu 舊唐書. Peking: Zhonghua shuju, 1975.

Kang Rongji 康榮吉, annot. *Lu Ji ji qi shi* 陸機及其詩. Taipei: Jiaxin shuini gongsi wenhua jijin hui, 1969.

Kao Yu-kung. "The Aesthetics of Regulated Verse." *The Vitality of the Lyric Voice*, pp. 332–85.

Karlgren, Bernhard. *Grammata Serica Recensa*. rpt. Stockholm: Bulletin of the Museum of Far Eastern Antiquities, 1972.

Keightley, David. *Sources of Shang History: The Oracle Bone Inscriptions of Bronze Age China*. Berkeley: University of California Press, 1978.

Knechtges, David, trans. *Wen xuan: Or Selections of Refined Literature*. Vol. 1. Princeton: Princeton University Press, 1982.

Konishi Jin'ichi. "Association and Progression: Principles of Integration in Anthologies and Sequences of Japanese Court Poetry, A. D. 900–1350." Trans. Robert H. Brower and Earl Miner. *Harvard Journal of Asiatic Studies*, 21 (1958), 67–127.

Krailsheimer, A. J., ed. *The Continental Renaissance 1500–1600*. Middlesex: Penguin Books, 1971.

Kristéva, Julia. *La Révolution du langage poètique*. Paris: Seuil, 1974.

Leitch, Vincent B. *Deconstructive Criticism: An Advanced Introduction*. New York: Columbia University Press, 1983.

Liang Ch'i Ch'ao. *Intellectual Trends in the Ch'ing Period*. Immanuel C. Y. Hsu, trans. Cambridge: Harvard University Press, 1959.

Liang Han wenxue shi cankao ziliao 兩漢文學史參考資料, ed. Peking University. Hong Kong: Xiongzhi shudian, 1962.

Liang Shi 梁史. Peking: Zhonghua shuju, 1973.

Lin, Shuen-fu, and Stephen Owen, eds. *The Vitality of the Lyric Voice: Shih Poetry from the Late Han to the T'ang*. Princeton University Press, 1986.

Liu, James J. Y. *Chinese Theories of Literature*. Chicago: University of Chicago Press, 1975.

———. *The Interlingual Critic*. Bloomington: Indiana University Press, 1982.

Liu Xie 劉勰. *Wenxin diaolong* 文心雕龍. Trans. Vincent Shih. *The Literary Mind and the Carving of Dragons*. Rev. ed. Taipei: Zhonghua shuju, 1970.

Liu Yeqiu 劉葉秋. *Zhongguo gudai zidian* 中國古代字典. Peking: Zhonghua shuju, 1963.

Loewe, Michael. *Crisis and Conflict in Han China*. London: George Allen & Unwin, Ltd, 1974.

Luo Genze 羅根澤. *Yuefu wenxue shi* 樂府文學史. 1931; rpt. Taipei: Wen shi zhe shuju, 1974.

Lynn, Richard John. "The Talent Learning Polarity in Chinese Poetics." *Chinese Literature: Essays, Articles, Reviews*, 5.2 (1983), 157–84

Marney, John. *Liang Chien-wen Ti*. Boston: Twayne Publishers, 1976.

————. *Beyond the Mulberries: An Anthology of Palace-style Poetry by Emperor Chien-wen of the Liang Dynasty (503–555).* Taipei: Chinese Materials Center, 1982.

Mair, Victor. *Tunhuang Popular Narratives.* London: Cambridge University Press, 1983.

Masuda Kiyohide 增田清秀. *Gakufu no rekisshiteki kenkyū* 樂府の歴史的研究. Tokyo: Sobunsha, 1975.

Mather, Richard. *The Poet Shen Yüeh (441–513): The Reticent Marquis.* Princeton: Princeton University Press, 1988.

Metzidakis, Stamos. *Repetition and Semiotics.* Birmingham, Alabama: Summa Publications, 1986.

Miyazaki Ichisada. *China's Examination Hell: The Civil Service Examinations of Imperial China.* Trans. Conrad Schirokauer. New Haven: Yale University Press, 1976.

Mo zi 墨子. *SBBY.*

Morgan, Thais E. "Is There an Intertext in This Text?: Literary and Interdisciplinary Approaches to Intertextuality." *American Journal of Semiotics,* 3.4 (1985), 140.

Nan shi 南史. Taipei: Chengwen chubanshe, 1971.

Nienhauser, William. "The Development of Two *Yüeh-fu* Themes in the Eighth and Ninth Centuries—Implications for T'ang Literary History." *Tamkang Review,* 15.1–4 (1984–1985), 97–132.

Okamura Tadao 岡村其雄. "Gakufudai no keishō to Fu Gen" 樂府題の繼承と傅玄. *Shinagaku kenkyū,* 35 (1970), 8–18.

Owen, Stephen. *The Great Age of Tang Poetry.* New Haven: Yale University Press, 1981.

————. *The Poetry of the Early T'ang.* New Haven: Yale University Press, 1977.

————. *Traditional Chinese Poetry and Poetics: Omen of the World.* Madison: University of Wisconsin Press, 1985.

Pi Xirui 皮錫瑞. *Jing xue lishi* 經學歷史. Rpt. Taipei: Heluo tushu chubanshe, 1974.

Pulleyblank, E. G. "Chinese and the Indo-Europeans." *Journal of the Royal Asiatic Society,* London. 1–2 (1966), 9–39.

Qi Ting-ting 亓婷婷. *Liang Han yuefu yanjiu* 兩漢樂府研究. Taipei: Xuehai chubanshe, 1980.

Quan Tang shi 全唐詩. Peking: Zhonghua shuju, 1960.

Rickett, Adele Austin, ed. *Approaches to Chinese Literature: From Confucius to Liang Ch'i-ch'ao.* Princeton: Princeton University Press, 1977.

Riffaterre, Michael. "The Interpretant in Literary Semiotics." *American Journal of Semiotics.* 3.4 (1985), 41–55.

———. *Semiotics of Poetry.* Bloomington: Indiana University Press, 1978.

Sargent, Stuart. "Can Latecomers Get There First? Sung Poets and Tang Poetry." *Chinese Literature: Essays, Articles, Reviews.* 4.2 (1982), 165–98.

Sawaguchi Takeo 澤口剛規. *Gaku fu* 樂府. Tokyo: Meitoki, 1969.

Scholes, Robert. *Semiotics and Interpretation.* New Haven: Yale University Press, 1982.

Seaton, J. P., and James Cryer. *Bright Moon, Perching Bird: Poems by Li Po and Tu Fu.* Middleton: Wesleyan University Press, 1987.

Shen Yue 沈約. *Song Shu* 宋書. Peking: Zhonghua shuju, 1974.

Shi jing 詩經, *Shisan jing zhu shu,* vol. 2.

Shi pin, see Zhong Hong.

Shisan jing zhushu 十三經注疏. 8 vols. 1815; rpt. Taipei: Yiwen shuju, n. d.

Shimada Kumiko 島田久美子. "Ri Haku no gakufu ni tsuite" 李白の樂府について. *Chūgoku bungaku,* 7 (1958), 17–53.

Siku quanshu zongmu tiyao 四庫全書總目題要. Ed. Wang Yunwu 王雲五. 1933; rpt. Taipei: Shangwu yinshuguan, 1971.

Song shu, see Shen Yüeh.

Sui shu 隋書. Peking: Zhonghua shuju, 1973.

Sunflower Splendor. Ed. Wu-chi Liu and Irving Yucheng Lo. Bloomington: Indiana University Press, 1975.

Tang shu, see *Jiu Tang shu.*

Teng Ssu-yu and Knight Biggerstaff. *An Annotated Bibliography of Selected Chinese Reference Works,* 3rd Edition. Cambridge: Harvard University Press, 1971.

Todorov, Tzvetan. *The Fantastic.* Trans. Richard Howard. Cleveland: Case Western Reserve, 1973.

Tong zhi, see Zheng Qiao.

Wagner, Marsha. *The Lotus Boat: The Origins of Chinese Tz'u Poetry in T'ang Popular Culture.* New York: Columbia University Press, 1984.

Waley, Arthur. *The Book of Songs.* 1937; rpt. New York: Grove Press, 1960.

———. *Stories and Ballads from Tun-Huang.* London: Allen and Unwin, 1949.

Wang Ch'iu-kuei. "The Formation of the Early Versions of the Meng Chiang-nü Story." *Tamkang Review*, 9.2 (1978), 111–40.

Wang Qi 王琦, ed. *Li Taibo quan ji* 李太白全集. Qing; rpt. Peking: Zhonghua shuju, 1977.

Wang Yunxi 王運熙. *Li Taibo yanjiu* 李太白研究. Peking: Zuojia chubanshe, 1962.

———. *Yuefu shi luncong* 樂府詩論叢. Shanghai: Zhonghua shuju, 1962.

Wang Zhong 汪中. *Yuefu shi xuan zhu* 樂府詩選注. Taipei: Xuehai chubanshe, 1979.

———. *Ssu-ma Ch'ien: Grand Historian of China*. New York: Columbia University Press, 1958.

Wen xuan 文選. Xiao Tong 蕭統, comp. Taipei: Shijie shuju, 1962.

Wenxin diaolong, see Liu Xie.

Wenyuan yinghua 文苑英華. Taipei: Huawen shuju, 1967.

Williams, Gary Shelton. "A Study of the Oral Nature of Han Yüeh-fu." Diss. University of Washington, Seattle. 1973.

Wilhelm, Hellmut. "The Bureau of Music of the Western Han." *Society and History*. Ed. G. L. Ulmen. The Hague: Mouton, 1978.

Wilhelm, Richard. Trans. Rendered into English by Cary F. Baynes. *The I Ching or Book of Changes*. 1950; rpt. Princeton: Princeton University Press, 1967.

Wong Siu-kit. *The Genius of Li Po*. Hong Kong: University of Hong Kong, Centre of Asian Studies, 1974.

Wu Jing 吳兢. *Yuefu guti yaojie* 樂府古題要解. *Baibu cong shu jicheng* 百部叢書集成. Taipei: Yiwen yinshuguan, n.d.

Wylie, A. *Notes on Chinese Literature: With Introductory Remarks on the Progressive Advancement of the Art; And a List of Translations from the Chinese in Various European Languages*. 1867; rpt. New York: Paragon Book Reprint Corp., 1964.

Xiao Difei 蕭滌非. *Han Wei Liuchao yuefu wenxue shi* 漢魏六朝樂府文學史. Chongqing: Zhongguo wenhua fuwu, 1944.

Xu Wenyu 許文雨, ed. *Wenlun jiangshu* 文論講疏. Taipei: Zhengzhong shuju, 1973.

Xue Shiqi. "Chinese Lexicography Past and Present." *Dictionaries*. 4 (1982), 151–68.

Yan Yu 嚴羽. *Canglang shihua jiaoshi* 滄浪詩話校釋. Peking: Renmin wenxue chubanshe, 1961.

Yang Weizhen 楊維楨. *Tieyai gu yuefu zhu* 鐵厓古樂府註. *SBBY*.

Yang Mu 楊牧. *You ren* 有人. Taipei: Hongfan shudian, 1986.

Yang Yinliu 楊蔭瀏. *Zhongguo yinyue shi gang* 中國音樂史綱. Peking: Yinyue chubanshe, 1955.

Yu Guanying 余冠英. *Yuefu shi xuan* 樂府詩選. Peking: Renmin shuju, 1954.

Yutai xinyong 玉臺新詠. Chengdu: Guji shudian, n.d.

Yu, Pauline. *The Poetry of Wang Wei: New Translations and Commentary*. Bloomington: Indiana University Press, 1980.

———. *The Reading of Imagery in the Chinese Poetic Tradition*. Princeton: Princeton University Press, 1987.

Yuefu guti yaojie, see Wu Jing.

Yuefu shi yanjiu lunwen ji 樂府詩研究論文集. Peking: Zuojia chubanshe, 1957.

Zheng Qiao 鄭樵. *Tong zhi* 通志. *SBBY*.

Zhi zhai shulu jieti 直齋書錄解題. Comp. Chen Zhensun 陳振孫. Taipei: Guangwen shuju, 1968.

Zhong Rong 鍾嶸. "Shi pin" 詩品. *Li dai shihua* 歷代詩話. 2 vols. Qing; rpt. Taipei: *Hanjing wenhua shiye youxian gongsi*, 1983, pp. 2–24.

Zhou yi 周易. *Shisan jing zhushu*, vol. 1.

Zhou Zhenfu. "The Legacy of the Han, Wei, and Six Dynasties *Yüeh-fu* Tradition and Its Further Development in T'ang Poetry." *The Vitality of the Lyric Voice*, 287-95.

Zhuang zi 莊子. *SBBY*.

Zuo Keming 左克明. *Gu yuefu* 古樂府. *Siku quanshu zhen ben* 四庫全書珍本. 12 *ji*, vol. 200. Shanghai: Shangwu yinshu guan, 1934–?.

Glossary

This is a glossary of graphs for names, titles, and terms. Graphs for items that occur only in poems or in cited passages, graphs that appear in the Works Cited or the Dynastic Chart, and graphs for common place names are not included.

ba zhen tu 八陣圖
"Bai bi gua" 白鼻騧
"Bai hu" 白鵠
bai hua 白話
"Bai tou yin (xing)" 白頭吟行
Ban Gu 班固
bao 報
Baoyue 寶月
bei ti 悲啼
ben ci 本辭
bian 變
bian wen 變文
"Bing che xing" 兵車行
Bo Juyi (722–846) 白居易
"Bo wei jin ming yue" 蒲帷鑒明月
bu 不
bu ru 不入
bu wei wen er zuo 不爲文而作

cai 採 采
"Cai ju pian" 采菊篇
"Cai lian qu" 採蓮曲

"Cai lian xing" 採蓮行
"Cai ling ge" 採菱歌
"Cai ling qu" 採菱曲
"Cai sang" 採桑
cai shi guan 採詩官
Cai Yong (133–192) 蔡邕
Cao Cao (155–220) 曹操
Cao Pi (187–226) 曹丕
　　[aka Wei Wendi]
Cao Zhi (192–232) 曹植
Cen Shen (715–770) 岑參
Cen Zhijing (fl. 575) 岑之敬
"Chang ge" 長歌
"Chang ge xing" 長歌行
chang tiao 長條
chang yang yuan 長楊苑
Chang'an 長安
Chen Lin (ob. 217) 陳林
Chen Shubao (550–604) 陳叔寶
　　[aka Chen Houzhu 陳後主]
Chen Tang 陳湯
chi chu 踟躕

chi chuang 赤幢
chou 酬
chou si 愁思
Chu ci chao" 楚辭鈔
chu si 初巳
"Chu zi Ji bei men (xing)" 出自薊
　　北門行
chui 垂
chui si 垂絲
chun se 春色
ci 詞
ci shi yuefu 辭實樂府
"Cong jun xing" 從軍行
Crown Prince Zhaoming (501–531)
　　照明太子 [aka Xiao Tong]
Cui Shi (fl. 710) 崔湜

da 答
dai 代
"Dai junzi you suosi" 代君子有所思
dai yuefu 代樂府
Dayuan 大宛
de (zhi) mo 德之末
diao 調
dong liang chen 動梁塵
"Dongmen xing" 東門行
du 渡
"Du chu chou" 獨處愁
Du Fu (712–770) 杜甫
du shu po wan juan 讀書破萬卷

Emperor Wu of Han 漢武帝
Emperor Wu of Liang 梁武帝
er bei 爾輩

fa 法
fan 反
fang dang 放蕩
fengming 奉命
fou 否
fu 賦

"Fu bing xing" 婦病行
fu de 賦得
Fu Xuan (217–278) 傅玄
Fu Zai (531–585) 傅縡
fugu 復古

Gan Yanshou 甘延壽
gang 釭
gao liu cheng 高柳城
Gao Shi (d. 765) 高適
ge 歌
geshi 歌詩
gexing 歌行
gu ci 古辭
gu feng 古風
"Gu feng" 古風
"Gu lang yue xing" 古朗月行
gu ti shi 古體詩
gu wen 古文
Gu yuefu 古樂府
Guandu 官渡
Guang ya 廣雅
guchui qu ci 鼓吹曲辭
"Guihe pian" 龜鶴篇
Gujin yuelu 古今樂錄
"Guo shang" 國傷

hai 海
Han xue 漢學
he (join together) 合
he (matching/harmony) 和
hengchui qu ci 橫吹曲辭
Hou Jing 侯景
hu 胡
Hu Zhenheng 胡震亨
hua 華
"Huaisuo shangren caoshu ge" 懷素
　　上人草書歌
huang 黃
Huanshaxi 浣紗溪

ji (continuation) 繼
ji (hope) 冀
"Jiang jin jiu" 將進酒
Jiang Yan (444–505) 江奄
Jiang Zong (fl. 575) 江總
"Jiangnan" 江南
"Jiangnan ge cai lian" 江南歌採蓮
"Jiangnan nong" 江南弄
"Jiangnan qu" 江南曲
"Jiangnan si" 江南思
Jiaohe 交河
jiaojiao 皎皎
jiaomiao ge ci 郊廟歌辭
jie 解
jie wu 節物
jin ti 金堤
jin ti shi 今體詩
jin wen 今文
Jin yue suozou 晉樂所奏
jindai qu ci 近代曲辭
jiuzi zhong 九子粽
juan 卷
jue wu 覺悟
jueju 絕句
jun 君

"Konghou yin" 箜篌引

lan 攬
"Lang yue xing" 朗月行
li 里
Li Bo (701–762) 李白
Li Fang (925–996) 李昉
Li He (790–816) 李賀
Li Qi (fl. 735) 李頎
"Li Sao" 離騷
Li Shangyin (813?–850) 李商隱
Li Shimin (597–649) 李世民
　　[aka Tang Taizong 唐太宗]
li si 離思
Li Yannian (fl. 100 B.C.) 李延年

lian/*liän (lotus) 蓮
lian/*liên (love) 憐
liang chen fei 梁塵飛
liang he 兩合
Liang Jianwen di 梁間文帝
　　[aka Xiao Gang]
Liang Yuan di 梁元帝
　　[aka Xiao Yi]
Liang you . . . wang 梁有 . . . 亡
liao/*lieu 聊
Liu Ji (1311–1375) 劉基
Liu Miao (fl. 525) 劉邈
Liu Shuo (431–453) 劉鑠
Liu Xian (Tang) 劉憲
Liu Xiaowei (Liang) 劉孝威
Liu Xiang (77–6 B.C.) 劉向
Liu Xiyi (722–842) 劉希夷
liu/*lieu (detain) 留
liu/*lieu (willow) 柳
Long 隴
lou 樓
Loyang 洛陽
Lu Ji (201–301) 陸機
lü shi 律詩
Lu Zhaolin (fl. 650) 盧照鄰
lun 論
"Lun wen" 論文
Luofu 羅敷

Mao Jin 毛晉
Mei Sheng (d. 140 B.C.) 枚乘
Meng Haoran (689–740) 孟浩然
Meng Jiangnü 孟姜女
Meng Jiao (751–814) 孟郊
Miao Xi (fl. 200) 繆襲
ming zhu 明主
"Mo mo" 默默
"Moshang sang" 陌上桑
mu 目
Mu tianzi zhuan 穆天子傳
Mulan 木蘭

neng 能
ni 擬
"Ni gu" 擬古
nong 弄
nong xiang 農祥

Ouyang Jin (Tang) 歐陽瑾

paixie changyue 俳諧倡樂
pan 攀
pang huang 彷徨
panqian 攀牽
panzhe 攀折
pian 篇
po sa 婆娑

qi fu 棄婦
qi zhi you qi 奇之又奇
Qiao Zhizhi (Tang) 喬知之
qiluo 綺羅
qin 琴
qing 情
qing fan er ci yin 情繁而辭隱
qing hua 輕華
qingning 青凝
qing yue 清月
qingshang 清商
qingshang qu ci 清商曲辭
qinqu ge ci 琴曲歌辭
Qiu Hu 秋胡
"Qiu Hu xing" 秋胡行
qu 曲
Qu Yuan (3rd century B.C.) 屈原
"Que tai yuan" 雀臺怨

reng 仍
"Ri chu [dongnan yu] xing" 日出
    東南隅行
ru 入
ruoruo 弱弱
Ruoye 若耶

se 色
Seng Zilan 僧子蘭
"Shan gui" 山鬼
shang 傷
Shang Fashi 尚法師
Shanglin 上林
shangliutian 上留田
"Shangliutian xing" 上留田行
shen 深
Shen Yue (441–513) 沈約
sheng 聲
shi 詩
Shi Chong (249–300) 石崇
Shiji 史記
Shi Yannian (994–1041) 石延年
shou 守
shu (writings) 書
shu bian 戍邊
"Shu dao nan" 蜀道難
Shujing 書經
Shuowen jiezi 說文解字
si/*si (thoughts) 思
si/*si (threads) 絲
"Si chou" 四愁
si zhu 絲竹
Sima Xiangru (d. 118 B.C.)
    司馬相如
song 頌
"Song bo pian" 松柏篇
Su Shi (1036–1101) 蘇軾
Sui Yangdi (580–618) 隋煬帝

"Tang shang ge xing" 堂上歌行
Tao Qian (132–194) 陶潛
ti 體
tian jia 田家
"Tian ma" 天馬
tian wen 天問
tianwen xue 天文學
tiao (minnows) 鰷
tiao (tendrils) 條

tong 同
"Tong que ji" 銅雀妓
"Tong que tai" 銅雀臺
tuo xiang 他鄉

Wang Bao (fl. 575) 王褒
Wang Changling (ca. 690–756)
　王昌齡
Wang Cuo (fl. 575) 王瑳
Wang Han (fl. 710) 王翰
Wang Jian (fl. 775) 王建
Wang Kangju (fl. 300) 王康琚
Wang Ruoxu (1174–1243) 王若虛
Wang Wei (ca. 701–761) 王維
Wang Yun (481–549) 王筠
wanqu 萬曲
wei (negation) 未
wei (on behalf) 爲
Wei Chengqing (fl. 700) 韋承慶
Wei Wendi (187–226) 魏文帝
　[aka Cao Pi]
wen 文
wen fu 文賦
"Wen fu" 文賦
wen tian 問天
Wen Tingyun (ca. 812–870) 溫庭筠
Wen xuan 文選
Weng Shou (Tang) 翁綬
wenxue 文學
Wenzhang liubie lun 文章流別論
wo xing yong yi jiu 我行永已久
wu (dance) 舞
wu (negation) 無
Wu ge 吳歌
Wu Jun 吳均
Wu sheng 吳聲
Wu Yue chunqiu 吳越春秋
Wuchang 武昌
wuming 無名
wuqu ge ci 舞曲歌辭

xi 兮
xi qu 西曲
Xi Shi 西施
xian guan jin shi 弦管金石
xiang 象
xianghe 相和
xianghe ge ci 相和歌辭
Xiang ma jing 相馬經
xiang si 相思
xiao 效
Xiao Gang (502–557) 蕭綱
　[aka Liang Jianwen di]
Xiao Hui (fl. 500) 蕭撝
Xiao Tong (501–531) 蕭統
　[aka Crown Prince Zhaoming]
Xiao Yi (r. 552–555) 蕭繹
　[aka Lian Yuan di]
xiaoshuo 小說
Xie Huilian (394–430) 謝惠連
Xie Lingyun (385–433) 謝靈運
Xie Tiao (464–499) 謝朓
xin sheng 新聲
xin yuefu ci 新樂府辭
xing 行
"Xing lu nan" 行路難
xinge 新歌
xiong qi 凶器
Xu Boyang (516–581) 徐伯陽
Xu Ling (507–583) 徐陵
xue 學
xue … ti 學 … 體
Xue Neng (fl. 850) 薛能
xue wen 學文
Xun Chang (fl. 420) 荀昶

yan 言
Yan Yanzhi (384–456) 彥延之
yang 楊
yang (vs. yin) 陽
Yang Wanli (1127–1206) 楊萬里

zhi (know/feel) 知
Zhi Yu (ob. 311) 摯虞
Zhou Danlong (644–674) 周丹龍
"Zhou lang yu sheng yao" 周郎玉
　笙謠
zhu bo 竹帛
zhu yan 朱顏

zhuo hui 濯穢
Zhuo Wenjun 卓文君
zi yue 漬月
ziliu 紫騮
"Ziliu ma" 紫騮馬
zuo 坐

Index

Printed and bound by CPI Group (UK) Ltd, Croydon, CR0 4YY

13/04/2025